My Book-Innit?

Wayne Reid

(a.k.a Ribs)

DEDICATION

"IT IS NOT THINGS IN THEMSELVES THAT UPSET US, BUT THE VIEWS
WE TAKE OF THEM." EPICTETUS

CONTENTS

ACKNOWLEDGMENTS

I want to especially thank my wife Laurel Reid for putting up with me and helping throughout the creation of this book.

Thanks also to the many friends that helped me on my way.

For my daughters Sian and Christina, my son Jordan.

And Dad.

Through this book, may you know me, may you remember and even forget.

TOO MUCH TOO YOUNG

I dream of an old building as vast as a car park, with sandy brown walls, floors and ceilings. It is dimly lit and there are many shadows. I enter cautiously through a doorway into what I now recognize as my childhood junior school, only it has changed, it is not the same as it was in those formative years. It is old and drab, the sounds of children have long gone. The building is derelict and eerie, neither lifeless nor living. I pass the large circular basin between the doorway and the two single cubicles in front of me. I am alone in the school toilets, listening intensely to the slow repetitive drip of the taps, the water clicking loudly as it connects with a stagnant puddle in the large stone basin. The entire room is filthy, cobwebbed and rancid from decades without use. Something else is here with me, still, hiding in one of the cubicles behind either of blue doors. Something unpleasant, lurking, waiting, hiding in the shadows and it knows I am approaching slowly, scared to the pit of my stomach. I know it is there and when I am close enough it will reveal itself. My heart thumps painfully in my chest, almost loud enough to be heard throughout the building, yet still I advance, my right arm outstretched to touch the blue laminate door. A painful swelling in my bowel reminds me of the fear in my heart, constricting my throat. I start to cry and simultaneously turn and run, run as fast as I can whilst gripped by the fear of the faceless entity now pursuing me, the fear that I may catch a glimpse of it, the face of my worst fear. The swelling in my bowel peaks and sears through me as I run, thin wet excrement drains out of me, my face contorts as the tears pour down my face, my legs sticky and hot, raw flesh rubbing against raw flesh. I scream and bolt upright, awake in a panic but not really awake, I am in between worlds, between sleep and waking, drunk and daydreaming but unaware of the difference. I still feel the scrutiny, the uncomfortable feeling of eyes watching me, waiting, hungry and ready to pounce.

These are my demons, and they are real, as real as the demons that took Adam, Jacqui, John and Little Tom. Led by their own hands into the long night beyond, whispering from behind the blue laminate door, just out of sight and sound but there all the same, waiting for me to open the door.

Vision

Vision like the truth pure and undiseased
Poisoned by a mothers' lies
Rolled from her tongue with ease.........

My earliest memories come from our time at Mardyke, a council housing estate built to house the families of the Ford production plant in Dagenham. The estate was built on wasteland near Rainham, Essex and immortalised in the 2010 film Made In Dagenham. Written by William Ivory, the film tells the story of the women who took on the bosses, the union, and the government to win equal pay for women workers, a battle still not fully won today.

The Mardyke estate in the film differs to that in my memory, the estate today is more how I remember it being. Grafiti, shuttered shop windows and abandoned cars being the norm. It was in this environment I spent my earliest years, aged 2, I was part of a gang caught on the roof of our block of flats having raided the delivery van behind the convenience store. When the driver went into the shop, we went into his van and ran away with a bounty of raw sausages, cigars and drinks. A neighbour reported smoke coming from the roof of our block and we were caught red handed.

I was 3rd born, my brother Leslie, named after our grandfather on my mother's side, was 5 years older and my sister Anne was born a year after him. Our father Ernie, a truck driver, was often absent from the home and that allowed us a certain freedom, until he came home and would often discipline us for our errant ways. This usually involved me being busted for letting down car tyres in the car park by inserting matches in the valves and watching the car sink onto it's wheel rims. I also had a habit of setting fire to things. I would set light to anything and everything I could, and when our mum, Alice, said she had a little brother or sister in her tummy for me to play with, I put a candle under her bed and demanded more chocolates from the box she had been given. This little misdemeanor led to me being sent to a psychiatrist for a short period, although Les claims to this day that it was him with the candle.

Another trait I had at this time was the habit of sleepwalking. Often I would be found wandering around the house in a trance like state, or talking gibberish acting out the dreams in my head. One night Dad heard the front door go and on inspection found me walking off into the boggy fields behind the estate, had he not come after me I have no idea what would have happened. The fields were full of deep muddy bogs, dangerous chemicals were illegally dumped on a regular basis and it was no place to be sleepwalking in your pyjamas.

I remember our last Christmas at Mardyke. I was too young to play my brothers' new game of Cluedo. Upset, I went upstairs and determined to run away and find a better life- a recurring theme as the years progressed, I placed socks on my hands and sneaked out into the snowy winter. By the time I'd thrown my umpteenth snowball, I decided it was time to head back, my fingers cold and damp, it was time for dinner. When I sneaked back inside I put the wet socks back in the drawer and went downstairs. Nobody had noticed my absence. Bastards……..

Joanne was born 1st February and before we knew it, we moved home to nearby Hornchurch. Dad was furious, Mum had got the council to move us into a house while he was away, he liked living at Mardyke but eventually came to realise he couldn't go back. The rest of us settled quite easily into our new environment, our house had a big garden, trees, 2 empty fields opposite a graveyard behind them, what more could we wish for? Oh yes, a dog, we needed a pet dog, or two, and a rabbit, and ducks….

It was the early 1970's, the country was in turmoil, strikes, power cuts, 3 day working weeks and weekends spent in the Working Men's Clubs watching Dad play drums. I got to taste more than lemonade and like most kids back then, would sneak the occasional bottle of beer out of sight of the grown ups. I liked the brown ale more than pale, but preferred mild whenever I could get it. Beer was good, even I knew that, but I never understood why the grown ups would stagger, fight and vomit their way through the car park before driving home. Maybe it was all the peanuts they'd eaten.

Settling into our new home also meant a new school. I was sad at leaving the school at Mardyke, we were half way through building a cardboard double deck London bus, and now that we'd moved, I would never get to drive it around the classroom or anywhere else. Our new school didn't have a bus, double decker or any other kind, but it did have a playground and it's own canteen. I soon made friends with other boys in my class and eventually forgot about the bus. We were too busy linking arms to form a long line across the playground, spinning round the line grew longer as we chanted -

"We protest, boys are the best!"

I was at the end of the line and as it pivoted round, getting faster and faster until I soon ran out of playground and crashed knee first into a bench. A large hole appeared at the top of my knee and blood poured down from it. I probably cried a lot, loudly too, but then again it was worth it just for the scar. It was the first of many injuries I would sustain at Hacton Lane Infants and Junior School. When we played rounders, I was more prone to catching the ball with my eye socket than my hands, a stunt that would see me laid prone on the field with a massive black eye forming. I would frequently fall off the climbing equipment, or jump off the wall where the older boys played cricket just in time to get hit in the face with the bat. One day a stray dog entered the playground, a group of boys were taunting it. I ran over and tried to stop them.

"Leave him alone or he'll end up biting you" The little shit bit alright, right down my forearm. I guess he was enjoying the attention and wasn't yet willing to be sent off home, unlike me, I was marched off to the school nurse and still to this day have never found out which one of us got the rabies shot.

Walking home one day I saw my Dads truck coming towards me by the railway bridge on Hacton Lane. The truck stopped and he called me over.

"Get in Son, you can come with me if you want"

"Where are you going?" I asked

"Germany" He replied, "Should be back in a couple of days" Back then we had no phone in the house, the only way we could call home would be to ring Jean, our next door neighbour, and ask her to get Mum on the phone. We headed to Dover and decided it was too late to disturb anyone. Dad bought a box of biscuits for me from the cafe in the port and before long we were aboard a very flat bottomed ship heading to Zeebrugge on a very windy night. I pissed and puked for England that night and had to spend the next couple of days wearing a pair of damp underpants and a merchant sailor's shirt given to me by someone on board. It was not a good look, but I sat bolt upright and proud in the truck, I was an officer, and I had the epaulettes to prove it. Being seasick did not faze me one bit, however, driving through Germany did. Not because I was on the wrong side of the road, but because there were no bombed out ruins. Convoys of soldiers on the Autobahn clad in green camouflage gear added insult to injury. My toy soldiers back home were a bluey-grey colour, not green. British and American soldiers were green, Germans wore blue, everybody knew that, except obviously, the bloody Germans themselves.

When we finally got home Mum was in the kitchen.

"Oh there you are, I guessed you might have gone with your Dad" Things were different back then I guess.

By the time I got into Junior School I had made friends with most of the kids in school. In the mornings I would walk to school with Matthew Wright, he lived down the street from us and we became Assembly Monitors. This meant we had to arrive early at school and prepare the hall for the headmaster's assembly. We would set up the record player, line up a particular track chosen for that day. Set up the projector, and the hymn and prayer books. At lunchtime I had another job, I was bucket boy (*no tittering at the back there...*) This involved scraping the leftovers of everyones meals into a bucket, stacking plates and placing cutlery in another bucket. My reward for this service was the undying love of the dinner ladies and first refusal on any spare meals and desserts left over after serving. This could often mean I would get 2 or 3 lunches and up to 4 desserts a day. I would just be leaving the canteen when the whistle blew and everyone ran back to class. Where all that food went I can't imagine, I never put on any weight but I was always fit, active and energetic.

Another close friend I made at Hacton Lane was Christopher Lacey. We were both keen artists, in fact his father was a cartoonist, he had a regular spot in a national paper. Chris obviously inherited his talent, but it wasn't enough, he wanted something more, so we hatched a plan that we would one day run away to Hollywood and become stuntmen. That day turned out to be a Thursday. We were walking home and decided this was to be the day. We left school and walked down past Hornchurch tube station, along the shops, thankfully Jean from next door who worked in the laundry was busy so we made it into Tony Burgess the Greengrocer without being seen. We invested all our savings, abou 5p at the time, on a bunch of bananas and headed off happy in the knowledge that they would see us through until we had walked the 27 miles to Southend. Chris had an aunt in Southend, and it was our plan to hunker down there until we were able to stowaway on a ship headed to Hollywood….. Now, you might be able to see a flaw in this, but to us, it was a foolproof plan, that is, until our feet started aching and we ran out of bananas and we hadn't yet reached Basildon. We decided to head back, and, in order to not get in any trouble, we hatched a plan to get a free ride home. We knocked on the door of the first door we came to and innocently asked for some water. The owner of the house obliged and asked us where we were going.

"We have to go home now" Christopher said, "We've just been kidnapped and jumped out of the car on the main road there"….. Nothing wrong so far….

By the time the Police had taken statements,dropped us home and spoken to our parents, the local press and our teachers, we almost believed it ourselves, in fact, it was only a couple of years ago that I told my father the truth behind that story, he had believed us all these years.

The following day Chris and I were paraded in front of the whole school at assembly. I thought we were busted but no, we were praised for our bravery and held up as a warning to the other students, that everybody needed to be careful out on the streets, walking home could be a dangerous affair.

The attention our "Kidnapping" brought us was actually quite nice, we were in the local paper and witnesses came forward to say they'd seen us being bundled into a car. No bananas were ever mentioned in the statements, strange that…..

Our Class was preparing for our christmas concert. Miss Sackville, our class teacher, was going through the preparations and getting us to rehearse one day when she stopped playing her guitar and called us all to stop singing.

"What was that noise?" She asked. "Everybody, start again, from the beginning"

We started again and her face took on a tortured look, through her thick clear glasses her eyes darted around, something was clearly upsetting her.

"It's coming from over there, you lot on this side" she pointed to our side of the group, "You lot, sing that again…"

Once more we began to sing, once more the pained look spread across her face, her top lip curled and I began to wonder why I ever thought she was a likely candidate for matrimony, the crush was being squeezed.

"YOU!"

I turned to look at the kid behind me only to remember I was in the back row.

"It's you." Her eyes suddenly burned through the beer glass lenses and the heat reddened my cheeks.

"Sing that again, on your own"

She wasn't wrong, I suddenly felt very much alone and vulnerable. As she began to strum her guitar I could hear the noise she had been searching for, it was coming from my mouth and I had no control over it.

"That simply won't do, that's awful. We cannot have you singing like that in front of everyone's parents. You will have to stand at the back and mime."

And so it was, that on the day of the concert I stood at the back and sang my heart out, silently, in the same way that John Redwood MP would later perform for the Welsh National Assembly, like his and my brains had been replaced by that of a goldfish.

"That boy's miming!" Said one parent to another
No shit Sherlock……

Miss Sackville left at easter only to return after the holiday as Mrs Clarke.

Cupid had definitely left the building….

Sex education in our school was a simple affair. The teacher dimmed the lights and we were made to watch a film about eggs and sperm. Diagrams of the internal workings of the male and female genitalia did little to interest me, but when Heather-who was sitting next to me, took my hand and put it inside her knickers, I suddenly found things a little more interesting.

Opposite our home were two other houses, and at the side of those were empty plots of land, each the size of a football pitch. We would often play out in the street,or in the alleyway between our house and Jeans' next door. Sometimes we would explore the fields opposite which were more suited for dumping unwanted furniture than playing football on. Myself, Martin Coombs and his cousin Maurice went to explore one day and discovered a wasps nest, you know what's coming right? Boys being boys we walked right up to the nest, which was in the right hand rear corner of the field to the left, not too far from home should we have to beat a hasty exit. Martin prodded the nest with a stick and dozen or so wasps flew out of the hole,I stepped back quickly.

"Here, let me have a go" Maurice stepped in and thrust a short scaffold pole he had found nearby, directly into the nest. I am not an expert, and even at the tender age of 7 or 8 as I was then, even I knew that was not going to end well. Maurice stirred the pole around in the nest and instantly all hell broke loose. I was already 10 or 12 feet away from the nest as a cloud of hundreds-if not thousands of wasps, angrily protesting Maurice's intervention of their routine, buzzed and darted in and out of each other in search of the culprit. It was like the insect version of a January sale on Regent Street, all for one and all for me. I stood rigid, absolutely petrified, cemented to the spot. Martin and Maurice screamed in unison, even before I could close my eyes they both ran past me, the huge cloud buzzing about them Their arms flailed, bodies twitched and voices screeched as they made their escape along the path and back to Martins' mum, Vera.

I stood still, a dozen or so wasps sniffing around me searching for the scent of fresh scaffold pole, any evidence that I had been involved, directly or otherwise in the destruction of their home. The pole was standing upright, still in the hole as I opened my eyes, unsure what to do next. Martin and Maurice disappearing across the road as the swarm thinned around them. Realising many would be coming back soon, I found the courage to run, as fast as I could.

By the time I got back to the safety of our house, my partners in crime had gone into next door, still screaming. It was a full 10 more minutes before they hushed. Someone called an ambulance and the boys were taken away for emergency treatment. I couldn't believe my luck at having not been stung, especially when I was later informed that they had managed to collect a total of 187 stings between them. I don't think they ever put another scaffold pole in wasp nest again but Martin and I did get ourselves into another bit of bother one holiday. There was an outdoor activities centre a few miles away from us at Ockenden, called Stubbers. We saw in the local paper that an adventure activity week happening and we wanted an adventure. We headed off on the big green 370 double deck bus and planned our day out, armed with nothing more than bus fare and a towel each for drying ourselves after the watersports.

"I want to sail a boat".

"I want to climb the rock cliff".

Neither of us had a clue how to do either, but it sounded like fun. We walked up the long path to the old house in the middle of the centre. It was a huge looking building, white walls and high ceilings, doors and windows looking out onto the numerous football pitches that surrounded the centre. It seemed pretty quiet and we walked around for 5 minutes before finding anyone.

"Can I help you boys?" Came a voice from behind us. We turned round and saw a bearded man with glasses and a wooly hat.

"We've come for the Adventure week and want to go sailing" I said before Martin got me tied to rope dangling over the abyss.

"I'm sorry but that was last week, you're a little too late".

He must have seen the disappointment spread over our faces.

"I tell you what though, if you would like to help out and tidy up this room next door, I'll see if I can arrange something for you".We jumped at the chance and were soon left alone picking up rubbish to put in a bin, moving things around and generally not knowing what we were really doing.

"Look! Matches, Fags and a bottle of wine-2 bottles" Martin held up his booty and we checked the coast was clear before having a sneaky swig of the foul tasting drink.

"Bleurgh! That's horrible, I don't fancy this anymore-shall we go home now?

"Yes, we'll come back next time" I agreed.

 With that in mind, we headed back downstairs and out the door towards the main road. As we walked up the path Martin was showing off his new trick. He put a match on the side of the box and flicked it away making the little stick ignite in mid air. Very impressive until one landed on the grass and started a fire. I used my towel to bash the flames out, Martin poured the wine but the flames fanned out quicker than we could move. There had been a severe drought and everything was tinderbox dry, as much as we tried we could not stop the fire as it spread, so we did the next best thing and ran away. By the time we got home a huge cloud of smoke could be seen for miles around.

"I hope that's nothing to do with you two" Mum said as we stood in the kitchen drinking squash. We said nothing, the smell of smoke on our hair said it all for us.

Before the developers moved in and built God's Waiting Rooms overlooking the cemetery, my brother Les and I saw a car pull up over the road. The driver got out and took a suitcase up the path, returning without it a few seconds later. He drove off, leaving his case somewhere near the wasp nest. We ran over the road and investigated, the case was there alright. We opened it and found a suit, the same as the driver had worn, however, this one had blood stains on it. Les took it to the Police station and returned with a receipt. If it wasn't claimed in 30 days, he could have it himself. It never was claimed, nor did Les go back for it.

I remember those fields for another incident too, when running through the grass in my plimsoll's and discovering a broken bottle. The glass tore into my left foot just below the inside ankle. I didn't really feel much but the amount of blood gushing from my foot was enough to have me carried off to the hospital. 6 Stitches later I was back home , foot up and resting. I still have the scar to this day.

Being number three of four I would always get my wardrobe courtesy of my brother's hand-me-downs. Ill-fitting trousers, shirts and soon to wear out socks. It happens to most kids, we accept the fact that we are destined to eventually have everything pass through us before going to landfill, the only option before society woke up to recycling or charity shop donations. By the time I had finished, there wasn't much left to donate or recycle, everything would be threadbare or torn. I was an energetic kid, forever tearing the knees in my trousers, ripping shirts etc. It was normal, it was play,or in the case of my cousin Carl, it was non-stop fighting. We would dive on each other at first glimpse, wrestling all around the house, tumbling downstairs, biting and slapping all the way.

In the early 1970's, industrial relations were pretty tense. Everybody was on strike at some point, which meant that when the bin men went on strike we had to burn or bury our rubbish in the garden. As kids we were all taught to use a garden fork and a shovel. We had all pitched in to dig out trees from the back garden, to dig holes for rubbish and bury dead pets. When our pet rabbit died we buried it in the garden. It was a beautiful black rabbit we called Velvet. Joanne was still very little and pronounced it as "Belvit". We dug a hole at the bottom of the garden and dropped the corpse in, no tears, no ceremony, it was a rabbit, a dead rabbit. Joanne hid upstairs all day crying but eventually came down later that evening when "Uncle" Alf came round. Alf was a big fella, a bit of a brute possibly. I always thought of Victor Mature in the film Samson whenever I thought of him. Jet black greasy hair, a permanent look of disdain on his face, he was a Romany, a gypsy by descent, and would often go fishing or hunting with my Dad. They were close friends and Alf would forever come around unannounced. This one night as the bell rang, Joanne rushed downstairs to let him in. The door opened and a scream ripped through the house.

"Belvit!" She cried and fled back upstairs.

Alf stood in the doorway, still holding aloft the black rabbit he had shot that day and brought as a surprise for our supper. I don't think she ever recovered from that shock, as for myself, I have never eaten rabbit since, mostly because I don't like the texture, nothing to do with the ghost of "Belvit", or the memory of Joannes blood curdling scream.

As I said, the digging of holes in back gardens was a regular event back then. Sometimes we would even dig a hole to find we had already buried rubbish in that spot, dig another and have to dig deeper until it was deep enough to accommodate all the rubbish we had to bury, including the stuff we had already buried. One day we dug a hole so deep we found an Anderson Shelter from WW2 that we didn't know was in our garden. These were the air raid shelters the locals would stay in at night during the Blitz on London. We were only a few miles from Hornchurch Aerodrome, where the Hurricanes were based and so would have been a prime target for the Luftwaffe. The shelter was covered over again an to the best of my knowledge, is still laying hidden beneath the old garden.

'Uncle' Alf had the dubious misfortune of working at the aerodrome as a digger driver, clearing the land for the development of South Hornchurch Nature Park. One morning his work mates went for their usual tea break and when Alf didn't show up, they went to investigate. His Digger was on tick over, sitting ashen faced in his cab, Alf pointed at the 1,000lb bomb on the bucket of his digger. The professionals were called in, South Hornchurch evacuated, Alf changed his underwear and midway through World Of Sport our house rocked from the vibration of the explosion, 3 miles away.

Another time we were digging in the garden an argument broke out. Anne, my older sister, was throwing dirt into the air from her shovel.
"Stop it" I told her, "It's going down my shirt"
The dirt and stones were falling on my head as she ignored me. Each time she would throw a load into the air it would

rain down on her little brother. A great pastime if you happen to be the older sibling, being the younger, not so good.

I held my garden fork level to her chest, motioning that I would kill her if she did it again. She did it again.

In a moment of frustration I turned and threw the garden fork into the ground next to her foot. When I say next to her foot, I sort of mean that was where it was meant to go. Where it actually went was into the ground at her foot, so much so that her foot was impaled by one of the steel prongs. I pulled the fork back out her foot and she wailed.

"Just you wait, I'm going to tell Mum what you've done" and hobbled up the garden path. A few minutes later she returned. "You're in big trouble now, I'm going to hospital now and Mum said Dad's going to sort you out when he gets home from work."

I have no recollection of my punishment this time around, however, it was probably more than just the usual slippering or smack across the bum with a leather belt. Whenever we misbehaved, or rather I misbehaved- it usually was me, I would be summoned to face Dad in the living room. He would either ask me for my version of events or direct me to go fetch his slippers from under the stairs. If it was bad, it would be a belt. I now look back and laugh at what must have been a ridiculous sight, Dad sat in his chair, me looking all forlorn, tears running down my face saying "Please don't hit me" whilst slowly walking, arms hanging limply by my side, out into the hallway, where I would open the cupboard beneath the stairs, step inside and without switching on the light (so as to drag the whole charade out as long as possible in the hope Dad would change his mind or die of boredom) I would grope around in the dark for his smelly, hard plastic soled, bottom stinging, footwear. Once located, I would carry them back to him, my bottom lip hanging on my chin, snotty nosed by now, still whimpering, I would hold them out at arm's length and when he took them, I would bend over his knee and take my punishment. In this day and age, it would be child abuse, in our time it was discipline, it hurt, but we accepted it. We did wrong, got slapped and went back to do more mischief, we were kids, it was our job to misbehave and it was ours parents' job to discipline us.

Growing up in our house was never dull, or not for long at any rate, we were forever visiting our relatives at weekends, or staying with our cousins when our Mum was in hospital, other people would come and stay with us for a night or two, sometimes weeks at a time, everyone helped everyone out back then, someone always available to babysit or put us up for a bit. We had many cousins, aunts and uncles, and whenever there was a family get together there was beer, lots of beer. As kids we would run around and play a lot, beer tasted like rusty water when we were too young, but eventually we would get a taste for it.

We were staying with friends in Caerphilly once. Left alone to babysit their 2 year old while the big people went to the Working Mens' club, we were surprised to find the little sod had opened a decanter and was trying to get at the drink inside. Thinking it would be a laugh we gave him some Rum to try, and then whiskey, and to be honest, all of the drinks in the trolley. It wasn't long before the nappy was off, the kid wandering around pissing all over the carpets, in his Dad's shoes and wherever he stood. He was like a hot water bottle with a hole in the middle, but mobile with it, gushing with every other step. By the time the big people returned, tanked up and carefree, he had virtually soaked everything in their living room.

After our scheduled break, everyone went home and I was left behind with Norman and Glenys.. They had offered for me to stay behind so that I could play with their nephew Kelvin Ruck, who lived a few doors down the street. Kelvin and I had become good friends and played rugby together everyday in the park or by the castle. I loved exploring the castle, climbing on the walls and imagining how things must have been when people lived in this magnificent place.

Kelvin played for his school rugby team, and for the local team, Bedwas under 12's. He invited me to come along to a match and I was excited to go. After a warm up, the coach offered for me to join in and before you know scored the winning try. Well, almost. I was there when the winning try was scored, in a picture in the local newspaper the next day.

Kelvin lived with his parents in a terraced house on a street filled with terraced houses. I was given his brother's bedroom to sleep in, it was a cold room at the top of the house, the bed covered with thick blankets and an eiderdown. There was no heating and the weight of the many blankets nearly crushed me each night. The bedroom was decorated with Royal Navy memorabilia. Kelvin's brother John, was in the navy, a position I would soon know as my own brother Leslie would eventually sign up. This week however, Les had other things on his mind.

Unknown to myself. I had been kept away from home because a local girl had been murdered on her way home from the Robert Beard Youth Club near where we lived. My brother happened to be of the right age to be a suspect and was taken in for questioning, along with probably most of the rest of the boys in the borough.

Coral Vidler had attended the Robert Beard Youth Club and left with a young man at the end of the evening. When she failed to return home her father reported her missing. Walking back from the police station, through an alleyway that lead home, he found a section of the fence broken and blood on the ground. When he looked through the fence he discovered the dead body of his daughter laying in the back garden of a house adjacent to the alley, he had already walked by and stepped in his daughter's blood on his way to the police station. Her killer was later found and imprisoned. I can never pass the scene without remembering the broken fence, the bloodstain on the floor and the name, Coral Vidler.

No matter what I did as a lad, I would always be overshadowed by my older brother, it's just the way it works. He was older and got new things, chose his way and I would have to follow. Except the night he laid in bed with a marble in his mouth, hearing him choke and being carted off to A&E put me off trying to copy that little trick. Clothes, school, Sea Cadets, Royal Navy, pension, death. I think that was the plan. Somehow it all unravelled. Growing up in the 1970's meant endless evenings in candlelit rooms, cold suppers or if the electricity was on we could watch depressing documentaries of Unemployment In The North, where empty docks lay silent, men woke each morning to spend the day as they had the previous however many, sitting on their stoops, smoking what they could afford to and wishing for a better life.

I used to cut the adverts out of the newspapers. Join the Army, Join the Navy, be a Policeman, Prison Officer, Pilot, anything that meant I wouldn't have to sit in a black and white suit,on a black and white stoop, smoking black and white fags on a black and white street. My street was colourful, my street had grass, children, blue skies and cars of various colours, shapes and sizes. I would cut out the adverts, fill in the application details and freepost them back to the advertiser. In a black and white room, somewhere in a black and white archive, lies hundreds of applications for a career, for a hope, for salvation, all signed Wayne Reid, aged 8.

Les had been in the Sea Cadets for several years and was heading for a life at sea. After his training, he when on to bigger and better things, starting as a radio operator he went on to be a something or other, doing stuff in places where stuff got done by people who did stuff, training others to do stuff and eventually being a someone, somewhere doing something that nobody is supposed to know about, but had to be done by someone, somewhere, and that someone was him, there. *If anybody else would like me to recreate their CV for them, please contact me through the usual channels.*

I decided at the tender age of 9 and a half years old, that I too wanted to join the Navy. Not for I this black and white life on the dole malarky, I wanted to live life to the full, get a job, a career, money, travel, adventure, seasickness and maybe even the occasional STD. All the girls love a sailor, they said, and I wanted to be loved.

Minimum age for joining the Sea Cadets was 10 years old, I was to wait 6 whole months before I could become a Junior Junior, but thankfully, because of my brother being a cadet already, I was allowed to come along too, but I could not get a uniform or officially take part until my 10th birthday.

Once I was old enough I got my uniform and joined the ranks. I chose to follow Les and became, in time, a radio operator. I learned the Morse Code and Phonetic Alphabet, eventually at my peak becoming the best Radio Operator in the Southeast. I won a scholarship to HMS Chrysanthemum and HMS President, the two training ships moored on the river Thames at Embankment. Now, they are in private hands, one is a floating restaurant, the other , I believe scrapped. My ability to send and receive morse code improved to the point where I could read at 23 words per minute, sending at 28. I scarcely believe it now, the speed at which I would manipulate a morse key, write a coded message, it was as if the signal ran directly through my ear to my hand without the distraction and delay of being filtered through my head. I was a machine, a very accurate, precise piece of machinery.

I somehow managed to become Cadet of the year and won a scholarship on T/S Royalist, the Royal Navy Sail training vessel. I was to join it in Portsmouth, at HMS Raleigh, and spend a week at sea learning the ropes,literally.

I arrived on board, having travelled alone by train courtesy of my travel pass. Back then kids would travel the length and breadth of the country unsupervised, we got where we were going, we were responsible enough to do so. Once my bag was stowed on my bunk, I was taken up on deck by the Bosun.

"First thing you have to do on board is climb the mast, all the way to the top. And when you reach the top" he smiled evilly, "-you have to go over it and down the other side-you don't go around it like some landlubber chicken, you go over the top, like a real seaman, or you'll do it again." This was his idea of welcome to my ship.

"Now, get up there and quick, I don't want to be doing this when it gets dark, and neither do you!"

Truth be told, I didn't want to be doing it then, I hate heights, always have, but I had no choice, I had to go up, and over.

The masts on the TS Royalist were about 100 feet high. To reach the first Yardarm you had to climb onto the gunwale, the bit that stops you falling over the side of the ship- or 'gunnell' as it is pronounced. From there you would climb the rigging to the first yardarm. The yardarm is the the cross member that the big square sails hang from. Climbing rigging may look easy enough on TV, but lifting yourself one step at a time on a rope ladder is not the easiest of tasks, the rope digs into your sole and your balance is thrown out. Many a seaman have been lost overboard whilst climbing rigging. Once at the first yardarm, you have to climb onto a small platform at the top of the rigging,this is made difficult as the gaps in the rigging get smaller as you get nearer the top. Once on the platform, another set of rigging leads to the next yardarm, some 25 feet higher. Finally, after the third and final yardarm, the last part of the climb is the final 20 feet to the top, up an almost vertical steel wire and rope ladder.

The masthead is a mass of rigging and navigational lights, none of which aide one's ascent or descent, at least, not in a controlled manner, losing your footing here is tantamount to suicide. At the top I fumbled with my hands, pulled myself up and with superhuman determination managed to get a leg over and down the other side. My heart was pounding in my chest, I really was petrified. I stupidly looked down to see the deck below but beneath me instead, was the murky water of the harbour. As the ship gently swayed in the breeze, rolling slightly from one side to the next, way up top I was swinging from one side over the water, to the other over the jetty, it was a motion I had never thought of before, the ship was berthed but way up there, 100 feet above the deck, it was like clinging onto an inverted swing, hardly moving at source, but savage at the extremity.

Once all the ships crew had arrived and been made to climb the mast, the Bosun decided who would work where on the ship. My job was to be second out on the first yardarm, this meant I would be positioned just over the side of the ship when we set or changed the sails. We were all finally welcomed aboard with bread and hot soup, chunks of vegetables floating in grimey water. And then it was lights out. We were rudely awoken at 4am, dressed, breakfasted and told to report on deck barefoot before we would set sail. It was a cold October morning and before we knew what hit us, we were scrubbing the decks with icy cold water, scrubbing brushes and soap. This prize I so proudly won was turning into a punishment. The cold air and even colder water from the hose turned our feet red, we were cold and in pain but had nowhere to hide, no sanctuary, only the Bosun's hard glaring eyes as he looked for slackers. Everything we did was scrutinised, we were tested and pushed at every opportunity. When it came to leaving harbour, I was given a special job to do. I was sent to the bowsprite and told to stand upright at the very end. Once we had cleared the harbour, and never before, I was to remove the ensign from it's position at the end of the bowsprite, pass it back to another rating standing behind me at the next halyard, and then climb back aboard. At no time was I to leave my post before we left harbour, or indeed, fall from the bowsprite at any time during the execution of my duty. I can honestly say, falling from the pointy bit at the front of a ship going forward is never a good idea, and I had absolutely no intention of doing so.

As we slipped our moorings and gently glided away from the jetty all seemed very comfortable. But as the wheel turned and the propellor dug into the water, I felt the ship behind me dip, I was standing on a rather large seesaw, rising up and down, almost touching the water one moment, and 30 feet above it the next. I clung on to the halyard for dear life. By the time the Bosun signalled for me to come back on deck I felt as sick as a dog but was immediately sent aloft to set the sails. 40 feet above the waves, swaying to and fro, standing on a thin cable, clipped to the yardarm. Below me, the waves, the ships deck and again the waves, swaying from side to side, all I could think of was how weak and ill I felt.

We unrolled our sail and descended to the safety of the deck. For the rest of the day all I could think of was not being sick, other cadets were already hanging over the gunwale feeding the fishes with the breakfast. When the call came for lunch I steeled myself and climbed down to the galley taking a seat at the end of the table. The smell of vegetable soup filled the cabin, but before I could taste a drop someone screamed. Another cadet had rushed up the ladder but before making it to the deck had emptied his load down onto the table beneath, splashing everyone within range, several of whom immediately vomited themselves and added to the suffering. I felt myself wretch and headed for the open deck, the vegetable soup far from my list of priorities. I would starve all week if I had to, but I was not going back below while we were at sea.

Eventually we all found our sea legs, we grew more used to the motion of the ship, the sounds, the smells and the nausea. We learned to deal with cold, hunger, sickness and the constant damp. For 5 days we sailed along the south coast of England, our seamanship skills improved, but alas, at the end of the week I failed to attain the Competent Crew qualification I had so dearly wished to return home with. It was a bitter pill, and I don't think I ever really recovered. I could sail dinghies, I was pretty good with a powerboat and an oar. I thought my time on Royalist would be a breeze, but it was much harder than I imagined, I was a wimp and a whinger on board, seasick and unable to reach even the basic level of competence. I was not ready for a life on the ocean waves, not yet anyway.

Back on solid ground life continued as it always had. Mum and Dad argued, visitors came and went, I would make Joanne cry saying we'd found her behind a blackberry bush. Les would punch me and make my nose bleed. Anne would flirt and dream of a life married to David Cassidy or The Fonze, or whoever was flavour of the month that particular month. Dad carried on driving trucks and taking us up and down the length of the country. We went to Sheffield a lot, Lincoln and

South Wales. One day we finished our last delivery and were ready for a bite to eat.

"Here skinnyribs"(*Dad always called me Skinnyribs when I was little*) he said giving me his last 10p coin, "-there's a baker's shop just around that corner, pop over and get us a couple of rolls or sandwiches. Something nice and filling, I'm starving. Thanks Son."

I ran around the corner and looked at all the goodies on offer in the window. Salad rolls, cheese sandwiches, doughnuts, cake and breads of all descriptions. Finally I saw them, big, round and filled with goodness. Dad is going to be so happy.

"Can I have 2 of those please?" I asked the lady at the counter.

"Of course you can, that'll be 8 pence please"

I handed over the big silver coin and she gave me 2p change and a bag with 2 big pink meringues with cream fillings…….

Dad was not impressed. It was a long ride home that day.

One of the most traumatic experiences of a young boys time growing up, has to be the transition from Junior School to Senior's. Leaving behind all the friendships that had been hard won, leaving the familiar surroundings, the regular route to and from school. Everything changes. With these changes come challenges, the making of new friends, reputations, survival.

I had applied to follow my brother to Abbs Cross School, with my second choice being Sanders Draper, where Mitch, Jeans' son, next door, was a student. Neither of these, nor my third choice- Anne's school Drury Falls ,were available to me. I was being sent to Harrow Lodge, a school I had never heard of, in a part of town I never ventured.

"That's a really hard school" I was told, "you have to be really tough there, they'll stab you in the toilets or behind the bike shed if they don't like you."

Darren Taylor, the first boy in our school to get a pair of Dr Marten boots, brown, 12 hole. He knew things.

"The 2nd year boys beat up the 1st year kids for fun, and there's no girls, it's boys only so you better not be a poof or they'll kick your head in."

What the fuck had I been signed up to. This couldn't be right, I was meant to follow Les, you know, good school, good grades, good job, laying in bed at night choking on marbles was meant to be the biggest danger in my life, not getting cut up in the toilet block.

I spent the whole summer toughening up. I punched every inanimate object I could, bannisters, doors, walls. I had to get hard, I had to be willing and ready to punch, to fight and survive. I practised my threatening stance, the look, snarl and slightly curled top lip.

"You wanna know?" I'd snarl into the bathroom mirror, waving around one of the many sheath knives Dad had bought home for me from his travels. I had one made from a deer's foot, a white resin handled blade designed to look like Ivory, a black handled knife with a Fleur De Lys emblem, and others. I stood there in my underpants waving the knife at my reflection, feeling tough and looking ridiculous without a single pubic hair on my body. "I'm hard I am, you wanna go?" The mirror never replied, the skinny boy with a face full of freckles, semi naked and flaccid continued to point his knife.

September came and I headed to my new school, in my new uniform with my new bag. Nobody got knifed in the toilet block but for the first few weeks there were scraps in the playground and outside the gates. Kids fighting their way up the pecking order. Proving themselves, proving to others who was tougher than this one or that. I managed to slip through gaps, I wasn't a threat or challenger, I wasn't one to be picked on either, I was nondescript, almost invisible but floating around the edges, I made friends and swore like the fucking hard bastard I fucking was. I blagged it.

We soon found or new groups, new friends. I became part of a crowd that would play very aggressively at break times. Eddie (Wag) Wager and Andrew (Meaty) Clegg would each pick a team. The game was called Runouts. One team had a minute to disperse, the other would then have to catch them and return them to a corner of the playground. Here they were guarded by 2 members of the other team. To catch someone you had to grab them and hold on, counting to 10 as they would kick, bite and punch you until you let go. Letting go meant having to repeat the process again and again, until finally, you had held onto them to the count of 10. To release other team members that had been caught, you had to get past the guards and touch your teammates who could then run free. I learned to count very quickly and loudly, ignoring the punches, clinging on so that I would not have to go through the process again and again. One day I was nicknamed a 'Human Shock Absorber'. No amount of punching could make me let go. Meaty and Wag took great joy at trying to batter the shit out of me in the name of sport, but I would take it, I held on, I found my niche.

Our games attracted many kids and was a great way to find out who was tougher than who. We made friendships that would grow and last all through our time at school, some still to this day. I became close to Meaty, we were good friends and I would sometimes go round his house to see him. We both played in the rugby team and were fearless on the pitch.

Meaty was a Prop Forward and I played Scrum Half. Games played against other schools often ended in brawls. At Great Baddow one very foggy winter morning, visibility was so poor we could do as we pleased off the ball, there were so many fights it was hard to know who was actually winning the match. Another time at our home field, we faced Brittons. Reputed to be the toughest school in the area they turned up with the biggest player I had ever come up against. This kid must have been 3 years older than us, he was huge, red haired and built like a brick shithouse with more pubes than King Kong. This guy was a monster. As much as we tried, we could not get into their end of the pitch, kick after kick of the ball ended with it coming straight back at us, our defence being tried again and again. The ball came into my clutch and I decided to run with it, dodging flying tackles left and right until a huge tree trunk of a leg sent me flying.

"Who the fu…." I began as I picked myself up, fists clenched ready to go. I looked at the beast in front of me and knew I had to finish this. I flew at him and was swatted away like a fly. Again I attacked and was smacked down. The referee jumped in between us.

"Do that again and you'll be sent off. Free kick to the visiting side for retaliation."

Do it again? Was he serious? He nearly killed me the first time!

We had a practise session one day after school, concentrating on tackling skills. I got sent home early after colliding in mid tackle with the underside of someone else's boots, my scalp split open and blood covered my face. I wanted to carry on but wasn't allowed and stepping onto the 248 bus I saw the reaction of the other passengers. Even the driver asked if I was ok, it was just blood, my face may have been covered with it but I felt fine and continued to drip all the way home.

Meaty failed to show up at school one day a year or two later. It turned out he had been in a car crash and had gone through the windscreen. He spent a long time in hospital having glass removed from his face and eyes. I visited him at home a few times, but his absence put a slight distance between us and we were never as close after his accident as before. We were still friends and had plenty of adventures together but I had drifted and found new friends.

Andrew Nunn and I were in the same class, 1H, the top class in our year. Each year had five classes, H, A R O and W. H was the top class and W bottom of the league. Somehow we managed to stay in the top form all through our academic years, no matter how much we messed up, we were still bright students. Andy and I became the bane of many a teacher's life. We would often be sent to the Head or Deputy head for misbehaving. Detention after school was a norm, as were the frequent smacks on the bum with a wooden bat or the cane. One day as I stood outside the deputy heads office whilst Andy was being disciplined, I counted the swishes of the cane. Whoosh 1, whoosh 2, whoosh 3, whoosh 4, whoosh snap-

"Aagh!" Andy howled, the cane had come down so hard on his backside that it broke.

"Get out!" yelled the teacher, shoving Andy out the door "-You, get in here and put your hand out"

The broken cane came down across my fingers and I yelped.

"Get out, and if anyone says anything, you say you got 6, and if you come back to me again anytime soon I will make sure you get the full amount. Now go!"

I didn't need to be told twice, I was out, Andy was along the corridor adjusting his belt and looking somewhat red faced.

"Fuck that hurt!" He said, "what did you get?"

"One on my hand" I showed him my throbbing fingers, "he said to say I got 6" I said smiling.

"You jammy bastard." I was, and I knew it.

Teachers at our school varied from the useless to the pretty inadequate, with the occasional semi-capable or even scary being the exception to the rule. Mr Samuels (aka Sammy) was our humanities teacher. A brilliantly knowledgeable man, he had once been on a TV show called The Sky's The Limit, where contestants would answer a range of questions in the hope of winning a holiday in Spain, Italy or Greece. The longer they stayed in the game, the further they went and the bigger the prizes. Sammy was so good he had to be bought out with a round the world holiday, new shoes, household items and a brand new British Leyland Mini car. But his downfall was his lack of social skills.

 Andy and I would often sit by the windows in Sammy's class. Whenever he wasn't watching, one of us would jump out the window, walk around the building and come back into the class.

"Where have you been, boy?"

"Toilet Sir, you said I could go"

Sammy looked confused behind his thick NHS glasses. He would often grunt something unintelligible and slink back into whatever book he was reading. Within minutes the process would be repeated again, and again. Quite often we would go into his desk drawer and take out his drawing pins before he arrived in class or at any opportunity when he had left the room. The pins would be placed on the seat of his chair or spread on the floor creating a defensive barrier in front of our desks. If Sammy came to get us, the drawing pins would go through his thin slippers and into his feet. Of course we would deny any knowledge but as daft as some teachers were, they weren't so daft as to let us get away with it. Whoosh, Whoosh!

 Harry Hawkins was our music teacher, I can't recall why we called him Harry, it wasn't his name but it was what we called him. I think we were in our second year when Harry introduced a student teacher to us. This poor soul was to train under Harry for his practical assessment. 12 weeks later he was to be tested and then assessed during our lesson. Yep, you know it couldn't end well.

The lesson prior to his assessment, we were allowed to bring in our own vinyl records to play. I brought in Never Mind The Bollocks Here's The Sex Pistols. David Hunter brought an ELO album.Someone else had Queen. Other records were brought in but the record player had been commandeered and that was it, we were playing the Pistols.

"Remember now boys, during our next lesson there will be an assessor present. You have had your fun today, please just be good for one lesson."

A couple of days later and the student teacher appeared with his assessor. Our whole class lined up in single file outside the music room, hardly a sound was made as we were led into the class and took our seats. The assessor took up a chair to the back of the class and our lesson began.

A full 5 or 10 minutes passed before notes were needed to be written on the blackboard behind our teacher. As soon as he turned around Andy and I swapped seats almost without making a sound. Behind us, a sheet of paper was turned and notes furiously scrawled onto an A4 pad.

Something was wrong. It was obvious in his nervous voice and the way his eyes darted about the class that he knew something was wrong, but still the student teacher continued bravely with his lesson. We all sat nonchalantly soaking up every word he said. We were a dream class. He turned once more to the blackboard and immediately 5 or 6 other kids swapped seats. When he turned back the confusion, anger and frustration were obvious. Behind us, the assessor's pen ran over and over his page, hastily scribbling his disdain for what was happening in front of him.

The third and final time he turned to the blackboard all hell broke out. Behind him, 8 or 9 boys had all piled onto the same 2 seats. As the would be teacher looked back, he was greeted with host of angelic, smiling faces. Butter wouldn't melt in our mouths. The assessor threw his pad into his briefcase and stormed out of the room, closely followed by the student teacher.

"You lot, stay here, don't move. I will be back!"

We never saw him again.

It was through Andy that I met my first girlfriend, Lynn. I had only ever asked one other girl out, a member of the GNTC (Girls Nautical Training Corps) which was Sea Cadets for girls. we had become quite friendly and asked her to go on a date,she agreed and gave me her address. When I arrived the following Saturday night to take her to the 'pictures', or cinema as some people call it, her mother told me she had already gone out with her boyfriend. I was gutted. Even Smiley Robinson, an older cadet who once fancied my Sister Anne, had better luck than that, he was actually dating Jo Brown, though when I met him on a 193 bus a few years later holding what I thought was an imitation hook, he told me how he'd played away from home, Jo found out and cut his hand off. I had only known one other person with a false hand, a young lad I met on a cub Scout camp. He had lost it when he was about 2 years old. His father had a butcher's shop and one day the little lad decided to put his hand in the mincing machine. Smiley wasn't so lucky after all.

Andy had met Lynn at the fair in Central Park, Harold Hill. They hung out together for a couple of weeks but Andy fancied her mate Debbie, and so said that I could date Lynn if I wanted. I was 12 years old and never had a girlfriend. What did you do with one? I had no idea, but I wanted to grow up quick and having a girlfriend was the way to do it. I had tried once, after my experience with Heather in our sex education class, to impress a couple of other girls. My classmate Nigel and I were probably 7 or 8 at the time,we were drawing one day, opposite 2 female classmates. Nigel told them to "Look under the table, I've got something for you". Intrigued, I looked too only to see Nigel holding his shorts open and his little ding-a-ling dangling in the shade. The girls chuckled, I thought they were impressed and so I thought I'd try it.

"I've got something too" I proudly stated, however, this time the girls responded with a unanimous "Urgh!" I didn't know why they chuckled at Nigel's and recoiled at the sight of mine, The only difference was that I'd been circumcised and he hadn't, maybe that was it, maybe I'd never be attractive to girls because I had been butchered. Things like that play on a boys' mind when he's little.

Lynn and I would meet up out and about at weekends at first, and then after school during the weeks that followed. When we were alone we kissed and fumbled.

"Use your tongue" Lynn said, "when you kiss me put your tongue in my mouth and move it around."

I did as I was told, I was growing up.

"Ouch!" That was obviously not how to undo a bra. "Have you never done this before?"

"Yes, but.." I lied.

By the time we finally got to be alone together indoors, I was ready. I was going to have sex for the first time in my life, if of course, you exclude those times I had woken up with wet pyjamas, courtesy of some very vivid dreams involving Cleopatra or Fenella Fielding on a chaise longue, and boy that woman could smoke.

We fumbled around with each other and eventually were ready to go. She laid on the sofa, her clothing undone, skirt about her waist. I laid on top and, well, laid on top. After a few minutes she asked if I was going to start pumping. "Pumping?" … I didn't even know she was sinking.

I Wonder

Have you ever stopped to wonder,
Sometimes where you're going,
Sometimes where you come from
Sometimes what you're doing?
Do you ever see the faces
Wonder if they see you
Wonder if they love you
Or wonder if you love them too?
Have you ever had to cry love?
Cry when you're only faking
Cry when your love is fading
Cry when your heart is breaking?
Do you ever feel you need me
Do you ever say you're sorry
Do you ever really feel me?
A river of tears for every lonely heart
Leaving me now you'll tear my world apart
But only if you leave me,
Only if you leave me.
Have you never tasted madness
Never let your soul go
Ever lost your memory
Ever found you just don't know?
Do you ever feel the pressure
Do you never let your feelings go
Ever had too much too soon
Ever felt you don't belong?
A million miles could change your world
Give you a chance that you deserve
But only if you take it
Only if you make it .

At The Edge

I was 12 years old, it was 1977 and the Sex Pistols came crashing into our home. I stared in amazement as I watched the Bill Grundy interview, captivated by the incredible noise that was Pretty Vacant. I had no idea what this was but I liked it. I had spent years sitting alone in the living room playing my parents records. I would play them again and again, catalogue them, set them out in order in their racks. Lord Rockingham's XI, The Shadows, Dave Dee Dozy Beaky Mick and Tich, Elvis, Judge Dread, Tom Jones, Bill Haley, Chuck Berry, Valerie Mitchell, all the musical education I could have needed. But this was new, this was nothing like anything I had ever heard before and I absolutely loved it.

It wasn't long before Les came home clutching Pretty Vacant and a Ramones single. He placed the records on the turntable and turned the volume up to the max. I watched in horror as he threw himself around the room, twisting, gyrating, bouncing up and down, off the sofa, off the walls, his head banging around uncontrollably. I was finally convinced that my big brother had lost the plot, he had cracked and as happy as it may have made me, Mum and Dad were going to be really mad.

The following day I found myself alone in the house and feeling inquisitive. I borrowed Leslies records and turned the volume to earbleed, back in 1977 earbleed was about the same level as an alarm clock, the metal wind up type that would scare you shitless from your slumber. I pressed the play button and as Steve Jones' guitar introduced the song I leaped in the air, drums crashed as I bounced off the furniture and screamed like I had any clue what John Lydon was saying. There was no turning back, I had discovered an adrenalin high I had never before known and I wanted more, much more, I wanted all of it. Sheena is a Punk rocker and so the fuck am I!

It was a good job Les had bought those records, I had no idea where to get them, they would just appear from time to time in the house. Now I could fully indulge myself in this new sound. Meaty, Andy Nunn and Mark Norris were all getting into it too. We would watch Top Of The Pops, talk about new releases and discover Smash Hits magazine. Punk Rock was sweeping the nation's youth and we were loving it. Everything that was before was now old and irrelevant, Punk was new, fresh and the voice of a generation. Not exactly our generation, we were too young, too middle class and from out in the shires, we were not the urban rats we aspired to be, but we were working on it.

Back at school, tensions were growing. As we grew from boys to boys with urges, desires and pubic hair, our playtimes grew more aggressive. Someone had found a bed sheet on the roof of the music room. It was brought down into the playground and use to throw boys up into the air. It was a great rush and everyone was laughing until one boy was thrown upwards and the call went out to let go of the sheet. The boy crashed to the tarmac and was carried off to the school nurse. The Deputy head came out and confiscated the sheet. As he turned around someone threw a ball at his head and before we knew it, all balls were confiscated. There was a great uproar and a hail of balls and stones were thrown at the staff as they retreated into the school hall. Once inside the teachers looked out of the windows watching for the perpetrators, their faces against the glass became targets for a barrage of stones. Windows of all sizes smashed and each time a member of staff appeared another hail of stones greeted them. Finally one kid picked up a huge piece of concrete and in full view of the staff, launched it from his chest. There was an almighty crash and the whole window frame fell into the hall. Within minutes, the Police arrived and kids were rounded up. For a very short time, we had ruled the playground, it was ours, and we were fearless.

News of our semi riot spread to other schools, talk was circulated of fights with other schools being imminent. They were coming this day or that. Some kids carried knives, others had sticks or bricks hidden about the school. One lad brought in a container of petrol to make molotov cocktails, but it ignited before he had the chance to make any, and he lost his eyebrows. School rivalry was always strong. Some kids couldn't get certain buses as they would take them past other schools we were in conflict with. Some kids made stuff up, and sometimes dozens of kids would appear at the school gates ready to go. Usually the police would arrive or members of staff would keep rival groups apart. For the most part, nothing would come of it, someone may get beaten up on a bus the next day or week, but full scale battles were rare.

My first proper punch up was in the park. A group of lads from the year above us took a dislike to the punks in the year below. Word got round we were to meet in the park at lunchtime. As we entered the park they were there, about 10 of them and an equal number of us. Naturally they had the advantage of being bigger than us, but we ran at them anyway. It was a free for all, fists and feet everywhere. I remember a big Chinese lad coming at me. All I could think of was the many Kung Fu films I had seen. I thought he was going to hack me to pieces with karate chops, so I jumped up and kicked his chest, punching his large round face on my way down. It all seemed to be over before it began, Meaty and Wag had made short shrift of the toughest of the other boys, and we were victorious. We had beaten the lads from the year above and for a while we were left alone.

Lynn and I were seeing more and more of each other, in every sense. We would spend as much time together as we could. After school I would go to her parents house and we would watch TV together downstairs, rushing upstairs when her parents went out, her mum had a evening cleaning job. Her Dad would take her and their 2 labradors out in the car, one would go to work and the other 3 would go for a walk in a park near Brentwood, leaving us a good couple of hours on our own,not really a good idea, but hindsight is a wonderful thing and kids being kids-I still didn't have any pubic hair, but I had learned how to pump.

We had been out one Sunday morning, visiting relatives somewhere, we did that most weekends, the kids would play or fight with our cousins, the adults would sit around being adults, talking about things adults talk about when their kids are throttling each other out in the garden.

"She started it!" Became one of my most used sayings.

"It was him!" *Prove it….*

Dad pulled the car up outside our house, close to the kerb he had barely put the handbrake on when the near side doors flew open. Over the road, Brian and his daughters were in their front garden. Seeing them, Joanne leapt out onto the grass and ran run around the back of the car. I was already out and by the gate when I heard it, the screech of tyres, the immediate sense of time in slow motion. I can still see the image to this day. Joanne's body, flying like a dejected ragdoll through the air, arms and legs unnaturally bent and flailing, moving slowly out of sight beyond the car parked in front of ours. She hit the tarmac and bounced, hitting it again, I saw through the next space as she came to a stop.

There were clouds of smoke,tyres had screeched and rubber burned hard on the road as one car after another stopped without warning. And the screams. There were so many different screams.

"Joanne!"

"Jo, no- not my baby!"

The sounds of my neighbourhood came flooding back. Time sped back up to normal and I ran out of the gate. It was a race to get to her first. Everybody else seemed to get there first and I didn't know what to do. Neighbours appeared from all around calling- "I've rung for an ambulance."

I didn't know what to do. Anne and Mum were with Joanne, Dad had the poor driver that she ran out in front of, by his throat, and I was told to put the kettle on. I dutifully went into the kitchen and put the kettle on. I mentally calculated how many neighbours and family would be needing a cup and decided that 12 was a good number. I lined the cups up and threw in the tea bags.

"Sugar....?" I paused, "How many want sugar?" I looked at the bag of sugar on the kitchen top and found no answer. Tears ran down my face as the reality of what had just happened sank in. I'd made 12 cups of tea and the ambulance was pulling away already, I should have only made 3.

Joanne was kept in hospital for a couple of weeks, her leg was broken but she was going to survive. Unlike me, I was late for a date and you know that never ends well.

It was about this time that Lynn became pregnant. I didn't know what to do, so I acted like it wasn't happening. Days turned into weeks,and suddenly it was pretty urgent.

"You stupid bastard." Mum had a way with words.

"It's not my fault, I ......"

It was my fault. I may not of had any pubes but I had definitely finished firing blanks. We left it as long as we could before telling anyone, and Mum was first. She made arrangements to see Lynn's parents and they agreed the pregnancy had to be terminated. We had no say, and to make things worse, we were not allowed to see each other again, ever. I was an animal, a vile despicable monster and I was never to see their daughter again. My own parents hated me. I was the black sheep of the family, an embarrassment. I was a child playing at being grown-up's, and my success was my failure. I was punished, shunned and despised. Lonely and all on my own to work it out. I spent hours wondering what I had done wrong. I knew we were too young to be doing what we did, but we were just 13 years old, kids. Everybody is a kid at some point, some stay that way longer than others, some grow up quick, some never do. I was having to process so much stuff mentally, trying to work out what was what. My life, my family, my world, the universe, God. Hell, if God really existed, why was he punishing me? But what if, what if?

I somehow found a train of thought that lead me to a realisation I have carried with me forever since.

An amoeba can have no comprehension of a double decker bus.

Think about it, something the size of an amoeba, a single cell life form, simply cannot understand what a double deck bus is, it is just too vast, too big for it to see or know, but yet it can live amongst it in it's ignorance. Just as we live on our planet, in our solar system, a little speck in the entire universe.

So what if, what if this big wide expanse isn't as big after all? What if this world was just a tiny dot, a blood cell in amongst the millions of blood cells in the vein of a little boy, sitting alone in his bedroom, not understanding the world around him? What if?

We wanted to be together, especially now, after the termination. Lynn was grounded, I was grounded. Life seemed to be pretty colourless for a while. Being denied, being ignored, being blamed for being alive when being alive was being denied. Guilt, shame and remorse were my only company, I had no-one I could to talk to. I was a randy little kid who knew no better, I had no way of dealing with the consequences of my actions, I hadn't been prepared for any of it, all I wanted was to do as my urges led, to have sex as often as I could, to have fun, to live and be left alone to live in the only way I knew how, doing things that brought me the greatest pleasure.

School time seemed to be filled with lessons I had no interest in. History was all kings and queens, battles and war. I would turn the pages in our textbooks to find things I wanted to know about, things I wanted to learn. Things like the founders of the Anarchist movement. Michael Bakunin. The true definition of Anarchy as a way of existing. Not the bastardised, petrol bomb throwing rioters that the media talk about, but the peaceful coexisting, the godless, ungoverned, self policing Anarchists.I would read what I wanted, then stare out of the window across the playing field, wishing for that freedom.

It would be 3 months before Lynn and I could meet again. I would call her when her parents were out. Then we started to meet and I would walk her home from school just to get some time together. I would bunk off early and get the bus to her school. Walk her the 5 minutes it took to get her home and leave. Each day we would take longer, eventually her parents realised why she was always so late coming home when they saw us at the bus stop. Then one evening as it was raining, they said I could come back in to the house. It was a start.

As soon as I was able to, I got myself a newspaper round. It was my way of getting some money to pay for things I wanted, records, clothes, and and I was soon to discover, something called a 'Gig'. I had no idea that I could buy a ticket and go watch my favourite bands play, I thought bands only ever played on shows like Top Of The Pops. Concerts were what orchestras played, bands played in school halls, Working Mens clubs and on the TV or radio.

There was an advert in Sounds, or maybe NME, Siouxsie And The Banshees were going to play Chelmsford Odeon and I was going to be there. I knew I could get the money now that I was working and having checked with Meaty and the other lads, collected their money and bunked off school one day to go to Chelmsford. I had never been before, but I knew the train from Romford would take me there.

I walked out of the station and having asked for directions from the ticket office at the station, I walked swiftly to the Odeon, an old cinema and sometimes concert venue. The Gig was over 16's only so I had already changed out of school uniform before leaving Hornchurch.

"Can I have 6 tickets for the Siouxsie gig please?"

"Are you over 16?" Came the reply through the glass. Shit, I hadn't fooled her, even though I'd been practising for this scenario all the way up here I obviously hadn't done a proper job.

"Of course I fucking am, I'd be at fucking school otherwise now wouldn't I?" I pulled a packet of cigarettes out of my pocket for full effect, put my hand in another pocket and pulled out a handful of coins.

The woman in the ticket box smiled. Her red lipstick spread from ear to ear. I hadn't fooled her.

"That'll be £12 please."

Six tickets, £12. Let me just savour this moment, SIX TICKETS-£12. Siouxsie And The Banshees, The Cure, John Cooper-Clarke and Spizz Energi. SIX TICKETS for £12, that's less than £2.50 each.......

We arrived at the Odeon and joined the queue to get in, looking every inch like 14 year old schoolkids dressed up for the night, all around us were punks in bright colours, dressed to thrill and kill. Make-up, hair dye and and attitude poured from every direction, in from the streets,, in through the doors and into our given seats. We were seated downstairs, near the back, in the middle of a row. All about us were hardened gig goers, people who knew what to expect, what to wear and what to say. I loved every moment. I wanted this to be the rest of my life. The atmosphere and camaraderie, the sights and sounds.

I remember seeing Spizz perform 'Where's Captain Kirk'. I remember John Cooper-Clarke doing 'I Married A Monster From Outer Space' and then The Cure came on stage. It seemed as if the entire room was dancing, everything came to life. We were stuck in our row of seats and watching from a distance, but we could see everything, we felt every note. Louder than anything I had ever heard before, even louder than my Sisters scream when I threw the garden fork through her foot.

When Siouxsie finally came on stage there was a rush to the front. Security guards blocked the aisles and stopped anyone else getting to the front before we could even try. Frustrated, I jumped up on my seat and stepped forward onto the seat in front, and again,and again. I got as close to the front as I could and stood on a seat throughout the entire set. Robert Smith of The Cure was back on stage, standing in for the recently departed Banshees guitarist. The audience jumped, danced and delighted at the blinding performance. Someone in the audience shouted "Fuck me Siouxsie!" Without hesitation, the 1st lady of punk responded with a powerful kick to his face. His night was over.

It took me about a week to come down from the gig, and almost as long to get my hearing back. I had a new love in my life now, live music. Real people with real instruments, playing live and loud in a room full of people like me, people who loved the music, desperate to change the world, incapable of making much of a difference but trying anyway.

My life now seemed to be one of conflicting ideals and standards. I wanted change but was headed towards conformity, I hated war but wore the uniform of system I wanted to change. I wanted freedom but was heading for a career of servitude. Conflict and contradiction were to be a huge part of my teenage years. For my thirteenth birthday I wanted a party. I invited friends and family, neighbours and anyone else that happened to be passing by.

"You can't have any alcohol" Mum said as I gave her a list of all the different drinks I wanted her to buy. It was basically a check list of every type of alcoholic beverage I could remember, most I had never even tasted or seen, but I had heard of them so therefore had to have them. This had to be the best teenage party ever, it had to be because it was mine. I wanted everyone to talk about it for years to come but had no idea what that usually meant. The things people would remember parties for were the music, dancing, drink, food, sex, fights, vandalism, police attendance, vomiting and not being able to remember what had happened the night before, I wanted it to be remembered for the fact that we couldn't remember it afterwards. Contradiction was certainly making itself known.

The party came and went, a few friends and neighbours came round. There was no sex, no fighting, no Hells Angels taking over the place before midnight, like they had done with Theresa's party once, next door. Mine was a damp squib, a room full of freckled teens drinking soda and eating trifle, singing God Save The Queen, and Milk And Alcohol while rolling around on the carpet like epileptic penguins on a sugar high. At least when we had our street party for the Silver Jubilee the year before, Anne was able to drink enough to be sick on the street on the way home. There were no street pizzas for my birthday, no graffiti on the walls, just a change in the tone of my voice and few blonde hairs in my underwear. I was becoming a man, allegedly.

Most weekends Lynn and I would go to Romford market and buy her parents' fruit and vegetables for them. One of my schoolmates, Mick, worked on the stall. I would get our order and pass him a crumpled £1 note. He would shove it into his money belt and give me change for a £10 note instead, he was a good lad was Mick.

I had long dreamed of a naval career, working at sea as a radio operator, it was a way out of a life of insecurity. Travelling from job to job, working for an unappreciative boss, slave to the system. As a Sea Cadet, I rose through the ranks and eventually excelled. I attended camps and training courses. Sailed anything I could clamber in and out of, capsizing most of them for the thrill of sailing too close to the wind. Clipped by my harness to a trapeze wire, water rushing over the side was the closest thing to flying I could ever experience.

I had several times attended the Remembrance Day parade at the Cenotaph in Whitehall, as a member of either the Guard Of Honour or the Sea Cadet Band. I spend time at Naval bases around the country, at HMS Raleigh I had only been on site a few hours before finding myself, amongst others, firmly in the bad book. We were caught red handed having a pillow fight in the dorm and were marched red faced and silent, wearing only our pyjamas from the warm still air of our accommodation block, to the cold wind and rain swept parade ground in the centre of the camp.

"You lot won't be thinking you're so funny by the time I am finished with you!" Our commanding officer barked. "This parade ground is a full one mile around, and you lot will now run that mile, not once, not twice but ten times without cutting corners, without even attempting to say one single word to one another. I will make you wish you'd never been born by the time I'm finished with you-GO!"

We did as we were told, it was freezing and miserable but we had been caught misbehaving and the military machine didn't appreciate that kind of behaviour. I place one bare foot in front of the other and paced myself on the long run around the parade ground. Cadets on the whole were fit enough to complete a task like this, but some were clearly struggling after the first few laps. At the centre of the square stood our all powerful officer, a man used to dealing with naughty underlings, badly behaved cadets and trainees. This man knew how to punish and he had us lot in his sights. After five laps it was obvious some were falling way behind. The worse performing cadets were pushed and bullied to run faster and faster. I kept my pace, steady as she goes, don't burn out. I had become quite good at long distance running at school, so for me this was pretty easy, it was keeping the stamina, keeping to a pace and not pushing too far, too fast.

On completing the last lap we were each greeted with the same question- "You boy, have you had enough now?"

"Yes Sir" came the response,again and again.

"Get back to your room and don't you dare make another sound until I say so."

This was too good an opportunity for me to miss. It was a cold wet night, well beyond 11pm and this man was standing in his shorts and vest. We had only our pyjamas on but the fact that we were running kept us from freezing.

"You boy, have you had enough yet?"

"No Sir" …… Oops. Throughout my life I have noticed points at which I made some really stupid choices, and this was one of them. I could have said 'Yes' and been sent to bed. But not me, no. I had to say "No Sir"…..

"Then keep going until I tell you otherwise" he spat back at me. It was to be another 5 laps later before he finally broke. I had spent the last 3 laps alone but for a very cold, very wet, somewhat pissed off officer who would now take every opportunity to berate me. My legs ached, I could barely walk or even stand by the time I got back to the quiet dormitory.

After breakfast next morning, I went outside the canteen and stood near the row of telephones trainees used to call their loved ones. At the end of the row was a guy, possibly in his twenties, a man, crying his eyes out. Crying because he wanted to go home. He did not want to be here anymore, and I caught a glimpse of what my future may look like. I knew that by saying "No Sir" I could have made myself a target. As a cadet, we were given a lot of leeway, had I been a trainee, not a chance.

Other courses we were sent on involved weekends away with some of my favourite people, The Royal Green Jackets. These guys were tough, no nonsense soldiers and I had a lot of respect for them.

We were on a night exercise, somewhere in Suffolk if I remember correctly. Separated into four teams, the aim of the exercise was to protect our ammunition box, which we had to hide in an allocated corner of the field of battle. Each team was split into two groups. One to defend the hideout, one other to head out in the dark and capture as many ammunition boxes as possible from the other teams. I was chosen to defend our position and bravely took my place laying in cold damp grass beneath a tree, looking out at a very dark field on a very dark night. I lay quiet and still for what seemed an age. From time to time I fiddled with my rifle, a standard trainee weapon of the time, Lee Enfield 303, with a pocket full of clips- blanks only, live rounds were only allowed at firing ranges. At my side, a handful of Thunderflashes, stick like explosives that would light up the sky for a few seconds, just long enough to temporarily blind the enemy. I lay in the grass imagining the German Wehrmacht advancing across the field. I was ready and waiting for them, I had the element of surprise and could pick of my targets as they approached, 100 yards away I could easily pick them off, they would stay out against the night sky, silhouettes I could easily pick off and they wouldn't know what hit them, who and where from. If they dropped to the floor I could throw a Thunderflash and blind them so they wouldn't see me as I lay in the grass reloading my rifle. Or so I thought.

Bang, bang,bang, bang, bang,bang fucking bang went the fucking bangs in the grass no more than six feet in front of me. "What the Fuck?"

"Stay where you are, you're our prisoner now" I lay with my face in the grass. How the hell had they crept up on me, how did they get so close without me hearing, seeing or smelling them?

"Where's your ammo box?" I told them of its whereabouts and a number of their party were despatched to get it. There was some more gunfire and they soon returned trailing the box behind them. The group vanished back into the darkness. As per the rules of the game, we waited a few minutes before heading off to attempt to steal someone else's box.

We came across a small wooded area and were greeted with gunfire, all hell seemed to break loose with shouts ringing out, rifles barked all around and Thunderflashes lit up the sky. Partially blinded by a Thunderflash going off in front of me, I saw a figure standing by a nearby tree.

"Freeze" I shouted, and ran forward pointing my rifle at my newly acquired prisoner.

"You stupid boy" boomed a voice I now recognised as belonging to the Commanding Officer of the Exercise. It couldn't have just been a cadet, a Green Jacket or some low ranking officer that might have kicked me in the bollocks for a telling off, no, it had to be the highest ranking officer out that night. "Stand still where you are and give me that weapon now!" My bollocking and humiliation were public and total. Rule 1. Never point a weapon at anyone.

I was starting to realise that I may not be cut out for military life, I mean, the sailing was great fun, obstacle courses and playing with guns was pretty cool too, but there was always this problem with discipline. Like the time I had to stand by myself next to our Commanding Officer at the end of the night. We were all assembled in the Cadets main hall, the nights training over, a few words from the CO and then Last Post. That's how it always went, but this particular night someone farted and I could not stop laughing, so I was made to stand out front and tell everyone why I thought it funny. Our entire company, Port and Starboard watches, officers and volunteers, Girls Nautical Training Corps (GNTC) and Marines, all looking at me as my cheeks flared red and my name put in the book of Defaulters. I was a bad boy.

As bad as I was I wasn't invincible. Mickey Barnard, a cadet two or three years older than myself and from a rougher neighbourhood, decided one night that I was to be beaten up, word came to me earlier in the evening that he and a side-kick were going to get me at home time. I knew Mick had a knife, I knew he didn't need it, he could take me anytime he wanted, but this night was his choice. As soon as we were dismissed and I stepped outside I felt a shove, a kick to my shin was sidestepped and I ran, and continued to run, long after the jeers and catcalls had disappeared behind me, I ran and ran. I ran as fast as my legs would take me, as far as my pride could sink. I was a coward, a chicken. I ran away and nothing would erase that feeling. I hated myself.

Outside of the Cadets, I was finding new music, new politics, new things that interested me other than sex and alcohol. I had been introduced to bands such as Stiff Little Fingers, Crass and eventually Discharge. Crass had a totally pacifist outlook. Their music was raw, their lyrics were sometimes threatening or at least provocative, their stance was always anti-war. As was the same for Discharge. Their demands for anarchy and peace came in a musical delivery reminiscent of 10 megaton thermonuclear explosion of its own. Stiff Little Fingers were from Belfast and sang about life growing up during the troubles. How could I reconcile my love for peace and the bands I was listening to, with my desire to wear a military uniform? The two were not good bedfellows. I could no longer claim my punk credentials if I continued to uphold the system, offer my life to the system that would gladly take it and throw me into the maelstrom. As long as I wore the uniform, I condoned the violence, the killing, the wars being fought by people like me, to enhance and empower those I had given my freedoms to. I was as much a part of the problem as the Generals, the Monarchies and the Politicians who fed men women and children into the war machine. I had to choose one or the other, I couldn't have both.

My parents were proud of my achievements in the cadets. Each year at award ceremony time I would come home with a clutch of awards for sailing, five-a-side football, attendance, or whatever I had done right the previous year. I managed to get Cadet of the Year and a free scholarship on T.S Royalist, I could be good when I wanted to. By the time I was 14 I was teaching other cadets morse code and radio communications. I was an Able Seaman and could progress no further up the ranks because of my age. I was to tread water for at least a year, a very long time in the life of a teenager. I began to miss cadet nights, stopped attending parades and other such things. My choice was pretty much made. I was to be Nobody's Hero.

School days were mostly spent in and out of trouble, Andy and I continued to play up whenever we could get away with it, even when we knew we wouldn't, we still misbehaved. One day, Sammy's little mini, his pride and joy, got lifted up onto the roof of a building. Other days it would be left in the field behind the school. It was light and easily moved, and everybody joined in the fun.

Our school was growing it's reputation in the area, we would often attend other schools to put right some wrong or other. Sometimes other schools came to us and there would be a standoff in the street or playground. It was during an away visit to St Edwards, a school on the London Road in Romford, that I first remember meeting O'Shea. He was in the year above us, brought in from some care home or boot camp for the criminally insane. Everybody was scared of O'Shea. The lads in the year above us were afraid of him, he was a loose cannon, primed and ready to go at any moment O'Shea was the stereotypical problem child, a skinhead who wore white sta prest to school. Even the staff were wary of him. There was no fighting at St Edwards that day, some bricks and stones were thrown, a few threats shouted at a distance and then the sound of police sirens coming from afar. It was time to leave and we all piled onto the 86 bus.

For some reason Andy and O'Shea didn't get along from the start. They both hated each other. Walking through the corridor in school one day O'Shea punched Andy in the face for no reason whatsoever. Andy didn't retaliate, he was bigger than O'Shea was but had no muscle, he wasn't really a fighter. A few days later as we walked through the school gates O'Shea appeared in front of us and again took a swing at Andy, he went down immediately and O'Shea turned to me.

"You can hit me if you like and I'll probably go down, but when I get up I'll hit you back, every time you knock me down I'll get back up until you go down and then we'll see how tough you are then…." I snarled in his face. A change came over his face, his fist lowered and he almost smiled.

"You're alright you are," he said, and we never had a cross word again.

Last I heard, around the time of the Falklands war O'Shea got sent down for 'Life' at Her Majesty's Pleasure. He picked a fight with a veteran on leave, when the guy didn't play along O'Shea waited outside the bar and ran him down with his car. He wasn't to be freed again until the Home Office declare him no longer a threat to society.

Another school fight was scheduled to take place in Harrow Lodge Park. It was between us and my brothers old school, Abbs Cross. Between the two schools was the park, home to Hornchurch Sport Centre and swimming pool, as well as Maylands, an all girls school with links to both Harrow Lodge and Abbs Cross, we all knew someone at one or the other. Quite often we would hang around outside the fence to Maylands, chatting through the wire with friends inside. I knew Sue and Natalie through Nat's brother Paul Barwell, who, although a year below us would often hang out with

Andy and myself. They went AWOL from school one day and I was going to go too, but I got seen by my Art teacher who reminded me I had my O'Level exam that day, and he hoped I hadn't forgotten. I had and somehow managed to blag a pencil from somewhere to do the exam. I left at lunchtime but still managed to pass the exam with an A-. Paul and Andy went to the West End and managed to be photographed and can be seen to this day on the cover of a compilation record called Punk And Disorderly (Volume 1). Andy is the tall guy to the front, Paul behind him is wearing a dog collar he nicked from Natalie. With them were a couple named Teed and Pascha.

In the late 1970's and early 80's a deadly craze was rampant amongst skinheads, punks and others in the UK. Kids would hide away in groups or sometimes alone sniffing glue from plastic bags. Toxic fumes in the glue contained an ingredient that cause hallucinations or 'glue dreams' as we called them. Continued use could cause the lungs to collapse or in the case of one of the lads in our school, Billy Mitchell, brain damage. He got a little carried away one day and began headbutting a tree, he was taken away for a brain scan and I'm not really sure they found one. This was only a short while before he thought putting Sulphuric Acid in our chemistry teachers cup of tea, was a good idea, it was only her assistant's quick thinking that saved her life, she knocked the cup out of her hand and Billy was suspended from school.

We were hiding in a group of trees one lunchtime, quietly sniffing Evo Stik someone had brought to school, when we were called to come over to Maylands, Abbs Cross were on their way, there was going to be a big fight, today. As we got to the fence we saw no sign of anyone from Abbs Cross. About 30 or so boys from our school were sitting around in the sun, jackets off, sharing niceties through the fence with the Maylands girls.

"So where's this fight then?" Someone asked.

"Same as the other day" I said, "there isn't one, they ain't going to turn up". I sat on the grass and immediately laid down to look at the sky. I was still high off the fumes I'd been sniffing and quite possibly watching some hallucination in the sky above us. Conversations around me continued for a while and I lay there, numb and carefree until a noise disturbed the peace. Across the park they came, dozens and dozens of Abbs Cross kids breaking the cover of trees at the top of the hill on their side of the stream. Shouting and screaming they came, 40- 50- 60, maybe 100 or more, at their head was one big lad, a skinhead in a crombie jacket running faster and faster down the hill.

"Come on you lot, let's kill the bastards" I shouted and jumped to my feet. I took out a whip from the inside pocket of my jacket and flailed it around in the air about me. The other boys with me seemed hesitant so I lead the charge. I ran downhill towards the stream, screaming and trying to crack my whip. Over on the opposite side of the bridge I could see the skinhead slowing to remove his jacket, we were heading into unknown territory here, this was going to be a real clash. I hit the bridge running and was back on the grass now heading uphill, this wasn't good tactically but I had no time to think about that, it was hit first-ask questions later. The skinhead at the front began to slow his pace. Unsure of what to do he looked around for a signal from the others, they had all slowed down and were looking to each other for confirmation or leadership, nothing was forthcoming. Almost as one, they turned and ran back up the hill, the skinhead put his coat back on and ran. He was 30 or 40 feet from me, I was gaining on him. Still calling, still cracking my whip.

"Come on lads, look at them run, fucking cowards, come on!" It was about two or three steps later that I slipped, my legs fell from under me and I lay on the ground panting for breath. I couldn't make it another step, I would have to let the others chase them back to their school gate. The others. I pulled myself up and looked around, I was alone on this side of the water, I had charged an entire school on my own, just me and my whip. And they ran away.

Word went around the area and for several months I would notice other kids looking at me strangely, like they knew who I was but I didn't know them.

Growing up in Romford was never easy. There was always someone who wanted to fight you if you looked different, stood out or were just easy pickings for one bully or another. I too was as bad as anyone else. I picked on a couple of kids in school because I knew no different. I remember having a go at Robert Rumbell one day. I don't know why I picked on him. He seemed a little too effeminate and that was reason enough. We had always been friends, before and after, but I have never understood why I had to pick on him. It was as if it was just expected, part of what you had to do. I saw in his eyes the surprise and hurt I'd felt when I'd heard Mickey Barnard wanted to hurt me, I thought we were friends, Me and Mickey, even though he hated me and my brother. He was a bully and when I looked into Robert's eyes, I saw myself running home from the Sea Cadets, running alone and scared and I somehow knew I had gone too far. I wanted to take it back but didn't know how to do it, how to say "Sorry".

There were many times I was picked on, beaten up or threatened just for dressing differently. So I was a punk, so what? You're ugly but I don't get in your face about it. I was going home from Lynn's one night when some drunks got on the bus. They were in their 20's, I was probably 15 at the time.

One of them started and before I knew it we were swapping punches, I had his head at my side standing on my seat, my arm locking him in place as I punched his face. My head was pushed back and one of his friends pushed a stanley knife against my face.

"Let him go" he said. I froze. The razorlike blade against my cheek withdrawn as I released him. He stood up and punched me in the face. I couldn't retaliate as the knife was still being held out at me. These men were big and tough.

"Three onto one and you still have to pull a blade" I sneered. They knew they'd lost. As the bus doors opened at Roneo Corner they turned to exit the bus, I jumped up and kicked the guy I'd fought in his back, he fell off the bus and the doors were closed quickly. The driver pulled away and I returned to my seat, a hand patted my shoulder, behind me a sat a biker, a big guy with a long beard and leather jacket.

"Good on you kid, you stood up to them, well done."

The bikers in our area were never a problem, they used to meet at the Bull pub in Hornchurch and were never a threat to the punks in the area, those of us there were. Mods and Skinheads were different. The Mods used to hang out at the bike shop next to the old cinema down the road from the Bull, walking past them meant having to cross the road. They would often jeer and take the piss but nothing too aggressive. One day on another Romford bus a group of 6 mods began to take the piss out of me, they were emboldened by their number. I stood up and walked over to the loudest of the group putting my face right into his.

"Say that again mate, and I will rip you apart in front of your friends" I turned to the next one, "-and then I'll have you, and you and you, the whole fucking lot of you."

The bus fell quiet and they got off at the next stop.

A few days after the incident with the stanley knife, I saw one of my attackers with his girlfriend. I was with Lynn and told her to stay clear as I walked in front of the guy who'd been so brave with his mates and a boxcutter knife.

"Remember me?" I said, glaring into his face. He tried to step aside and again I blocked his way.

"What's his problem?" Demanded the girlfriend, telling him to stand up to me. "Why won't you have a go at him?"

I stood rocklike in his way, he sidestepped again and pulled his girlfriend away with him. Humiliation complete.

Dealing with skinheads was a different matter. The car boys would jump out of their motors, punch you then drive away, they would always run once they'd hit you. Skinheads would continue to fight until the adrenalin was gone. If you went down, they'd carry on hitting and kicking you. There were 3 main groups of skinheads in our area. Romford skins were a ragtag bunch, some from our school, some from others. Mark Burns was one them. An ex-punk he knew everyone and everyone knew Mark. The Dagenham skins were mostly ex-punks too and they were normally ok with us. Those that weren't, were the Harold Hill skins, they were nasty horrible pieces of work for the most part. They were not particularly hard, but there was a lot of them and they weren't the most intelligent of people either. Andy took up boxing following an attack by Harold Hill skins. He was beaten with a baseball bat and was in a bad way for a while. Something in him changed then, he started to become more aggressive as a way of defending himself, but it started putting a distance between us.

There was a fair in Central park two or three times a year, I would never go as it always ended in violence, someone would get stabbed or beaten up by another gang, it was enough to put you off your candy floss. Travelling home from Lynn's house involved passing the park on the bus. I could see the lights of the rides and would always look down to see if any of my school mates were getting on the bus as it stopped. I looked down one night to see an ocean of bald heads.

"Holy Fuck" I thought, "- I'm going to die."

Some of the skinheads looked up and saw me, I could see this wasn't going to end well. They began to kick the unopened doors and bang on the windows. 40-50 Angry skinheads were not my idea of pleasant travel buddies, nor it seemed the bus driver's. He put his foot down and pulled away without opening the doors. The sense of relief that washed through me was incredible. I felt as though I had escaped certain death.

We pulled into the next stop and were greeted by another gang of skinheads. The doors opened and I sank in my chair as they climbed aboard. I steeled myself for the worst, expecting a punch or kick at any moment but nothing happened. The top deck filled and a few more stood in the gap between the seats. One lad sat next to me.

"Mind if I join you?" He asked.

"No mate, help yourself" He was already seated. "Been to the fair?" I asked.

"Yes, we came up to do the Harold Hill, they're a bunch of cunts, had a go at one of my mates the other week, he was on his own in Romford and they gave him a good hiding, so we came to repay the favour, they shit themselves".

The next gig I went to was Stiff Little Fingers at Hammersmith Odeon, the same venue where David Bowie announced the retirement of Ziggy Stardust, breaking the hearts of tens of thousands of dedicated followers. It was only a few days after I'd been injured in a fight at school. My ribs had been bruised by a lad in the year above us, he held me down after a brief struggle and kicked me in the side of my chest, I thought my lungs had burst. On our way to the gig

Mark Norris repeatedly prodded my chest and giggled as I winced. My nickname was born out of this teasing, and the fact that as a little kid my Dad would call me Skinny Ribs. I was to be known from this time on as 'Ribs'.

I loved the energy of SLF, Jake Burns' voice rasping with angst and passion, here was a man who really meant and felt every nuance of every word. The music was loud and fast, the stage performance full of energy and aggression. This was teenage frustration, raw and in your face. This was my life, my love, my passion on full display and I never wanted it to end. The next time I saw SLF was at the Rainbow. They recorded a live album called 'Hanx' and if you just happen to turn the volume up as Fly The Flag ends and Alternative Ulster begins, you may just hear a solitary voice screaming at the top of my lungs "Ulster!"

We had started a punk band of our own, as most kids did back then. Four schoolmates taking on the world and we meant to win. I was elected singer, the perfect role considering my earlier achievements at Junior School. I managed to pencil a handful of songs and would scream them energetically into my £15 microphone. I had continued with my paper rounds in the morning before school and following the disappearance of my leather jacket, I had started working in the evenings with Lynn's mum. We cleaned the toilets and offices at the Ford Motor Credit Company in Brentwood. My jacket had been a christmas present, but after I painted the names Siouxsie and SLF on the back to advertise my allegiance, the jacket vanished one day. Mum said Dad had cut it up into little bits in the back garden and then burned it. I was angry and Dad and I fell out big time. I worked to buy my own clothes now and began to put zips and pins on everything I could. Dad caught me sewing zips on the back of my school trousers one night, he lost his temper and lashed out, perforating my ear drum. We stopped speaking and life at home soured. I was ignored, blanked. I felt dejected, unloved and unwanted.

I spent hours in my bedroom, playing music and making my very own tartan bondage trousers- just like the ones I'd seen down the King's Road, only slightly tighter. You know when you lay a pair of jeans down and cut the material around them, stitch back and front together and make your own trousers, yep, 2 dimensional red tartan bondage trousers, complete with continually tearing crotch built in.

Justin Pearne was our elected drummer, he couldn't play and his allegiance was questionable. He finally left the band after I confronted him in the playground at school. Lynn recognised him as one of a group of lads who'd propositioned her in Romford one day. I punched him on his head and rebroke the hand I had broken in a previous fight with Paul Lyne. Another six weeks in plaster and a warning from the doctor.

"Do it again and your hand will be damaged for life, it hasn't had chance to heal properly, and is already permanently weakened. Not more fighting, you need to learn to wrestle or keep your temper under control".

My temper was in need of calming, I knew it, but had no idea what to do. Everywhere I turned people wanted a piece of me, I had to fight back, I had to survive in this environment and survival did not mean running away. Survival meant standing your ground, believing in the things you stand for. Taking a stand to make a difference, create change.

Justin was out of the band and Paul Barwell stepped in to take his place. He bought my Dad's drum kit through an agreement brokered by Mum, £200, not the £1,000 they should have been. Andy was our bass player. He spent countless hours practising to play,his fingers ripped on the unforgiving strings would often bleed. It didn't help that he bit his nails, chewing them down to the quick, a habit he shared with Lynn, it looked painful and often would turn my stomach. Lynn and Andy shared the habit, they both chewed their nails like that. They remained friends all through my relationship with her, sometimes to my detriment. One night at Paul and Natalie's flat I found myself alone in the living room with The Yobs christmas album blaring noisily from the stereo. We had been drinking and I hadn't noticed the others leave the room. I found them in Paul's bedroom, all three laying on the bed, Lynn with her clothes in a mess and Andy kissing her. I pushed the two of them aside and laid claim to my girlfriend. Something told me she was actually enjoying the attention and wasn't pleased I'd disturbed them. I was never to feel fully comfortable in that relationship again. Insecurity would remain with me for years to come.

Meaty was our lead guitarist and pretty much the driving force behind the band. He was a pretty good guitarist and introduced us to another local band, Vertical Hold. They had previously been called The Nylon Zips, and we'd seen them play in a church hall in Harold Wood a little while before the Siouxsie gig in Chelmsford. We all became friends and would go to each others parties, gigs etc. Following my attack on Justin, I had stopped going to band practices. To be honest, I don't recall being invited to any and after a while thought I too had been replaced. I had heard of a gig coming up at The Windmill Hall in Upminster. Vertical Hold were supporting UK Decay, and our band was to open. We went under the name of PreMenstrual Tension. I busied myself photocopying flyers at work in the evenings. I must have printed off a couple of thousand and handed them out at gigs in London, as well as to other punks I met out and about.

On the day of the gig Lynn and I arrived a little late. PMT were already on the stage playing.

"Where the fuck have you been? Get up here." Meaty yelled through the microphone. I didn't know I was still in the band, I didn't know I was meant to be performing, and didn't know what the hell I was doing. We howled our way through an awful set of Sex Pistols songs and a couple of my own. Songs I had written on little scraps of paper suddenly coming to life in the real world, juvenile maybe, but mine all the same.

You're still a child, you're only 15
Still a child don't care where you've been
Still a child in their eyes
Still a child that their money buys....

Funny how I can still remember that all these years later.

The set descended into an awful mess. Someone let off a fire extinguisher and the rest of the show was nearly cancelled. Fred Previous managed to talk the caretaker round and Vertical Hold took to the stage. It was a great gig for us locals, when UK Decay came on the room seemed to erupt and fill with music and strobe lights. Abbo, the bands singer and frontman performed an amazing set. I danced my little cotton socks off that night, it was (to me at least) a total success.

The Windmill Hall is situated in the park at the top of a huge hill leading down to Upminster Bridge and Hornchurch. Opposite the park is the windmill itself, painted white it stands proud above the borough and could be seen from miles around. Upminster park was also the hangout of the local Upminster Punks. Kirk Reid and his younger brother Jamie, Drugs, Womble, Dogend and others. For a while I would hang out with them, listening to Adam And The Ants songs on an old tape player, drinking beer and wine even though we were all under age.

Jim, (AKA Womble on account of having had a testical removed) turned up one evening with a bottle of Southern Comfort. I had already had a bottle of wine and was keen to get drunk. He offered the bottle round and I had the first go, greedily pouring about a third of the bottle down my throat.

"Fucking hell," he exclaimed, "Do that again."

The golden brown liquid burned my throat and warmed me instantly, it wasn't a cold night but my insides were now on fire. I took back the bottle.

"Watch this, watch this-everyone, come on, do it again". I poured another third of the bottle into my stomach and smiled, a warm buzz swept through my head. I held out the bottle but Jim refused it saying-

"No, you finish it, come on, fucking hell everyone, watch him finish it" All eyes were on me as I swallowed the rest of his drink. I twisted sideways as a cheer went up, threw the bottle across the grass and then……

Often, people who have died or had near death experiences talk of a white light, of calm and serenity amid the chaos all about them. This was my experience.

My only memory following the throwing of the empty bottle, was of being aware of myself, seemingly alone, naked and horizontal as if on a hospital trolley, but I felt nothing beneath me. I felt nothing around me other than being surrounded by an intense white light drawing me feet first towards an ever brighter source. My arms were out as if crucified laying on my back and all around me was calm and silent. The serenity of this sensation can never be overstated, I was blanketed in warmth and love, shrouded with silence and could want or think or feel for anything. I was totally at the mercy of this feeling. Gliding ever closer to whiteness. No drug, no earthly sensation could replicate the depth of perfection in this moment.

Bang! I was back. Surrounded by noise and movement, like having that falling dream when you are asleep and you bounce back to being awake, this was like that but 100 times worse. I hurt. I hurt in my stomach, my head, my face. I didn't know where I was or what was happening, but everything was so loud and my head was killing me.

"You stupid bastard." Mother's voice stood out above the maelstrom.

"You gave us quite a scare young man" I opened my eyes and saw a nurse next to my mother. "The police brought you in during the night, we had to pump you out and get your heart beating again, but you're a strong lad, you'll survive, but don't be getting yourself in that state again".

I was released from hospital later that day. Mum took me home and I went straight to bed for about 2 days. I was worn out and totally oblivious to what had transpired. As I slept, I later found out, Mum went to Hornchurch police station and managed to persuade them it was better that the whole incident was forgotten. No charges were pressed from either side. I had no clue what had happened but was able to piece together the following.

After throwing the bottle away, I became very loud and raucous, singing and swearing like a trooper. I attempted to start a fight with some Rockabilly Kids that hung out with us at the park. Eventually, a member of the public called the police and a van was despatched. I was pinned to the floor, screaming "Who killed Liddle Towers?" and "Police, Police, Police Oppression" as I wrestled with the officers. It took four of them to hold me down and cuff my hands behind my back. My friends looked on helpless as I was lifted from the ground and thrown head first into the van. My final act of defiance was to kick a policeman square in the face. As he went down, three of his mates jumped on me, one sat on my head, another my chest and the last cuffed my ankles.

I can say nothing of what happened next as the only witnesses were the nursing staff at the hospital when I arrived. However, somehow I "fell over" in the police station, vomited and choked on it. When I arrived at A&E I was covered in bruises, head to toe, with the biggest swollen black eye I had ever had in my life. My heart had stopped as a result of choking on my vomit and I was brought back from the edge.

Alone in my bed I dream of our house. Standing on the landing at the top of the stairs. There are thick cobwebs everywhere, dust covers the bannister and the furniture is covered in white sheets, just like in the movies. The house is dying and we are all gone. I step off the landing but instead of falling I fly around the hallway, alone, drifting, on my own.

Wild And Wandering

I left school in 1981 with one O'level and three CSE's. Not a bad result considering my long periods of absence, not only did I break my hand twice, I also had the misfortune of having an ingrown toenail. This is where the nail begins to slay outwards and cuts into the soft skin at the sides. It usually infects and is quite painful but can be treated by having the nail removed and allowing it to grow back again. Each time I had this I could blag six weeks off school. On the third occasion I presented myself at Oldchurch hospital to have the nail removed. Once cleaned the toe would be injected on either side with an anaesthetic, this was the most painful part of of the procedure until it wore off and the pain of the operation itself kicked in. My doctor this time seemed a little impatient and wanted to get me out as soon as possible. A nurse cleaned my toe and just as he was about to nick me with his scalpel I jumped up.
"Woah, hang on I haven't had my jab yet!"
"Calm now, you're a big boy and I'm sure you can take it"
"No I fucking can't" I fired back at him, "I know what it's like when that stuff wears off!"
 Unhappily he prepared the anaesthetic and injected both sides of my big toe. I felt it expand, blowing up like a balloon. It was painful but familiar as this was how it had felt the other times before. Suddenly there was a sharp pain, one I wasn't used to. The doctor had cut a slit in my toe and before I knew it was ripping out my toenail without waiting for the anaesthetic to take effect. I let out a mighty howl and fell back on the bed. I could scream no more through the pain in my foot, I was silently writhing , squeezing the last bit of life from

the thin bed sheet that had been covering my body. The nurse came over to me and tried to console me, for ten long minutes I was in excruciating pain, but as the anaesthetic told hold and the pain subsided she was at last able to dress my wound. I never saw that doctor again, I don't know what became of him, but I hope it was slow and very, very painful.

I made good use of my time off by sitting in the bathroom with a bottle of TCP and a stud earring. Once the stud was through the middle of my nose I relaxed and left it to heal for a few days. Once I was ready, I put a small hoop through the hole instead, it was sore for a while, but it looked so good.

I had been accepted into Barking College Of Technology, on a bakery and Food Technology course. Having long since given up on the idea of joining the navy, I knew I had to find another career. I had done well at Home Economics in school, it was a subject that covered cookery, house-making, and all manner of life skills necessary for surviving the modern world. I don't know if kids have an equivalent today, judging by the lack of basic common skills and sense I see in most post school teens, I doubt it .

I kept my paper rounds going through summer and worked the evenings still in Brentwood. However, once I started at college I hung up my newspaper bag, never to return. It was time for some other youngster to learn the value of work and money, I was off to learn a real job. I did well at college, it felt much better than school and Lynn was accepted on the same course. We were spending more and more time together and that time was starting to have an effect on our relationship. She seemed to become more sullen, more aggressive and moody. She would have frequent headaches, and flare up suddenly blaming the migraines. I tried to ignore this but found myself getting quite depressed at the future I could see ahead of myself. Maybe I should have joined the navy, maybe she would have been happier with Andy, maybe I should just shut up and get on with the story.

One day in the canteen I started talking to a punky looking student I had seen a few times at the college. She told me she was in a band. I'd seen her boyfriend arrive to pick her up a few times,he drove an old bedford van and parked outside our classroom. She said his name was Sid and he was their drummer, manager and roadie.

"Rubella Ballet" Had I ever heard of them? I had seen the band's name in the press and she too was kind of familiar. Well if I get chance I would make a point of going to see them, and hopefully do a better job than when I went to see Joy Division -or was it Wasted Youth? I didn't bother checking the exact address of the venue and spent an evening walking around Liverpool Street when we should have been on Liverpool Road. A couple of weeks later Ian Curtis committed suicide.

I was quite poor in those months, I didn't qualify for a grant or a bus pass. My £5 a week child allowance was taken by my mum as board, even though I spent more time at Lynn's than I did at home. Les was gone, he'd joined the Navy and was loving it. Anne was due to marry and I made her wedding cake. I wasn't allowed at the church but I was allowed at the reception afterwards. I was still the black sheep, mostly absent and rarely missed.

I still managed to go to several gigs while at college, mostly in London, but also at The Greyhound in Chadwell Heath, I remember seeing Manufactured Romance there one night, one of my favourite bands, playing on my home turf.

A few of us from our area went together to the Rainbow for a punk all-dayer. A lad I knew at college, Dave got into a fight with some skinheads. They broke his nose and before anyone knew what was happening the venue almost emptied. I had just put my leather jacket on a pile on the floor and asked Lynn to keep an eye on it while I went to dance down the front. The term Dance is used very lightly here, dancing is what other people do, what we did was more like body slamming and punching each other with fists and elbows, a delicate blend of ballet and brawling to music but there were no steps, you just had to smile as the punches came and went. I took a few steps toward the front of the crowd just as they turned and took lots of steps toward the exit. Arms out in front of myself, I swam against the tide until the tsunami was gone.

"Oh shit!"

In front of me, from one side of the venue to the other, was a line 5 or 6 deep of the ugliest bunch of mermaids I'd ever seen in my life. Hundreds of skinheads stomped towards me and I was all washed up and alone on the empty beach. Behind me,every sensible person with more than half inch of hair was heading out into the foyer.

"Come on you Punks" went the call, "come on!"

"Come on then" Said a familiar voice coming up from behind me. It was Mad Max, a mate I'd travelled to the gig with. Together with Tim and Del who worked as security at the 100 Club and other venues, these guys were not only well known, but not to be messed with. Expecting all hell to break loose, I watched as the skinheads opened their line and walked past us, like walking around a solitary tree in the park, we were left to dance as they continued to threaten the rest of the audience. Max was eventually lifted up onto the stage, at some point soon after, he had managed to break his back.

During our Easter break I had managed to secure a couple of weeks work in a bakery in East Ham. RD Beautyman and Son had placed an advert in the British Baker, a trade magazine I had subscribed to. After a week on confectionery, I was asked if I could, or would stay on.

"You don't need to go back to college, you can stay here and gain some experience, when all those students leave they'll all be fighting for the same few jobs, who's more likely to get it, the one with experience, or the one with the bit of paper in his hand?" Rod Beautyman convinced me to stay, plus I was now earning £90 a week, I was loaded.

I left college with immediate effect and was soon presented with the problem of transport. So long as I was on Confectionery I was to start work at 6am, but Rod wanted me to help out on Bread. This meant a 4am start time and Friday night I would have to start at 10pm and work through until about 10 am, sometimes later on Saturday mornings. This suited me fine as most gigs I wanted to go to were either Tuesday night at the 100 Club or Sunday night at the Lyceum. Other nights I could go to other venues if I wanted, but Friday night wasn't an important night on my calendar.

In order to make the 4am starts I needed to drive. I immediately applied for my provisional license on my 17th birthday and began taking lessons. I was also helped by a neighbour, Lesley Maskell would get up at stupid o'clock in the morning and take me to East Ham. As I became more proficient she let me drive her car and winced whenever I crunched a gear or braked too heavily. Without knowing it, Lesley was giving me the greatest gift of my life. The ability to drive, the freedom that would follow could never be overestimated, it really opened up the world for me. To this day I am truly thankful to her for her generosity.

Within a few weeks of starting I bought my first car. A MK3 Ford Cortina, big, boxy and red. I was the happiest man alive the day I was able to remove the L plates.

The Ford was not to last long though. Bought for £70, I began to lose faith in it when the gear stick came out in my hand. We were on our way to the Lyceum one night, the car was full and I pulled away from the lights by the Bank of England. I went to change from 2nd to 3rd gear when it happened and I panicked.

"Put it back in and whack it to make it stick" Suggested Steve George from the back seat. Steve was Vertical Hold's singer and being a few years older than me he had more experience and about this sort of stuff. I did as he said and it worked, but a short while later it did the same thing again. I no longer trusted my car and sought a replacement soon after. A gold painted Talbot Sunbeam Alpine. She looked sporty, sounded like a tank from inside but had no room in the back. For a couple of months I was Jack The Lad, but the car cost a fortune to insure so I traded it for a Hillman Estate.

I had only had the Hillman for a week or so when Lynn and I went off for a holiday. I'd hired a caravan at Great Yarmouth and we were going alone. No siblings, no parents, no work. Just us, the beach and the bar. What could possibly go wrong?

It was now September 1982. Other than attending gigs whenever I could, between working and 'Going steady' with Lynn, my life seemed to be pretty dull. I wasn't happy at home, I liked my job but something wasn't right. Lynn was working in the bakery with me now on confectionery. In hindsight I should have not got her a job with me. It was too much. I had no breathing space. My life was going nowhere. We had spoken of getting engaged, buying a house, white picket fence, 2.3 pets and a caged child, maybe holiday once in a little while in the sunshine, maybe spend our evenings like her sister Sue, sprawled on her sunbed, or arguing over how cold the roast potatoes are.

As I drove to Yarmouth I knew something was in the air. I was getting down and disheartened with the life I saw around me. Andy had left school, left home and gone to live in a squat in Camberwell. He was living the life. Drink, drugs, gigs, girls and nobody to answer to. He now had a room in Earls Court, a basement flat he shared with Wilf, Tich and Danes. Me, I had a Hillman Estate.

Relations at home had gone down the pan steadily over the years. I had rebelled and gone astray, not led astray, I was an active participant in my own self destruction. Andy, Steve West (who was a one time neighbour of Andy's), and myself spent more and more time out of school. Steve had introduced us to a new kid at school, Adrian White (aka Chalkie) who lived in St Leonards care home by the bus station. The homes are now upmarket housing, but when we were at school they were filled with problem kids.

Adrian was a young black kid from the streets of Bethnal Green. He introduced us to Reggae music and 'The Herb'. We would give him our pennies and he would disappear for a few hours to the back street snooker halls of the East End, returning later to teach us how to roll a joint. The first time I tried it I was sick, but I liked it too, I liked anything that took me out of my reality, away from my frustrations.

One day, we were in the graveyard when Adrian ran over to an old lady tending a grave, he scooped up her purse and ran off. Within minutes the police caught us and we were all nicked. We were put on probation for 2 years just for being present, Adrian got 3 months in juvenile detention. If there is one thing I have never recovered from, it is the shame and guilt of that day. I have always struggled with knowing that I was a part of that shameful act. I don't blame anyone else, I was there, I accept that fact. Our parents had other views, and once they got together, we were not allowed to see each other anymore, each blamed the other and relationships soured, stretched and broke down amongst the finger pointing. The truth was, we were all to blame, we had all lost our way at some point.

I had also pushed my parents' buttons by getting a tattoo. I had just turned 16 and borrowed my brother's birth certificate. For a whole £5 I had a skull and crossbones permanently etched into my upper right arm. Mum went ballistic saying Dad would kill me if he saw it. She also said he'd kill me when I cut my hair into the punk Mohawk style for the first time. Whatever I did resulted in the same response, pushing a stud earring through the centre of my nose and swapping it for a sleeper.

"Wait 'til your father sees that, he's going to kill you, you stupid bastard-what have you done that for? You used to be such a good looking boy" *Yeah, yeah,yeah.*

After a few days of relaxing in Yarmouth, spending money in arcades, walking around town and hanging about in the cabaret bar on the campsite, I found myself daydreaming more and more. I was watching people around me, seeing how they interacted and moved. I became aware of having never really had a normal relationship. Never feeling relaxed or free, I had always had Lynn on my arm, always had a second shadow. After school, at college, at work, at gigs, at home. I was starting to feel a claustrophobic sense of panic. The thought of a mortgage, 25 years of more of the same, more work, more arguments, Lynn's migraines and me being told what I can and can't do.

We were in the cabaret bar one night and the lady compere asked where everyone was from. There was a big shout from most of the audience- "Coventry". The city's Jaguar workforce were on annual leave and had descended on Yarmouth en masse. She went around the audience asking questions and making us all laugh. On the opposite side of the dance floor sat a family of four. Mum, Dad and two daughters. The elder daughter had caught my attention. She seemed about my age and moved comfortably around the room whenever she got up. Whenever she did, my eyes followed her, watching her ease and grace, she was happy through and through, the polar opposite of how I felt in my life.

The next day we passed them in my car, a happy family doing things together, happily. Our eyes met and I thought I detected a smile. A smile. Nobody ever smiled at me, people swore at the ugly kid in the leather jacket, with his tattoo and silly haircut under the peaked cap with it's skull and crossbone badge I had taken to wearing. People sneered at the ring through the middle of my nose, the gold studs protruding from my nostrils, the dozens of pieces of silver hanging from my ears. Nobody smiled at me, not in my world.

I saw her again that night in the bar. I watched her as my stout went slowly flat in its glass. I saw her sit, stand, talk and walk. No second shadow, no black cloud over her.

"Are you OK?" Lynn asked, interrupting yet another day dream.

"Yes, I'm fine" I lied, "Do you want another drink?"

"Yes, same again"

I walked to the bar dragging my black cloud behind me.

The next night was our last night on holiday. We ate the last of our bread and soup and headed to the cabaret bar one last time. We took our usual seats near the dance floor, a place we could watch the show and observe without being roped in to the festivities. I looked around and saw that the family I been watching all week were not there. It was still early. I went to the bar and got our drinks. When I got back to my seat they came in through the door and headed once again to their usual table. I felt a wave of relief.

I don't recall the entertainment that night. Maybe there was a comedian, a juggler, a magician, King Kong in a Tutu singing "I love to love but my baby just loves to dance", I don't know, I was watching the other side of the room.

I remember only the thoughts in my head at the time. Why was I doing this, what is so special about this one young lady, she wasn't a punk like me, she was straight, she had her hair in a simple wavy cut, blonde and thick, beautiful in a particularly English way- whatever the hell that was meant to mean. There was something about her, something I needed to know. I was transfixed and as the minutes passed, the time to go our separate ways came closer.

It was nearly time to go when I saw her get up and head to the door.

"I'm going to the toilet" I said, rushing from my seat. I felt Lynn's eyes upon my back as I headed out the door to the toilets and exit. Beyond the door I was out of sight and there, right in front of me was, whatever her name was.

I went straight up to her. I had never had to break the ice before. Never had to chat a girl up or say something to get their attention. I felt naked and vulnerable, I was scared and fumbling for something to say I tapped her on the shoulder.

"Do us a favour, tell us what your name is".

She turned to face me, a faint twitch across her face gave way to a warm but confused smile.

"It's Debbie" She said, "Why?"

I had no idea what to say. Nothing. I stood before her as useless as I had ever been in my life. Nothing came to my mind, and I just looked at her sweet face.

"Thank you" I pulled away and headed into the gents toilet.

"For fuck's sake, you stupid fucking idiotic fucking useless bastard fucking idiot!" The voice in my head was not a happy one. "You didn't even get her surname".

A few short hours later, we drove out of the camp and headed towards the A12, the road home. It was a clear mild night and I wanted to get home early before the traffic got too busy. Just outside Colchester the car spluttered to a halt. I checked everything. 4 tyres, lightbulbs, HT leads, spark plugs,petrol gauge says we have quarter of a tank, man in the moon says"It's a long walk home-should have joined the RAC dickhead".There was nothing to do but wait until morning when we could call Lynn's Dad to tow us home.

I sat on the bonnet of the car watching the stars. There were millions in the clear sky, a shooting star flit across the heavens and I swore it was a UFO, I'd never seen either before but I would tell everyone I could it was a UFO.

"What are you doing. Why are you going home, back to that misery, if you want to change you have to make change, you have to do it? You have to make it happen, you have to get up and go. Why didn't you ask her, why didn't you tell her you wanted her, because you do, don't you? You want out and don't know how to do it, Andy did it, you can too. Call Andy, get out now".

My car had recently been resprayed. It took a few hours for the mechanic in the garage I'd bought it from, to discover the length of masking tape that had fallen into the fuel tank and blocked the filter, starving the engine and bringing the car to a spluttering halt.

I picked the repaired car up from the garage and called Andy.
"I'm leaving home, mate, can I come stay with you?"
"You won't leave, you're full of shit".

"I have a plan" I told him, "I'm going to do it, if you don't want to know it won't matter, I'm going anyway, I've had enough".

I met Andy and his girlfriend Tich, at Dagenham East tube station, as we drove to Great Yarmouth I told him about my plan and the girl who'd inspired me to do it.

"We just go to the reception office, get her phone number and I go find her". Simple.

Arriving at about 2am meant sleeping in the car, which was actually part of the plan anyway. One of the benefits of having an estate car was the extra space in the back. Andy and Tich probably had a better night's sleep than I did, as I was across the front seats with the gear stick competing for morning wood of the year award. We had parked near the beach and didn't have far to go far for breakfast. Hot eggs, bacon and beans, tea and toast, a veritable feast and it smelled a damn sight better than the inside of my car.

We ambled around the seafront but eventually headed to the caravan park, after all, it was why we were there.

"Can I help You?" the receptionist asked.

"Yes, I don't know if you remember me, but I was here a couple of weeks ago" The look on her face said yes, she recognised me. "Anyhow, I'm looking for someone I met here". I told her I had left my job,home and girlfriend.

"I'm afraid the office is closed until Monday, but if you give me some details I'm sure we can find her. Now what is her name?"

"Debbie"

"Debbie what, what's her surname?"

"I don't know".

"Ok, what caravan was she in,was she in one of ours or a tourer, we have 2,000 caravans but they are all numbered"

"I don't know". There was a pause.

"Alright, an address, where was she from?"

"I don't know, but you've gotta help me".

"I'm sorry, but there is NOTHING I can do, I have nothing to go on, I cannot help you"

Her words were like a kick to my stomach. This can't be it I thought. Andy led me outside.

"Come on mate, we'll sort something out, there's a pub over the way there, let's get a drink".

We'd been sat in the bar of the Iron Horse for about an hour, going over our options. It was decided we would go back to Earls Court, we could drop Tich off at Maldon on the way, she wanted to visit her parents. As we were finishing our drinks, a familiar face entered the bar. The female compere from the cabaret bar.

"Wait here" I said, before dashing off to catch the compere. I introduced myself much as I had at the reception office, and yes, she remembered me. It was a good job there weren't many people looking like me in Norfolk at that time.

"So I was thinking, that maybe you, seeing as you might have a bit of influence over there, might be able to help me out a little, I'll buy you a drink if you like, you know if you can help".

"Look, I'm not saying I can, but I find this whole thing very romantic and IF I can find anything out for you, I will try the best I can. The office is shut tomorrow, so go back at 10am Monday morning. If I find anything, I will leave a brown envelope at the desk for you".

I returned to Andy and Tich, smiling like a Cheshire cat, with a ring through his nose, studs in his nostrils and the biggest tin of sardines on the planet.

We spent the rest of the weekend driving up and down the seafront, shooting people with a pea shooter Andy got from a souvenir store. We went to watch an over 18's film at the cinema that Andy said was brilliant. A 3D porno, all I remember was an oversized pair of breasts reaching out to me, and a load of oranges bouncing down a stairway as they spilled from a brown paper bag. This wasn't likely to be winning any oscars anytime soon.

On the short pier was a tattooist. To kill some time I had another tattoo done. Andy and Tich shaved the sides of my head and we drank a lot of beer.

Monday morning we arrived at the reception office. I had begun to realise the futility of the exercise and expected nothing, but there on the desk was a brown envelope with my name on. Whoever she was, the female compere, she could have had no idea how much this meant to me. That envelope was stuffed full of hope, of dreams, of adventures unknown. It was the key to my future. A simple brown envelope, with 4 telephone numbers from the Coventry area.

We headed back later that day, not because we were in no hurry, but we were almost skint. We had to wait until night time to syphon the petrol I would need to get to Coventry. We stopped in Colchester and I found an alleyway leading to a house with a car outside. I stepped through the gate and approached a car by a garage. Just then I heard voices coming down the alley. I ducked behind the garage, next to a long chain that would normally have a big dog shackled to its end. The gate creaked open. Suddenly aware I was in the shit big time, I tried to tiptoe around the side of the garage but my knee collided with the petrol can I was carrying.

"Who's there?" A voice called out, "Hey you!" I ran as fast as I could down the garden straight towards a 10 foot high wall. Throwing my can over the wall I leaped as high as I could, my fingers gripping the top of the wall. For once in my life, the pains and endurance of military assault courses actually paid off. Behind me I heard footsteps and the deep gravelly bark of an Alsatian guard dog. I pulled myself over the wall and landed with a thump on the other side. In front of me was my fuel can, all was not lost. I picked it up and ran for my life back to the car. We all ducked down and lay silent as someone ran past no noticing the Hillman estate with the steamy windows. Once he was gone, I started the car and headed out of town.

We dropped Tich at Maldon and headed to Earls Court. I slept on the floor of Andy's room and met Danes and Wilf in the morning. Danes had answered Andy's phone to me a couple of times and did not look as I had pictured her by her voice, she was an ex-skinhead with very plain jane features. Wilf was pretty much how I pictured him, but instead of a normal Mohawk haircut, he wore his hair in two fans, always sprayed and immaculately coiffed. Andy took me round to meet Major at his squat on the Warwick Road. I could stay as long as I wanted, anytime I liked. The place was a mess, semi derelict but there was water and electricity, neither of which were being paid for.

I decided to leave for Coventry that night, but first, there was a gig at the Moonlight Club to go to. Just around the corner on the Talgarth Road, lived Lou and Claire. Andy and I sat in their room as they dressed and did their hair for the night. We went to the gig and afterwards I dropped them back home, then headed north up the M1. I had never been North up the M1 in my life except in my Dad's truck as a kid, so it was a relief to see a hitchhiker standing by the side of the motorway.

He was a teacher, his car broke down and he needed to get to Birmingham. I took him to Watford Gap services and bid him farewell after a quick cup of coffee.

Coventry was only 17 miles away now, I caught a glimpse of it's lights in the distance from the M45. Once in town I found a quiet backstreet by the city centre called Starley Street to park, climbed in the back and slept through until morning.

Next day I made several attempts to contact the names on my list. One girl remembered me and when we met, I could see it wasn't who I was looking for. Another, said it definitely wasn't her. The third never answered the phone and the fourth was a dud number.

Driving around Broadgate later that afternoon, I saw two Punk girls and pulled over.

"Hey, any squats or anywhere I can stay around here?" I asked.

"You can stay at the Punk flat in Wood End with us if you like, Rich won't mind"

They jumped in the car and directed me to Bell Green.

"You'd better leave the car here, it'll be safer". We walked the last half mile to Wood End in the twilight, I wondered what I had got myself into, this place was like Mardyke on steroids, big, semi-vacant and scary looking blocks of flats sat on fields of short grass, you could sense the abandoned mattresses and burnt out car shells before you saw them. In the shadows lurked fear and aggression, violence was only a whisper away, watching from behind dirty net curtains.

Rich Mulligan was the official tenant of the flat he shared with a whole posse of loveable characters. He was a couple of years older than me, totally colourblind and would often squint to see past his own nose. He was immediately likeable and when I asked him if I could stay he had no hesitation.

"Just give me £2 a week from your dole and it's no problem"

On my way to the flat I noticed the two girls in the back of the car exchanging looks. Mich and Anne-Marie were silently talking about me.

" I think Mich likes me" I said, "What do you think of my chances?" Rich laughed out loud and patted me on the shoulder before walking out the room,

"Oh I think your chances are pretty good" He was still laughing.

As it turned out, Mich did like me, a lot, and a lot more often than I had even thought possible and for the next few days, I had no idea if it was day or night.

We lived in one room, Mich and I, Craig and Marie, Steve Brophy and his girlfriend Belinda. Other people came and went, like Lucy, and Craig's sister, a 13 year old punkette Samantha sometimes staying for a few hours, sometimes days on end. While most Punks at the time sported Mohican/Mohawk style haircuts, Craig had his cut sideways, an odd choice but pretty unique at the time. Visitors to the flat regularly included Adam Bradbury, Dagsy, Colin, Pugsey, Little Tom and Munchkin. The list was seemingly endless, as were Rich's girlfriends. I had never before met anyone like him. He would spend all night in his room with one or sometimes two girls, go out in the morning and return with another, only then to see her off in time for another to visit for the evening. The man was a legend, Punk Rocks' very own Ron Jeremy.

In the bathroom a pile of filthy clothes festered in the bath, they'd been there since the Romans left and would probably survive a nuclear strike, as for the toilet, well, some things are better left unsaid. I sat in the living room one night and penned a song, just incase I joined a band.

3 Spires

3 Spires in the dark of night fingers point and voices lie

The Suns' on the rise it's oh so nice on the streets.
Sky blue city that looks so nice,
Lady on the horse won't you be my wife
Take me far away from this land I've come to know.
Take me to another land,
A dream I know with golden sands
Take me far away from this world I've come to know.

Rich's flat was a maisonette, a two bedroom dwelling with upstairs bathroom, the kitchen and living room were downstairs and there was a balcony looking out over the green to the front of the building, beyond the road, and just past the Doctors surgery and Fish'n'chip shop. My first visit to the chippy was a steep learning curve. I was used to London portions and when I was given the biggest bag of chips I'd ever held, I bit my tongue, stepped outside and showed Brophy my 2 for the price of one prize.

"No mate, that's the same as I got, that's normal round here".

What wasn't normal was calling bread rolls batches. I shall step back now and let you argue it over, let me know when you've reached an amicable conclusion.

If I had arrived a week earlier, I could have witnessed one of the cruellest pranks of our age. It is still talked about in some circles even today. Sharif used to ride his bike to the flat in the morning, leaving it in the living room for safekeeping while he went to school. One night he arrived to find nobody was home. The door was open and he stepped inside calling out to his absent friends. He went into the living room where the stereo was blaring out the Queen song, Bicycle Race. He looked around and found himself alone, just himself, the record on the turntable and his beloved bike hacksawed into a dozen pieces in a shopping trolley.

"YOU BASTARDS!".

There were many pranks played at the Punk flat. I was told only a day or two after meeting him, that Little Tom had died. Rich even took me to the top of a car park in town to show me where he'd fallen to his death, even the dirty mark on the floor below where he'd landed. I wasn't the only person to fall for this. Everyone had been told of Tom's demise at some point. Even Rich's Swiss girlfriend, Brigitte was sad to hear of his departure. She had been home in Switzerland for a few months and returned one day to the sad news. The following morning Lucy was in the kitchen making tea and toast for Rich and Brigitte when there was a knock at the door. Not knowing any different, she let Tom in and asked him to take the tray of tea's up while she finished the toast. The scream that emitted from the bedroom when Brigitte saw him was loud enough to wake Dagsy, and he lived at his parents' house 3 miles away.

I stayed in Coventry for a couple of weeks before going home to collect my clothes and personal effects. I'd written home to say I was ok and living with friends, before I left I told Mum I was staying at Lynn's, and told her I was staying at Mum's. By the time they realised something was wrong I was long gone. I took Mich and Anne-Marie along for the ride, we spent a night on the floor of my classmate Ray Collins' bedroom. Mich and I slept on the floor while Anne-Marie kept telling Ray that if he didn't quit with the 'Ten Fingered Bra' thing, she would beat the living daylights out of him. Ray survived the night but that was the last time I ever saw him. He was killed soon after on his scooter, coming home from The Greyhound in Chadwell Heath. Someone jumped a red light and Ray had no chance. I recently visited his grave, he is laid almost next to my Grandparents' grave in Romford. On our way back I managed to crash my car by running it into the back of a stationary vehicle. With no other option we bunked the train back to Coventry and had chips for supper, again.

Brophy invited me round to his mums' house to watch the evening news. We didn't have a TV at the punk flat and earlier that day a film crew had got a whole load of punks to walk around town while being filmed for Midlands News.

It was funny seeing all my new friends on TV, Lucy, Rich and many others looking a mix of bewildered and awesome. They only had a few seconds on screen but it was enough to make the walk to Potter's Green worthwhile. On the way back we decided to stop for some grub, chips. Brophy led me to the chippy and as we entered some other lads began to mock us. They stepped outside and seemed to be waiting for us. Sure enough, as we left the shop there was a gang waiting for us. I saw a couple of guys hiding in shadows as we walked by, two more up ahead, the guy who'd initiated it was off to our side with another, we were just about surrounded when one of them stepped forward. We ate some chips.

"You're in the wrong place, you filthy bastards"

The chips were actually very nice.

"You want to have a go do you?"

Brophy was hungry, he kept eating his chips.

"Fucking cowards!"

I threw my chips on the floor and turned to face my aggressor. He was expecting a response but hadn't thought I would have a pair of tin snips and a large screwdriver at his throat before his next breath.

"Take your little gang of boys back to the cesspool you came from before I cut your fucking throat out, and don't you ever call a punk chicken again, or I will come back and rip your insides out- you understand?" He understood.

They retreated slowly and I turned round to see Brophy standing there, eating his nice warm greasy chips.

"You dropped your dinner mate, but well played".

A band I liked at the time, The Exploited, recorded a song called Sex And Violence. It would have been more apt and true to life if they'd called it Chips And Violence because in 1982 there was more violence outside chip shops than any bedroom I'd ever heard of. The Parson's Nose on Corporation Street was a no go zone on a weekend night, even Pete Waterman the famous music producer and train collector, one time Coventry DJ, his description of Coventry City centres' "Rivers of Blood" was of the street outside the chip shop on Broadgate, scene of many a dispute between hormonal young men and women. Rich and I were waiting our turn to order when a voice piped up behind us.

"'Scuse me mate, but, you from London?" I turned to see a semi-friendly looking face behind me. He'd obviously read the bit on the back of my jacket that said 'London Punx'.

"Yes mate" I replied, expecting him to ask if I knew so-and-so as so often happens when away from one's hometown.

"You're from London, and you're here?" A wave of ugliness and faux confusion spread over his less welcoming face.

"Yes, I've just moved here."

"You're here, but you're from London? So why is it that you're here and you're from London, but when we go to London we always have people fighting us?" Like I was meant to be the font of all London based knowledge and psychology.

"Well, when you go to London what do you go for?"

"Football" He replied getting closer and closer to my face. I now knew what he was after and where this was going. Rich had already got our chips and I took the opportunity to step away from the village idiot behind me. I liberally splashed vinegar over my meal, before adding way more than my weekly allowance of salt.

"So how come…..?" He was starting to get really boring now.

"Well what d'you expect when you go to football matches? There's always fights between rival fans." Trying to state the blindingly obvious to this guy was a waste of time, he wanted a piece of me for no other reason than where I used to live.

"So I reckon I ought to be teaching you a lesson for coming here when you're from London….."

I pushed him out the door onto the street,if it was happening it was going to happen outside. Rich was with me, so I knew I had back up to take on this moron's so far speechless mate too, if he decided to do more than just sneer idiotically from behind Mr 'This is my town and I say who can and can't be here". He went out backwards and I was right with him, unlike my chips which were now on the shop floor. We faced each other off in the road, Taxis beeping as they tried to pass, black cabs and West Midlands Buses running behind schedule as we danced in their path. I clenched my fists and prepared for the onslaught but he was leaning towards me, his right hand behind his back. It was less handbags at dawn and more like wet nappies across the sandpit, only his nappy contained a deadly surprise. In the back of his jeans, tucked into his underwear he carried a knife. I knew this not just from his stance, but because I found out later from Mich that he lived in the same care home she was meant to reside in.

"His name is Jez and he's a fookin' head case" she told me,
"You're lucky he didn't stab you".

"Big man are you with a blade in your hand?" I sneered as we danced in the road.

"Come on then, you fuckin' cockney punk bastard" Probably somewhere, there was at some time a band called The

Cockney Punk Bastards, and they probably called their first and only album 'Come on Then', I doubt it did well.

"I ain't fighting you while you have a knife in your hand"

This shocked him.

"You wha...?"

"I don't give a fuck what you say or do, so long as you have that knife I ain't fighting you, and you're a fucking coward for having to carry it in the first fucking place. Come on Rich, we're leaving". Rich looked up from his chips and we started to move.

"You can't just walk away you chicken, come back and fight..."

"Fuck you" I shouted, "You're a fucking coward and you know it, I'd beat the living daylights out of you if it weren't for that knife, prick!"

I never saw him again after that incident, I did hear he got sent down for a couple of years for stabbing someone, but he deserved it and more for making me lose my chips.

I had been with Mich for a few weeks when one day when we were in town we bumped into her Dad. She was 16 and under a supervision order, that meant she had to either stay at home with her parents or in the care home she had been sent to. She stayed at neither and didn't want to.

"Are you coming home tonight?" He growled

"Fuck off, no" She replied, I stayed out of the conversation.

"Are you going to the home, and why aren't you at school-and you, who are you?"

"Just fuck off and leave us alone" Mich was not destined for a job in the diplomatic corps and neither was her father.

"I'm telling you now-I'm going to get the police onto you you and make sure they take you back to the home..."

We walked away but kept looking back, only to see him approach a police officer and turn to point at us as he explained the situation to him. Mich ran first and I followed. The policeman called and then started to run too. As fast as our legs would carry us, we ran across Broadgate and down the subway next to the big department store. Mich was still ahead of me when we reached the bottom of the slope and turned right, she could sure run when she needed to. I followed behind moving as fast as I could in my Jackboots and three pairs of heavily ripped,worn and soiled trousers, it was all the rage to wear more than one pair as they began to fall apart, us punks, we were way ahead of the game when it came to fashion. The copper was now at the top of the ramp as I reached the bottom, about 200 yards in front of him. I turned back round and hit the corner in full flight only for the world to momentarily stop. Everything went into slow motion. I was virtually frozen in mid stride, my legs spread wide as I hung in the air, my mouth gaping. For right there,on that corner I nearly ran into her. Debbie.

Our eyes met and for a moment I thought she recognised me and smiled. I thought she knew this was more than just chance or accident, this was....

"Oh bollocks!" I yelped, reality hitting me as my front foot hit the ground, frustration slapping me in the face as I knew I couldn't stop. The policeman was bearing down on me. I had to run.

As we lay on the mattress back at the flat, I tried to explain what had happened. I had come to Coventry to find this girl, without even knowing she actually lived here. I knew now she did, I had seen her and now I had to find her. Brophy honked up a huge blob of phlegm and spat it at the ceiling where it hung, threatening one day to come back to earth.

"I have to find her, it's what I came here for" I explained.

Mich got up and went to Rich's bedroom. For the rest of the evening I lay alone as Mich and Anne-Marie made as much noise as they could with Rich. Craig sat in a corner giggling to himself, he'd been out all day picking mushrooms and nobody was getting any sense out of him tonight. Brophy spent the night as he always did when I was there, slapping his belly up and down on Belinda's at twice the speed of light.

Suddenly there was a noise, the front door, and then up the stairs. I looked as the door opened and in flew Animal. I say he flew in because he seemed to be airborne and did land with both feet from swinging into the room on the edge of the door. Animal was everything you'd expect from a kid with a name like that, he was loud, he was bursting with energy, self assertive and full of life. We hit it off immediately. I had only just met him and yet I felt we had been brothers all our lives.

I saw Mich in Broadgate the next day, I had decided to go to London for a couple of days to get away from her and there was a gig I wanted to go to. She asked if I was coming back to be with her again and I told her honestly, no, I needed to find Debbie now and it wouldn't be fair. Without hesitation she punched me in the face, jumped on me and introduced my face to the pavement. She didn't take rejection too well, I had heard that before, someone had warned me about her temper. I didn't fight back, she was a girl, and now an ex.

Someone had the bright idea one night that we should streak around Wood End. At that time it was a regular event at cricket, tennis and football matches. Attention seekers stipping off and running around butt-naked in public either to publicize an injustice or seek short term fame. Without hesitation, we were all running off into the night starkers. Nobody paid any attention, it was just them mad punk rockers off their heads again.

Animal and I got out of town as soon as we could. We'd been invited to Burton-Upon-Trent and took the train, we also took the shopping trolley that had been used in the flat as a washing basket. We emptied out Brophy and Craig's crusty unmentionables and wheeled the trolley out while the coast was clear. At Burton we were stopped by a policeman 50 yards from the station. He wasn't a happy policeman, but we were happy he was just finishing his shift.

"If you two are still in this town tomorrow night when I get back on shift, I will nick the pair of you, now get out of my sight, you've got 24 hours to get out of town".

As it turned out we were gone the next morning. We were taken to Derby and told we could stay with a couple in their flat. She was a rather large lady and was also about 8 months pregnant, her husband, a tall thin guy was incredibly welcoming and let us use their home for the next few days. I cannot for the life of me remember their names, but they were the friendliest couple you could wish to meet, and if you're reading this, if you know them, then Thank You for having us, and by the way, whatever it was it wasn't me, it must have been Animal, I would not have done that, whatever it was that he did, because it couldn't have been me, I wasn't there, it was him.

We hit the town centre and because we were staying a few days, bought a sack of potatoes, a catering size tin of beans and a kilo tub of margarine, a veritable feast to keep us going while we were there. We also bought a postcard and mailed it back to the guys at the flat. The message was simple.

"I've run away and I won't be coming back", signed The Shopping Cart.

With our post and shopping done, we hit the pub and soon found ourselves in the company of -amongst others, Martin, the singer from the band Anti-Pasti. We were hobnobbing good and proper.

Then came some devastating news, Blitz, GBH and some other bands were playing in Digbeth the following night. With or without our potatoes, we had to be there. We thanked our hosts and the friends we'd made in our short time in Derby and headed over to Birmingham, leaving our beans and potatoes behind. The Margarine we took as we needed it back home. Unfortunately, half way through the gig, the plastic tub caved in under the weight of a dozen leather jackets, 2 backpacks and doubtless someone's stray boot. Margarine spread all over the floor of the Civic Hall. Punks and skins of all shapes and sizes slipped and fell this way and that, it seemed nobody could stay upright for long. The dance floor was like an ice rink on amateur skaters' night. If you were at that gig and reading this, NO, I am not paying your cleaning bill.

I stayed at the squat in Earls Court with Major, Danes came around and hung around a lot with us, she tagged along, we were close, just friends keeping an eye on each other, staying warm and clothed all night under a single sleeping bag. Major had moved to London from Loughborough, Leicestershire. He was always pale skinned, ill-looking, anaemic. He had just about the longest Mohawk in London and the side of his head bore the tattoo of an eagle holding an Anarchy symbol. Just before I met him, Major had been involved in a video role for The Strangler's. He was the guy with the big red mohawk in the Strange Little Girl video, along with a whole group of other punks .He was famous.

Upstairs were a couple of Queens, the funniest, most outrageous guys I had ever met in my life. At first I was weary of them. I had no experience of gay men ever in my life before, I had never knowingly met any, and had been brought up on a diet of homophobic hypocrisy, not by family as much as society in general. Watching Larry Grayson on TV was as close as I had been to one of these mythical creatures. Once I met them though, they found out I was straight everything was ok. We knew our boundaries, they took the piss out of everyone, every moment of the day and I was no exception, I was lauded at every opportunity and I loved it, I loved their humour and that they cared not for societal norms. Theirs was a life of fun and frivolity.

Someone had been out early one morning and stolen a bag of bread rolls from the doorstep of a shop or hotel. We ate all we could and the rest were thrown at passers by in the night time. We hid behind an open window and them bombarded people below as they passed by on the street. The Queens were particularly good shots at this, and would come out with the greatest of comebacks should anyone not take kindly to the joke.

Other people came and went, friends, punks, straights, druggies and dealers. I was making friends on an hourly basis and had no regrets about having left home, or leaving Mich. It was in the squat I first saw anyone shooting up heroin, smack as it was called then. It happened a lot, and before long I was helping my friends to inject when they became too frantic. My calm disposition helping to control their panic at not being able to do it themselves. Not being a user myself, I could see their frustrations taking over and talk them down.

We survived mostly on dole money. About £15 a week at the time, but most people had something else going on. Some were prostitutes, rent-boys, drug dealers, thieves and scammers. Sonia was a prostitute. A beautiful black girl from the midlands, she sold herself for money for heroin, so she could get through the day. The one act feeding and exacerbating the other. Which came first, the prostitute or the junkie? For a short while I looked after Sonia, I would wait outside hotels, make sure she came out on time and in one piece, she bought me food, drink and drugs from time to time. We had a mutual respect for one another and in another life would maybe even have been a couple, but not here, not now. I would get money begging, or from people wanting to take my photo, which happened quite a lot back then. All over the world were photos of punks in London smiling or acting up, sometimes posing for that extra 50p, £1 or whatever we could get. The King's Road, Chelsea was a great place to earn money from tourists and other camera wielding civilians in need of some culture.

I arrived alone at the benches and sat on the back of a seat, Danes had gone to Kensington Market with Andy and Tich. Within a few minutes some other punks took up the seats around me. A girl with long green hair sat in front of me. She put her arm around my leg and began stroking my thigh. I replied in kind, stroking her hair and the back of her neck, and although we hadn't seen each other before, it was obvious we were now very good friends. After a while we all got up to move on. I'd got a couple of pounds in my pocket now and was happy to go back to the squat. Standing up, I saw what I hadn't been able to before. The girl with the green hair was green from head to toe. Green hair, green eye makeup, green nails, green leggings and Dr Martens. I had pulled a fucking Leprechaun.

"I'm going back to the squat in Earls Court" I said, hoping she may have somewhere else to be.

"I'll come with you" she said in a Geordie accent. I'd pulled a Geordie fucking Leprechaun, the only one in existence.

I woke up next morning and immediately pulled my clothes and boots on.

"Where are you going?" She asked, still naked in my sleeping bag. I may have been a gent the day before, but I had no intention of becoming this girls' regular boyfriend.

"I'm going out" I replied standing up "-going to find myself a girlfriend".

She jumped up and threw the nearest thing she could find at me. I ran to the door and down the wooden staircase, plates, cups, glasses smashing all around me at she screamed "You bastard!" while threw just about the entire contents of the room at me. I heard James, Paul and Major all laughing as I headed out the back door. I spent the night getting drunk at the 100 Club. I don't remember who played or what happened next, only that I woke up in a large room with a high ceiling. Outside the sounds of traffic and beeping horns. Nothing felt familiar, my head was fuzzy and I couldn't remember a thing. I turned on my side and almost jumped out my skin to see a young woman with a pink Mohawk laying next to me. I didn't know who she was, I couldn't recall ever seeing her before.

 She stirred and woke, a smile spread over her face as she saw me. Whatever had happened, I thought, it wasn't so bad. Then she began to talk. I couldn't make out what she was saying, it was odd, I could hear her voice but the words made no sense to me. They rolled and rose, up and down, almost musically, it was a foreign language, it was Italian. I looked at the thick curtains on the windows and saw bright light shining in through the gaps. The traffic, the horn blowing outside. I was convinced, I had woken up in Italy, but how? I had no passport and as far as I knew, now means to get home. I was in the shit, properly, in the shit. How was I going to get out of this? I tried to communicate with the girl beside me, but to no avail, she spoke no English and I, no Italian. It was hopeless. Eventually the bedroom door opened and in walked a familiar face. Soldier, carrying a tray of tea and toast.

"Thought you might fancy some of this, man you were a state last night, had to bring you home for your own good" He explained, "Valentina here said you could stay with her, you two were pretty funny to watch last night, both pissed as farts."

It was another two days before I went back to Earls Court and the Green haired Geordie. Knowing my return may be greeted with flying crockery, I stepped lightly up the stairs listening for any voices. Sure enough, I heard them. She was in bed with James and she was definitely not crying over my absence. The relief was total, I was still a free man.

We had received a letter from the court saying the Bailiffs would be coming to remove us from the property next morning. We naturally ignored the letter and were rudely awoken by the smashing of the street door, followed immediately by the back door caving in.

"Bailiffs!" went up the call. Major grabbed a baseball bat but hadn't even got out of his sleeping bag as the bedroom door came crashing in and several large men in black jackets set about smashing the sink with an iron bar.

"Out, out the lot of you, before we fucking smash your heads in-move, you dirty fuckers"

I grabbed my sleeping bag and headed down the stairs. All around me was pandemonium. Bailiffs smashing everything they could, toilets, bath, bannisters, doors, cupboards. Nothing was spared, everything was smashed to little bits and no doubt we would be blamed for it.

I never saw the Queens from upstairs again, they moved to another squat somewhere and that was that. Major stayed behind to find another house to squat while I headed back to Coventry with Paul and the Green Haired Geordie-whose name we had discovered by now was Kaz. James had gone to find somewhere to stay in Hammersmith and in his absence Kaz had taken up with his mate Paul, a sometimes rentboy from Kensington.

Instead of going to the Punk Flat, I went to see Big Dave. Dave was an ex-biker who lived up the road from the Punks. He had a flat on the top floor of a block on Deedmore Road.

Dave said we could stay for a couple of nights or as long as we wanted, he was pretty easy going and I got on well with him.

The Dead Kennedys were playing in Brixton, and I wanted to go. I took Paul and Kaz into town and we met up with a load of other friends. By lunchtime it was time for me to head down to London.

"I'll see you all in a bit, just going to get my coach ticket" I announced to nobody in particular.

"I'll walk down with you" said Paul, leaving Kaz with a very happy looking Big Dave. Once out of earshot, Paul said

"Can you take me with you? I want to get some money from my Dad, I'll give it back to you at the gig, I just have to get away from her-she's doing my head in". I agreed, and once again found myself sneaking out of town without telling.

The Dead Kennedys gig was filmed for TV that night and was a blinder of a gig. Paul was good to his word and met me in Brixton with the money I'd loaned him. We stayed in a squat nearby that night, some other punks having offered us somewhere to crash.

I went back to Harold Hill to visit Paul and Natalie. Paul had got himself a scooter and we wanted to go for a ride but had no fuel so we waited until dark and went out to get a suitable container and attempt to syphon some. There was a chip shop nearby and behind it there would be plenty of used oil cans. We picked through a rubbish bin and found the best of the bunch, a 25 litre can with a lid and no dents or holes. Walking back to Paul's flat we were stopped by police in a patrol car.

"What have there then lads?"

"An oil can, found it behind the shops there, just wanted to put some oil in it, Paul needs to strip his bike down and we need something to drain the engine oil into" I lied.

"Theft from a council bin, sorry son, but you're under arrest".

Paul was sent home with a warning not to play with ugly boys that hadn't washed for a week, I was cuffed and taken to Romford Police station, given a blanket, a room with no view and regular updates on the investigation of the decade. At around 2 AM the chip shop owner did not want his can back. At 3 AM the representative from the council did not not want to press charges. At 4 AM the manufacturer of the can, a company in Germany apparently, also declined to press charges. At 7AM, I was served breakfast in my room and shortly afterwards, released back into the public, having been kept out of mischief all night.

I went to see Andy. He'd seen Major and told me he was back in the squat again so I went to see him and stayed at the squat before returning to Coventry.

Kaz had now moved on to Big Dave. They were a couple and for a short while, everything was fine. Dave eventually had enough and put her in his old Renault 4, driving her to her parents' house in Middlesbrough.

"She's your daughter, you can have her back" he said leaving her on their doorstep.

I wrote a letter home to Mum, telling her I was ok and had moved in with Dave. I now had an address she so could write to me. I was also away from Mich and didn't have to eat any more paving slabs. I stepped out of the Post Office in town, licking a stamp as I put it on my envelope. As I looked up I saw her walking past with her parents. Debbie. I froze to the spot as she walked by, smiling, walking away. Something in me came to life and kicked me into action, I ran up behind her and tapped her on the shoulder.

She turned to face me, a surprised, stunned look on her face. I looked back at her, not knowing what to say, and then

"Do me a favour, tell me what your name is".

"I told you before" she said, "it's Debbie".

Not only was it her, but she remembered me. The guy from the cabaret bar, at the caravan park in Great Yarmouth a lifetime ago. She remembered me, my face, my clothes, my pierced nose and everything else, she remembered me and right there and then, that meant the whole world to me.

"Come on Deborah" interrupted her father, "come along now". I asked for her phone number or address and she wrote both down on a piece of paper I found in my pocket.

"We'll be home later-about 4pm, call me then, yes?"

"I will" I promised, and let her go.

Instead of waiting for them get home, I called the number she'd given me, it rang and rang, nobody home, it was her number, it was her address. I went to Pool Meadow bus station and asked some schoolkids how to get to her address.

"I know Debbie" one girl said, "she goes to our school".

I waited outside her house for their return, sitting on their garden wall. In this day and age it would have been classed as stalking or some other infringement of somebodies' human rights, but in 1982 it was a real life fairytale. Debbie appeared at about 4pm, as she had said, with her family, the same group I had seen in Yarmouth. I wasn't allowed in the house, so we sat outside talking, on the garden wall. I told her all about my journey and how having seen her I had to leave home and everything else behind to find her. She told me she had noticed me back in Yarmouth and was somewhat intrigued. She liked me too but we were from different worlds. This didn't put us off, we saw each other as friends for many months. Eventually losing touch, but never forgetting.

I was in a charity shop a few years ago and came across some 7 inch singles she had written her name on. The records had belonged to her in 1982/3, they were her favourite bands at the time. I bought them and put them with my own, a little bit of the fairytale, a glass slipper left for me to find.

I first met Barry through Andy and Major. Barry had had an awful upbringing, his mother was addicted to barbiturates and would feed them to Barry to keep him quiet. Everyone knew him as Tuinol Barry. He had a short Mohawk haircut, a red rose tattooed on his cheek and the lyrics of the Sex Pistol's song (God Save The Queen), We Are The Flowers In Your Dustbin- tattooed on his forehead. I hung around with Barry for a while, he was a good laugh, and a nutcase too, we all were to some degree or other. Barry's problem was his reputation. It was believed he was as hard as nails, his tattooed face set the scene before he had a chance to speak. Whenever he was off his head on anything, drink, drugs no matter what, he wanted to fight the whole world, and would often let the world know about it too. There were a few times I had to calm him down before something got out of hand. Sober, straight, he was a pussycat and a good friend, but he wasn't scared of anyone even though, for all the song and dance of it, Barry couldn't fight his way out of a wet paper bag, as he even said so himself.

I'd bought a new car, £12 from Mike Jones, Andy's mother's boyfriend, now husband. I drove to Earls Court with a friend from Seven Kings called Rags. We picked up Barry and Andy and headed for Coventry. We had no money for food or petrol but managed to beg enough at the services to get there. At each stop there would be a race between ourselves and the waitresses for the unfinished plates of food. We spent a weekend in Coventry, Barry had brought some 'sweeties' and it wasn't long before I had to babysit him before we all got beaten up. On our way home, the car broke down in Northamptonshire and we called the RAC. Major thought it would be a good idea to make it look worse than it was so he pulled off the HT leads and threw them into a field beside the motorway. A passing cop saw this and pulled over. We were cleared, but I was ticketed for having no tax on the car, I would get a summons in the post.

The recovery guy turned up and laughed when he saw the car with only one lead on the plugs.

"If you put the others back on, I'll tow you home, but like this you're not going anywhere".

Reluctantly Major fetched the leads and we were towed back to London. There was nothing wrong with the car, we'd just run out of petrol.

I took Barry round to meet Lou and Claire who had a flat on the Talgarth Road. In no time at all Barry and Lou were an item and when Claire moved out, Barry moved in. I would frequently visit them whenever I was in London, we'd go to clubs, gigs and generally hang out together, we had some good times together. I always had a soft spot for Lou, she was one of the nicest people anyone could wish to meet. She had a beauty about her, and spoke with a well bred, almost posh accent. She also swore like a trooper and could fight like one too when provoked, she was a genuine person who loved her friends and would do anything for them.

I was heading back to Coventry and had a few hours to kill, so decided to go see my mate Paul at his bedsit in Kensington. I knocked the door and waited for it to open.

"Hey Ribs, good to see you man, come in". I stepped inside and he lowered his voice. "I've got someone here at the minute, but we're all done, we're going out in a bit but you're more than welcome to come in" he said.

"I just popped round for a cuppa, off to Coventry in a bit so I won't stay long"

"Yeah, that's cool mate, come in, I'll put the kettle on". Paul walked through the bed/living room into the kitchen and clinked some mugs together. I stepped into the room and saw another man half out of his bed. He'd had time to put his tracksuit on and introduced himself a little too energetically. I held back and let him know that I was not there for his enjoyment. Paul did what he did for a living, which was none of my business, he was a mate and I was here to see him while passing, I was not an added extra. There was a pause and his smile waned a little, then from under the bed came a tiny labrador puppy.

"Oh my god, he's so cute!" I said reaching out to pick up the little pup.

"Get back under the bed you little shit" There was a slap and a yelp, the pup went back under the bed, I went into the little kitchen to see Paul.

"I don't know who your mate thinks he is, but if he touches that pup again I'm gonna rip his fucking head off, I mean it mate, when I leave here I'm taking it with me".

Paul reminded me they were going out, the pup was staying and he promised to leave his key under the doormat. I stayed in the kitchen, drank my tea and left.

Ten minutes later I was back, the key under the mat got me in, and the pup was liberated. We went straight to Victoria coach station and on to a new life in Coventry.

Having the extra mouth to feed was suddenly a burden. I bought a big bag of dog biscuits and hoped they would last until my next dole cheque arrived. As it happened, the biscuits lasted longer than the human food and Dave and I found ourselves with an empty pantry two days before payday. We had become used to cutting things close, it was a part of life on the dole, running out of money and food before the next giro arrived. We laid in the living room in our sleeping bags listening to Boy's Don't Cry all night long. We tried not to but ended up tesing each other with descriptions of all our favourite foods. Starvation was getting the better of us. Dave changed the record, we had three at the time, Boys Don't Cry by The Cure, Meatloaf's Bat Out Of Hell, and Stiff Little Fingers- Inflammable Material. He put on the SLF album and I went into the kitchen, an idea had come into my head and I had to act on it. I looked in the cupboard and found a jar of marmalade, it was half empty but enough to act as a sweetener. I checked the ingredients on the dog biscuits, flour water and a whole list of vitamins, additives and other things I'd never heard of. I decided to grind the biscuits down, add water and marmalade, boil it and hey presto- we would have porridge, or something resembling it. There was nothing to grind the biscuits with except an old house brick we used as a doorstop for Spazzy the Pup to get in or out of my bedroom.

I ground down the biscuits, Spazzy wasn't impressed, nor was Dave when I told him I'd used his marmalade, and neither was I when I realised how disgusting it tasted, and the extra chunks of brick from grinding the biscuits in the saucepan did little to help the texture or flavour.

Spazzy and I parted ways soon after, I couldn't look after him and a friend Shaun, who lived nearby, took him for his sister Mandy to look after. Spazzy only lived a few short years, he was epileptic and was eventually put down.

Whilst sitting on a wall in town one day, I was approached by a couple of girls. They were art art students and wanted to take my photo for a project they were compiling. I say no worries and asked them about their college.

"It's called The Butts, and it's pretty cool. You should come hang out at the Student Union, it's a good laugh and you'd get on with everyone there". I promised to pay a visit and collect a copy of the photo they'd taken, and sure enough, the Student Union became a welcome alternative to hanging around in the cold in town.

Christmas was coming and I had been invited to stay with my sister Anne. Her husband had landed a job with a printing firm in Aston Clinton, near Aylesbury,Buckinghamshire. I packed my sleeping bag and headed off to London once again.

I jumped the train to Aylesbury and when I arrived was topped by an inspector. He'd been waiting for me following a tip off from a ticket inspector I'd managed to evade on the train. I was given a choice, £10 fine on the spot or get dragged off by the police and given a £100 fine in court. I reluctantly handed over my last £10 note and walked all the way to Aston Clinton. Anne was working in the pub near their house, she kept me in beer for a few days. Tim and I spent some time getting to know each other, talking about music, women and life in general. We went out for a walk in the woods, taking his air gun to shoot fish and rabbits, we killed neither but I did manage to shoot myself in the calf accidently squeezing the trigger without the safety catch on. It stung for a while and left a red mark, but no permanent damage.

I had arranged to meet a girl on the Kings Road, day after boxing day and had planned on going to a gig at the Lyceum the night before. Discharge, GBH, AntiPasti and others if I remember correctly, so I needed to get back into London. I checked with the bus station, there were no buses and no trains running on Boxing Day so I decided to hitch a lift. I left early in the morning and walked to the main road. Noticing there wasn't much traffic, I decided to walk a bit down the A41 towards Watford. Surely someone would stop and give me a lift, it was Christmas after all. I walked, my arm out and thumb upright in the usual manner but to no avail. I kept walking and walking finally arriving at the Lyceum about 8pm. My feet were raw in my jackboots and to top things off, the gig had been changed. The original line up had been pulled and replaced by The Meteors, King Kurt and a couple of other bands I wasn't particularly keen on seeing. I'd walked 40 miles and was in agony, all I wanted now was to sleep.

I'd met another Wayne outside the Lyceum, he was the drummer for a band called Riot Squad I'd never seen. I knew him from staying at his squat in Brixton and told him I wasn't going in to the gig after all.

"Me neither" said Wayne, "what are you gonna do instead?"

"I'm going to Earls Court, there's a squat there we can stay in and tomorrow I'm meeting someone on the Kings Road".

"Mind if I tag along?" He asked, "I don't fancy Brixton tonight".Unable to walk any further, we caught a bus towards Hammersmith. By the time we reached Chelsea I was in agony.

"I'm getting off at the graveyard mate, I can't make it to Earls Court and if I do, I won't be able to walk here tomorrow". Wayne agreed and we got off the bus, crossed the road and settled down in our sleeping bags between the graves.

"Wakey,wakey sleeping beauty, time to get up and be gone". I opened my eyes to see 2 policemen standing over us, it was daylight, and time to get up apparently.

For breakfast I pulled out a tin of new potatoes, another full of peas and baby carrots and a tin opener. We had 2 spoons but no cooker, so we poured the vegetables onto a gravestone and ate them cold.

My date never turned up in the end, so after hanging around all day on the benches, I went back to Earls Court and finally took my boots off. My feet were red raw, blisters on top of blisters had taken layer after layer of skin from them, my thick socks were caked in blood and ooze. It was going to be a long time before I walked any long distances again.

Later that day Major gave me a spoon on which he'd cooked himself a hit. I licked the spoon and swallowed the filter, within seconds I felt a warm waxy sensation in my head, my mind went numb and I puked over the floor before collapsing in a heap where I lay. I was out for the count. I had entered a gateway to another world, where nothing mattered, nothing except the desire to relive the same sensation day after day. It was infinitely more powerful than the white light I had come so close to in the hospital bed a couple of years previously. This was darkness, hollow, empty nothingness with only one way out. I lost that entire night to darkness, and I soon wanted more.

I had been visiting The Butts for a while and got to know many of the students there. I had starting dating a girl called Melina, Smelly Melly I would call her. She had dark hair and olive skin, her mother was Greek and her Father English. We were more like close friends really, never getting to the point of heavy petting let alone undressed. For the 6 weeks or so we were together, I hadn't even taken my boots off. She told me that her father would know when she'd seen me as he could smell me on her clothes. I always had a lot of respect for her, for some reason I thought she deserved better than me, and she did. Melina was a student at The Butts and helped me get to know everybody else there. At weekends we would go to The Lanch, The Lanchester Polytechnic Student Union, where there were always bands playing in one of the halls or an alternative, punk and new wave disco. I saw many bands here, some gigs I still can't remember to this day like The Sisters Of Mercy. It must have been a really good night. The Lanch became a regular haunt for me whenever I was in town.

The Sex Gang Children played one night and a massive fight broke out behind me in the audience. People seemed to be just piling on top of one another, everybody punching downwards. I leapt in and started pulling people off, there were dozens of them, all from out of town, all of them having a go at getting to whoever it was at the bottom of the pile. I kept digging and with the help of a couple of other people managed to finally clear the scrum, there at the bottom, side by side, were Al Cockerell and his girlfriend, Jill Phipps, 2 locals still having a go at the bottom of a pile of 40 or 50 outsiders, fearless to say the the least.

Through Melina I met Helen and Clare, two art students who dressed in the Rockabilly style of the 1950's -60's. I admired their style and soon became very good friends with both. Melina and I parted company, the day after I had her name tattooed on my arm, I never regretted it, we carried on as friends but never able to have a relationship together, that same old problem, two different worlds but only one planet, and I had not yet come to terms with relationships, I was perpetually insecure with a very low sense of self worth. I thought I was ugly, unwanted, unloveable and all too often, uncontrollable. Helen and I became an item and had a long on and off relationship. To be honest, I was probably a bastard to get along with. I was way too loose a cannon to be kept in place by anyone or anything. I was perpetually drunk, stoned or stupid in my behaviour but Helen would always accept me, always say "That's Ok" when I guess, I really wanted her to say "No, don't be fucking stupid, you're better than that".

I received a tax rebate out of the blue, £121.00 which seemed like a small fortune then. I said nothing to Dave, having virtually moved out of his flat by that time and staying with Animal and his mum. We had become almost inseparable and he let me move in following an incident with Lambsie one night. Lambsie was a lifesize wooden cutout of a sheep, probably a display or promotional piece that Dave had found and brought home to the flat (along with the set of temporary traffic lights he'd acquired, flashing red, amber and green all night long for about a fortnight before we threw them out the window through lack of sleep).

Dave and I had gone out for a drive one night in his little Renault 4. He had no tax, no MoT and no insurance, I doubt he even had a licence, but quite often we would head out after dark looking for mischief. One night we ended up at Corby Services and deciding to sit at a table in the restaurant I noticed a yellow tablet in front of me.

"Is this yours-did you put this here?" I asked him.

"No, what is it?" I recognised it as an Ativan, something I had had in the past, nights where I would black out and wake up in Islington with people I barely knew, for example. I quickly swallowed the pill before Dave could get it out of my hands, after all, he was driving and I didn't have a clue how to get home, let alone drive with the Renaults dash mounted gear stick. By the time we got home I had started hallucinating. Little people were waving at me through the gaps in Lambsie's wool. Lambsie was talking to me, her mouth moving up and down as she chewed tufts of our carpet and the breeze flowed along her wool exposing more little people waving at me to help rescue them. Lambsie was possessed and there was only one thing for it. I headed to the Church on Deedmore Road and begged the vicar to exorcise Lambsie. The vicar would not, and I daren't go back to the flat as long as Lambsie was there.

Within a week of moving in with Animal, I was at the doctors collecting valium and cream for my scabies. I don't where the scabies had come from but the cream saw it off, the valium was meant to help me sleep but was used more widely as a recreational treat.

When my rebate arrived I called Animal to come quick. "They've made a mistake look, they've paid me too much"

"That's a tax rebate, but if it is a mistake, we better cash it quick, before they stop it". With that in mind we ran to the post office and cashed our giro's, Animal had £27, I had £121.

"Right then" I said stuffing the cash in my pocket, "where are we going?"

"Margate" Said Animal. We'd been to the Fair a couple of weeks previously and met some girls from Margate. One lived in a pub run by her parents and said we were welcome anytime to come down, though we would have to stay at a friends house.

We stopped by to grab Shaun and Jason (Toady) on our way to the off licence at Bell Green. I bought a gallon bottle of scrumpy for each of us before getting the bus into town. By the time we reached the Inter-shop, we'd finished the scrumpy and I got 4 bottles of sherry, this we drank on our way to The Butts. Once there we took Helen, Clare, Lisa and a few other people over the road to the pub for a pint before we left. We were about half way through our drinks when the barman came over and pointed at me.

"You, I've told you before, you're barred, now get out of my pub" I had never been in the pub before as I rarely had the money for pub priced drinks. There was a bit of a fracas and before I could get out the door someone threw a glass at the bar, all hell let loose and we ran out as fast as we could. We went back to town and got more drink from the Inter-shop. Then headed to Pool Meadow bus station for our tickets. The students said goodbye and went back to college, leaving myself and Animal to be seen off by Shaun and Jason.

It wasn't long before the police arrived, 2 minutes before our bus was due. Shaun had been reported for urinating against the bus stop and we hadn't noticed him do it.

"You lot, up against the wall" ordered the first officer out of the car. We were searched and separated, interrogated one at a time.

"What's your name, Date of birth, where are you from?" The first three miscreants answered the same and were told to

"Fuck off home". I was the eldest, only one year above the others but enough to single me out for special attention.

"Right you're nicked for Drunk and Disorderly" With that I was immediately handcuffed and thrown into the back of the car.

"You can't arrest him" Animal protested, "He's got my ticket!".

"You want to go with him do you?" replied the officer,

"We're going to Margate" protested Animal, and just then, the cuffs were on and Animal landed on top of me in the back seat.

"You can't fucking nick us, we're going to Margate" I cried, they didn't care, they weren't going to let us on the coach like this, they were taking us in because of Shaun.

Standing at the charge desk one of the officers took notice of Animals long white pointed winklepicker boots.

"Do your feet go to the end of your shoes?" he leered.

"Does your head go to the top of that helmet?"

We were definitely not going to Margate.

It was Helen's birthday and a band had been booked to play in The Butts student union hall. The Screaming Dead were from either Gloucester or Cheltenham, and were an instant hit with Animal and myself. The fact that their bass player had his head painted green was an instant fascination for us and we quizzed him about it afterwards.

The following day we went into town and purchased our own green face paint, black eyeliner, lipstick and blusher. We perfected our look and headed out into a very unready world. In 1983 it was shocking enough to see people with mohawks, pierced noses and raggy clothing, to see people walking around in daylight with their heads painted green was unheard of. We were freaks, totally out there, people would stop still like they'd seen ghosts of those they'd lost years before. Some would grab their children and pull them in close, cover their eyes, cross the road to get out of our way. People who may on other days have attacked us, stood with their mouths open wide, unable to process what they were seeing. Even punk friends who'd seen it all before hesitated when they saw us. We truly stopped traffic.

The Screaming Dead played again, a week or so later in Worcester. Animal and I were there and we spent the night with the band after the gig. Next day we hitched home to sign on at the jobcentre, still painted green.

There was a coach trip to London coming up. It had been organised by an Alternative Clothes' shop on Far Gosford Street. We had our tickets and were duly painted green for the occasion. Unfortunately we were so drunk that the coach driver threatened to leave us on the hard shoulder of the M1.

Someone intervened on our part and we were taken to a nightclub somewhere in the West End. I recall being in the doorway arguing to be let in, I was on my knees with the doormans' kneecap between my teeth. Animal pulled me off and we walked away.

"I've got an idea" I said, "Let's go to Margate".

We bunked the tube to Upminster Bridge and then walked back down the track to jump over the fence onto Hacton Lane. We were so busy talking and singing to each other that we never heard the British Rail express train. Something caught my attention and I looked back just in time. I shouted to Animal, who was just behind me and we both dived sideways onto the embankment. The train passing by only inches from our feet, travelling at about 90 mph.

We popped in to see Mum and spent the night sleeping on Leslie Maskell's sofa, her kids both scared and inquisitive about the men with the green heads.

Margate was a blast, we slept in a converted shed in someone's back garden and lived on chips and donations from the local kids, all friends of the girls we'd met in Coventry. We couldn't stay long as once again, it was time to sign on at the job centre back home. We walked out of town just as it started to rain. By the time we got to the main A299 road we were soaked through. A car pulled up at a junction in front of us, just as the driver was about to pull onto the road we jumped into his car uninvited.

"Cheers for the lift mate" I said, knowing full well he had no intention of picking us up. "If you can drop us by the M2 we'd be very grateful". He was only going to the next turn off and once again, we were out in the rain. We finally made it to the services later that evening and spent a couple of hours slumped under the hand dryers in the gents to try to dry off. A friendly trucker took us to London, we were dropped at Highbury corner and bunked the train home to Coventry.

I made it to the Kings Road one day, my head green and hair sprayed upright. Even the punks found it hard not to stare. Traffic almost stopped and buses tilted, as passengers on the upper deck rushed to one side to get a better view. In 1983 people were still shockable.

Andy and I were seeing less of each other now. He'd moved on from the band we had formed together at school. Meaty continued to play in a new line-up, now called Rigor Mortis. Andy had joined a band called Brutal Attack, playing to a much harder edged audience. Mostly skinheads, some punks, each gig was a potential battle zone, even Andy said he was frightened sometimes. Eventually, he succumbed to his fears and shaved his head. He had a new best friend too, Lance, and I found myself liking them both less and less. I hated the direction he was going, I couldn't bring myself to see any of his gigs, his political stance had virtually taken an about face exchanging anarchy and peace for brutality and oppression. Violence and hatred seemed to have taken over, his sense of humour was all but gone and I found it harder to recognise the friend I had grown up with.

Living in Coventry meant I could keep some distance from that side of things, but being in Coventry had it's down side too. I would dip in and out of depression, I fantasised about the white light and would do all I could to get stoned, one way or another. I had been getting Valium from my GP and would use that to wipe myself out from time to time, waking up having no recollection of the hours before. I came round alone in the flat one day, and pushing myself up from my mattress, felt a warm sensation down both arms. My forearms had been cut to ribbons, my left wrist had a gaping wound, blood poured from within and I ran to the phone box holding it together.

When the ambulance came, the technician gave me some advice on route to the hospital.

"Next time, cut up the vein instead of across, that way it'll work".

I couldn't believe what she'd just said.

"I wasn't trying to kill myself," I said, "I don't know how this happened!"

"Sure you didn't".

My wounds were dealt with, I had 6 stitches in my wrist and a mile of bandage up both arms before sent on my way.

Guardian Angel

You're waiting by the door
Though you know I'll never answer,
I've seen your face before
All my life I've been a chancer.
You stand there in the cold,
I sit here warm but tired
Waiting as years pass by,
To slowly feed your fire.
Though I shan't rush-I know you're there,
Your presence is so real,
So wait for me Oh silent one,
Until the cold I feel.

Happy House

Having put myself on the housing list as soon as I could, it wasn't long before I was offered somewhere to live. A maisonette on Bittern Walk, Wood End. No more would I have to wonder where I would live, no more did I have to put up with whatever was offered. I had my own home now.

During my time at Big Dave's flat, I wrote to Lynn and told her where I was. She jumped on the train and came to find me. In a scene straight out of a spoof comedy she passed me on a bus heading to Wood End. I was going in to town and thought I was seeing things when I saw her on the top front seat of the 21 bus. She hung around a few hours and then went home, returning a week or so later when I promised to meet her at the station. When she arrived I was too drunk to stand up straight and had to be helped home by Lucy and Lynn. When I awoke the next morning she was gone again.

Eventually she returned when I got my own place and moved in along with Lucy, Animal and from time to time various other characters. Lynn began to assert herself a little too much and it was obvious we could never be together. We stayed friends and she settled into a new life in a new town with her new boyfriend, Jason Connell. 'Jay' seemed to appear from nowhere, he was a friend of someone Lucy knew and was suitably weird to fit in with the rest of us. Another friend of Lucy's, Bone, was an on-off girlfriend of mine, we had a very casual relationship with each other, almost like an accidental habit, we must have both liked each other, but we never went beyond occasional lovers. Sometimes she lived with us, sometimes she went home and we wouldn't see her for ages, a little like me buggering off to London on a whim whenever I fancied it.

Soon after moving in I managed somehow to get Vertical Hold a support slot at The Lanch. The lads agreed to the gig and came up in a minibus. I offered to put them up for the night and they arrived bright and early in Wood End. So bright and early that I was the only one awake. I showed them into the flat and offered to make drinks, Lynn and Lucy appeared from their slumber and came downstairs. Steve George had brought his girlfriend Mags, who I adored. I had known them for years and always had a good laugh around them. Steve was the band's singer, Mark Routledge played guitar, Paul Drums and Fred Previous was their bass player. We were just settling in and I was showing Steve the view out of our windows, when the living room door flew open. In bounced Animal, stark bollock naked but for a pair of cowboy boots and a handful of throwing knives that he quickly dispatched at the dartboard on the opposite wall. Mags screeched and hid behind Steve, laughing her head off at the site of this naked knife thrower, Steve however, was less impressed and asked him to put some clothes on. Nobody could make an entrance like Animal.

The gig was a success and I spent the evening happily dancing along to the familiar sound of songs like 'Rubber Cross' and 'Biohazard', songs I'd heard many times over the last few years. I didn't know it, but this was to be the last time I saw the band play together.

Someone else had moved in with us, Bab. A small Collie cross dog that Lynn and Lucy found wandering. He allegedly followed them home without any prompting- which I always doubted. He was a beautiful dog with a loving temperament. Jet black fur but for a white tie mark and collar, toes and tip of his tail. Within a few days we dyed his collar and the tip of his tail Pink. Bab loved it, he was a huge attention seeker and would run up to people in the street, stop in front of them wagging his tail and smiling, literally lifting his cheeks and smiling, everybody loved Bab, and Bab loved everybody.

Back in London, Major had been evicted from the squat for a second time. He now had a flat on the Talgarth Road, just along from Lou and Barry. I came to visit and the door was opened by a lad from Liverpool I'd never seen before. We sat up talking all night, Major didn't return until the following day. I asked him about the cigarette packets he'd stuck to the wall, hundreds of empty Marlboro packets covered the chimney breast and adjacent walls.

"I hide my stash in one, but only I know which" he said smiling, "having so many to choose from makes it harder for anyone else to find". That I could believe.

I popped in to see Lou and Barry, as always, they were really pleased to see me. Lou once said that what she loved about me was that I was the most macho man she'd ever known, without being in the least bit macho. She said I wasn't false, I had no image or mask I'd hide behind, I was just me, and I guess that summed me up, even today, I hear her voice, that dry slight rasp, with a very well-to-do accent and huge opened mouthed laugh, and it makes me smile. Lou was right, I was and am myself, just me. Then, now and always-innit?

We hung around in the flat for a while, drank some beer and shared the valium I'd brought with me. I had decided to pop in on Gary and his wife, a couple of Goths who lived above a shop on North End Road. Back then we didn't use the term Goth, we had no idea of a differential between punks and Goths, they were just punks with make-up and better looking girlfriends. I often went to see Gary when I was around, he was the only person I knew in the area with a TV set. It was here in their flat, that I saw for the 1st time the familiar face of the guy I'd met at Paul's bedsit, singing on Top Of The Pop's, wearing the self same tracksuit and long blonde dreads as he did the day I liberated his puppy. This time however, there was to be no Top Of The Pop's, no TV whatsoever.

I left Barry and Lou and remember walking part of the 300 yards to the corner of North End Road. After that, nothing until I came to my senses walking through a bus station. Nothing around me seemed familiar, nothing. I had no clue where I was, what day it was even. I was totally lost and had a strange sore feeling in my neck. I put my hand up and found a safety pin stuck into my flesh. I'd pierced my neck with a large safety pin and it felt quite sore.

I spotted some punks tucked away in the corner of the bus station and crossed over the bus lanes toward them. They were sniffing glue from plastic bags and I asked if I could join in. Taking a few breaths from the bag I'd been given, I turned to the group as they looked at me inquisitively.

"So whereabouts are we?" I asked,

"The bus station" came the reply, followed by an all inclusive laugh at the stupidity of the statement.

"I can see that (*Einstein*…), what bus station, where are we?"

My accent and not knowing my own whereabouts must have been something of a curiosity, so was their reply.

"Exeter man, we're in Exeter".

What the fuck……

"And what day is it?"

"Saturday".

Top of the Pop's was on Thursday nights, it was now Saturday and I had been teleported about 200 miles across country with no idea what had happened in between. I left the locals with their bags of glue and headed to the ticket office. I had just enough money in my pocket for the coach back to London, but no matter how hard I tried, I could not recall the missing hours, or how I made it so far from home.

"Where did you get to?" Barry asked, "I thought you were coming back the other night".

I told Barry and Lou of my adventure, they'd gone to see Gary on Friday and he told them I hadn't arrived, he hadn't seen me for a couple of weeks.

I was back in Devon a few months later to visit a girl I'd become friends with, BeeJay. I'd met her in Wood End one day, why she was there I had no clue, but I hitched down to Honiton to see her. I arrived in the evening, quite late, and managed to get a quick drink before the pubs shut. I wandered up a hill overlooking the town and set my sleeping out next to a hedge, the lights of the town below me, with just the sound of the sheep nearby, I curled up and slept for the night. Next morning I set about trying to find her. I met a couple of lads that knew her and said she would be at work now, she worked for a newspaper in Exeter and would be home on the train about 5.30pm. I was invited round to where one of the lads lived and when we entered his room I was in for a surprise. As all kids did, he had a collection of photos, newspaper cuttings and posters on his walls. Something caught my eye and I saw an image of Major in one of the pictures. I looked closer and there were other people I knew in other shots too, and then I saw myself, a photo of myself, with Major and some other punks on the benches on the King's Road, only it wasn't me, it was my face, a similar jacket, my face but no tattoos on my bare arms. This was not possible. I could not have been in this photo without tattoos, but it was my face, and Major, I was shocked, and very stunned to realise that I had a double, and he knew my friends.

It wasn't long after returning to London, that Barry thought it would be a good idea to go down the King's Road. Lou used to hang out there regularly but had been a bit of a hermit lately, anyway, she also needed to get some hairspray.

The idea was that Barry and Lou would shoplift the hairspray from a busy chemist shop, but they had to be careful as Barry was on parole, one can of hairspray would get him a 6 month holiday at the nation's expense. As we entered the shop, I became aware that we had been followed. I looked back out the window and sure enough, two uncomfortable looking guys with short haircuts were watching our every move. Lou and Barry were being a little too obvious in their deliberations and I knew things were going bad. I stepped outside the shop and straight up to the two cops.

"Got a spare cigarette or 10p I could have, either of you?"

That was all they needed. I was shoved to one side, pulled and pushed face against the wall, my hands pulled behind my back and quickly cuffed.

"You're under arrest for begging, sonny, we've been watching you,we knew you were up to no good". They were so busy with me they didn't notice Barry and Lou slip out of the shop with half a dozen cans of Elnett.

I was walked, hands cuffed behind my back to Chelsea police station, where I was charged with Begging and put in a cell overnight. As I was processed I was required to empty my pockets and place the contents on the desk.

"Anything else before we search you?"

"No, that's it" I lied. I had forgotten about the little wrap of speed Wilf had given me the night before. I felt it in my back pocket but had left it there in the hope they wouldn't search me, and now it was all I could think of. Thankfully there was no search and I was put into a cell on my own. As soon as the door slammed shut I took out the wrap and snorted it's contents. Despite being told on several occasions to lay down and get some rest, I paced the cell all night and appeared before the magistrate just a little too wide eyed and bushy tailed. I was fined £2 and released back on the streets.

Back with Lou and Barry we came into contact with the police once more. We'd come into possession of some dodgy £20 notes, most of which had been passed on without any problems, but this one evening, coming back from the King's Road, Lou asked someone for change as he got out of a taxi. The guy gave her two £10 notes and she thanked him before he walked into a convenience store holding the note to the light. We ran off and were back at their flat laughing about it when the doorbell rang. Lou answered it. It was the police. Lou had been assaulted a couple of days earlier and made a report to the police, an officer was on his way round to update her on their progress when the call came through on the radio. He couldn't believe his luck as he came into the room and saw us sitting there like butter wouldn't melt in our mouths. The epitome of innocence.

We were taken off to Hammersmith Police Station and held in separate cells for the next 2 days. Lou had received her giro the morning of our arrest and swore the note had come from change she'd received in a chemist shop. The staff in the shop knew her and said she had been in using a £50 note to pay for her purchase. We kept to our story and nothing could be proved, Barry once again saved by the skin of his teeth. Lou didn't cope well with being incarcerated, she threatened to kill everyone, she threatened to hang herself with her bra, she threatened to scream and scream until she was sick and I had to shout through my cell door to calm her. Barry was in a different cell and could only hear me, not Lou, so between the two of them I had my work cut out. We were eventually released without charge, oddly enough, they said nothing about the wraps of contraband they found in the police van as we were being taken into custody.

I continued to travel up and down the M1 spending days on end in either Coventry or London. My door was always open to anybody needing somewhere to stay. Sometimes I would return home to find people I'd never met asking who I was when I walked in.

"I'm Ribs, this is my flat, who are you?".

There were never any bad times at the flat, nobody came to attack us, unlike the Punk Flat which was often the scene of some violent incidents involving people who didn't live there. Locals who didn't like punks living amongst them.

Mark Norris, my friend from school who'd given me the nickname Ribs, came to visit one time and we shared some acid with him. He'd never had any before and probably never since. We spent the night in fits of giggles and wandering around the fields behind the flat. Strange beasts and monsters following our every move. At one point we crossed a footbridge over the M6 motorway and as we felt it sway from side to side, Mark looked a little less than happy about it.

Killing Joke were playing in Birmingham one night and we all headed over. We had been drinking prior to our arrival and it wasn't long before Lynn and Lucy needed the ladies. We were in a queue of about 300 punk rockers waiting for the venue's doors to open and nowhere to hide for a pee. Nowhere except behind the one solitary car in the car park opposite. I assured them nobody would be able to see them modestly squatting behind the car and desperation eventually led them over the road. As soon as they crouched down the solitary figure of the vehicle's owner walked up, climbed inside and as a roar of laughter went up from the queue, he drove away leaving the two girls in mid flow and red faced. Sometimes, you just have to have to smile.

I had been looking for a tattoo for the side of my head. Several people I knew already had them, each individual of the others. I met a French tattooist, a punk lad who was living with someone I knew, they invited me to their flat and as soon as I walked in I saw what I had been looking for. A picture amongst the others called out to me from their living room wall, a skull in a burning shroud. Without hesitation I asked if he would tattoo my head and he duly proceeded to do just that. The pain at times was awful but once he'd started I had to let him finish, I had to bear with it- for the final result would make it all worthwhile.

Drink, drugs, sex and Rock'n'Roll were all we ever needed. It was our lives. We were aimless and unproductive as human beings, but we were happy in our house, our lives meant nothing to the outside world, and the outside world meant nothing to us. Animal and I came and went as we pleased, we were our own masters, our own worst enemies too, eventually our proximity and differences took their toll.

Animal and I began to drift. He had brought a motorbike into the flat and it was taking up most of the living room. Lynn, Lucy and Jay wanted it gone, they also wanted Animal out of the flat all together. He was my mate, but even some days I tired of his boundless energy. For me though, I finally had enough when he'd helped himself to food from my pantry. His mother lived 5 minutes away and he could always go home for a meal, I had no such safety net and when it was gone, I went without. Sometimes Lucy would take me to her mother's place in the next block of flats to feed me. She had been a lifesaver to me so many times, I don't know that I ever really thanked her. We would sit in their kitchen eating and talking for hours on end. Whenever her mother came in I would freeze. They would talk about things in Polish and I had no clue what they were on about, but with the harshness of the language I really believed she was having a go about me being there eating their food, AGAIN!

Animal eventually moved out, he left his bike behind and after a couple of weeks I thought he intended leaving it for good. I bumped into Big Dave and told him about it one day. That was my first mistake, my second was to say OK when Dave said he'd burgle my flat and take the bike.

Obviously this didn't go down well with Animal, I hated myself for having thought it could ever have been any sort of a good idea, I had just wanted the girls off my back, the bike gone and some peace and quiet.

The peace and quiet was abruptly shattered about a week later when my front door was kicked in. A dozen or so skinheads stormed into the maisonette smashing everything they could. Others grabbed my records and left as quickly as they'd come back into the dark night. I had heard the door and jumped out of bed. My initial reaction was to protect the girls. I remember throwing a stool down the stairs at the intruders and chasing after them as they left, but even though I recognised some of them, there was nothing I could do. I had invited this upon myself by agreeing to Dave's stupid idea, this was the price I had to pay.

A couple of days later, in town, I was approached by one of the lads I'd recognised. He told me he was on his way to sell some records, I could buy them if if I wanted to but when he opened the bag I could see clearly they were mine, they still had my name written on them. Humiliation complete.

Animal got his bike back, Dave arrested and I spent less and less time at home, eventually moving into a house on Princess Street, Paradise (*No really, there is an area of Coventry called Paradise…..*) with an ex-prospector from the Satan's Slaves Motorcycle Club.

I first met Fritz in the Brewer & Baker pub, it was the regular haunt for us punks at the time, Rich DJ'd in the back room at weekends and we paid our 10p to get in and drink watery beer with the Irish folk who seemed to live in the pub full-time. Nobody was ever told to leave that pub unless they were thrown out, usually we were all locked in, especially when a fight broke out. I walked in one night just as Mich's brother Griff smashed a beer glass into Al Cockerell's face. All hell broke loose and Griff was forcibly removed from the pub.

Fritz had just got out of prison and fancied Lucy. Lucy did not fancy Fritz and I was stuck in the middle. Things turned out ok in the end and Fritz and I became good friends, eventually sharing the house on Princess Street, Greg Chapman, a friend from The Butts, moved in for a while too, he was out most nights door to door picture selling , but left the house after a disagreement with Fritz. Fritz went through a phase of waving his sheath knives around and threatening to kill people. He had been stabbed in the back himself when he left The Slaves, that was normal procedure, but Fritz was not the stabbing sort. He threatened me one night and I told him to do it.

"Come on, stab me them, but do it proper-right here through my heart". He looked down at the long knife in his hand and mumbled about having to get the blade sharpened.

It wasn't all grim, some nights we sat up playing Hangman, for the laugh. We ended up going to the nearby Police station at 2am to inquire about the correct spelling of Porage, Porridge...... *There was no google back then kids.*

Fritz and I had been speeding for about three days, laying on our opposite sofas in the living room listening to a heavy metal compilation album, Axe Attack. Motorhead and Girlschool pumping the adrenalin round and around our heads, the speakers vibrating to the bass and the neighbours wishing we lived elsewhere, anywhere but there. I felt the temperature suddenly drop in the room and outside in our back garden, a figure appeared and seated itself on the wall, only it was not so much on the wall as where the wall should be. I looked closer and saw the outline of it's frame, a hooded cloak covered its body, something behind its head glinted-a scythe, and then it lifted its head to look at me. I was looking straight into the face of the Grim Reaper. I asked Fritz to shut the curtain behind him, went into the kitchen to make a drink but collapsed on the floor shaking and crying uncontrollably, my nerves had reached their limit, my body and brain pushed too far now spasmed and twitching uncontrollably. I was done.

Once again I found myself at Major's flat on Talgarth Road. We were becoming close friends and thought it was time we became brothers, blood brothers. Major got penknife out and slit his thumb, blood oozed from the wound. I did the same and we pressed our thumbs together, our blood mixing. We were now brothers, watching out for one another at all times. Upstairs were a load of German punks who'd just arrived and were staying for a while. With them were a couple of english girls who had spent some time in Coventry.

I didn't realise it at the time but remembered later, I had met one of them, Maz, in the Brewer & Baker. She had dated my mate Naz for a while. Maz & Naz, a bit like Ribs & Bone, sounds funny the first time you say it but don't go buying a hat, it might not last that long. Maz was also known in Cov as 'The Oxford Bag', not the best moniker but it wasn't mine.

I got along ok with everyone and was surprised a few weeks later when Maz and her friend knocked on my door. Maz was poorly and they needed somewhere to stay for a bit. Fritz and I put them up and after a week or two they were gone again.

Unfortunately for me, I had gotten too close and was soon showing the same symptoms as Maz had, the same jaundiced look that Major would sometimes display. I went to my GP and was sent for a blood test. Two weeks later I returned for the results.

My doctor quizzed me about my drink, drug and smoking habits. I was honest with him and always am, no doctor can ever fix you if you lie to them.

"I'm afraid the truth is this" he said, "if you carry on as you are you will not make it through to the end of next year. You have Hepatitis A and B. You have to stop smoking, drinking, taking drugs and eating fatty foods. If you do as I say you may live for maybe another 10 years, but at this rate you will be lucky to live beyond the next year".

It was December 1983, I was 18 years old and had only one year left to live.

No words can ever undo that. None whatsoever.

I step into the dark hallway, all about me is black and silent except for the rustle of plastic wrappers littering the floor. My feet scrunch and crackle as I step slowly forward. There is a faint light coming down the stairwell, a skylight or possibly a hole in the roof letting the daylight through, only it feels dark,like night time, like a dark dream I can never escape, returning again night after night. I touch the black bannister and feel the dust of all eternity clinging to my fingers., cobwebs hang in corners of the ceiling and between the spindles on the stairway, many are missing, others twisted and disabled out of place hanging loose and threatening in the dark, their existence given away by the light reflecting from splintered fragments. One step, then two. A pause and twist of the neck straining for sound but nothing echoes other than the breath from my lungs. Another step and rustling of plastic, step after step to the next landing. It was here, this was our landing, these were our rooms, the scene of our laughter and games, our hopes dreams and fears, this was our squat, our home when we had no other and only each other. This was our sanctuary, our playhouse and prison. The place we lived and some even died. In the dark I stand alone, the only life in a world I no longer know, alone and silent but for the drip, drip, drip from the bathroom down the hall. The handle is stiff and creaks, it is cold beneath the dust and as I turn it I know what is inside. I have been here before. I have seen this room so many times and each time I am chilled to the core. I open the door slowly. Across the room, near the window, the blind leaks in the night sky, it's slats tattered and broken. All about me the sound of echoes, drip, drip,

drip. The water is cold, still but for the odd ripple, gliding from the drop as it hits the water across to the lip of the rim. And still she lays there naked. Her head lays backwards to hide her face in a shadow. Her chest is bare and only partially submerged in the dirty water, her arms spread out either side of the bath and nothing has moved, nothing has changed, she is dead in the bath, her skin leathered and drawn. Still she lays there, waiting to be found, waiting for someone to notice, but nobody ever sees her, because nobody sees my dreams.

WILD BOYS

I fully accepted that I was here of my own making. I had no illusions that I was my own worst enemy, and for that I was to pay the ultimate price. I was to going to die, my life was over, wasted before it had truly begun.

"What does he know, he's only a doctor?"

I took the lid off a bottle of vodka and drank the contents neat. I was going out alright, but I was going out on my own terms. I had put myself here and now I had to pay for it.

I decided to move to London, there were too many people in Coventry I loved and did not want to see me go downhill. In London I was anonymous, one in several million and my life mattered very little in the grand scheme of things. I was a lowlife, a waster wasting away in an ocean of wasted chances, squandered dreams and misery. Nobody would miss me, nobody would mourn and cry at my departure, only another dead runaway, bagged and tagged before lunch, forgotten even before the big breasted tea lady in the corner cafe pours her first cup of the morning.

I moved into the house next to where we had previously squatted. Major and his girlfriend Willow, had a room on the ground floor, other people lived upstairs and in time, I took over the basement flat. Willow had moved down to London from Nottinghamshire or South Yorkshire, possibly Barnsley or Wakefield area, we were never too sure of where people came from as most of us were running from something or someone, we would often have to guess by accents or the stories they would tell of the pasts they hadn't forgotten.

Raggitty was a well known face on the scene. I'd seen him around at gigs and out and about for years, usually with his mate Moggy or Ray (Little Sid) but most memorably on the Sid Vicious Memorial March, Feb 2nd 1981, when he kicked a shop dummy that had been taken from outside Reflections, along the Kings Road just as the police arrived. He was carted off straight away and the rest of us ran to regroup. One girl had been hit by a car and it's driver set upon by some of the punks, hence for the police attending in force. He and his girlfriend Fiona stayed with us for a while, they had suddenly arrived homeless and we all lived together as one big family.

Gary, who I had gone to see before my unexpected trip to Exeter, got me helping him out on an evening paper round. I got a few extra pounds in my pocket but it only lasted a few weeks. Most days were spent in the pursuit of drink, drugs, cigarettes and money. Begging was a 24 hour business for Major and I, and London was the ideal place to do it. People would give us coins for coffee, cigarettes, tube rides, whatever we asked for. There was also money to be made from our looks, having our picture taken could mean we had enough cash to go to a gig or buy more drink. When our dole money came we would immediately spend it on booze, filling a bucket with whatever we could get and dipping our glasses in until all was gone. We became very close, sharing everything we had and behaving like feral kin. We had each other's backs at all times, and were together most of the time up to some no good deed or other.

We were walking back from a gig in Fulham one night and Major thought it a good idea to steal a car. Somebody had left their doors unlocked and before I knew it, Major being an opportunist, jumped into the driver's seat. He pushed a scissor into the ignition,turned it and started the engine. I jumped into the passenger seat.

"I didn't know you could drive" I exclaimed.

"I've been doing this for years" he said, then promptly showed me he'd never been taught how to drive properly. The engine screamed and and gears crashed as he tried to move us down the road without using the clutch pedal. He hadn't switched the lights on and within minutes we were the talk of the town, a distant siren blaring closer and closer. Behind us I could see the reflection of a blue light on buildings and urged him to get a move on.

"Fuck, the police are coming, I wished you'd said you couldn't fucking drive, we're going to get caught in a minute".

Major hit the accelerator and and the engine screamed in second gear. He raced forward unable to find the courage to go for third, but deciding a moment too late to take a left turn. Instead of shaking off our assailants, we bounced sideways up a kerb and the car crashed into a brick building. I shot forward and headbutted the windscreen before bouncing back into the seat. The car rebounded off the wall of a bank and settled next to another vehicle. I couldn't get out of my side of the car, the door was against the other vehicle. Turning to Major I called for him to get out of his side but he was already out, laying on the bonnet. I jumped out of the car as soon as I could get across the seats with Major's size nines on either side of the steering wheel. The police sirens were getting louder as I pulled him from the bonnet of the car. He was stunned, winded and had only a few small cuts and bruises. We ran off as quickly as we could, but we had been seen by someone in a phonebox over the road, I saw the outline of someone approach after the crash and feared we were soon to be busted. We limped home through back streets and alleyways as quickly as we could, both bleeding and bruised, neither wanting to get caught. The following evening we got a visit, not from the police, but a local dealer I shall call Bob.

"You pair of fucking idiots" he said looking at us. "You're lucky Uncle Bob is around looking out for you. After you fled the scene last night I had to spray the car with WD40 to get rid of any fingerprints-'cos I knew you two were too stupid to think about putting any gloves on!"

"It was you in the phone box over the road?" I asked

"Yes, I'd just dropped someone off and was ringing the taxi office when you pair smashed into the bank" he smiled, "so I got the spray out of my car and saved your necks before the old bill arrived. Of course, I told them you ran off the other way knowing you'd be heading here, so next time you pull a stunt like that, put some gloves on and you" he looked at Major, " take some driving lessons too!"

Bob was a frequent visitor to most of the punks, Goths and weirdo's in the area. He prefered to deal with us than the skinheads or straights as he'd been a rocker and a hippy himself in the past. Our rebellious natures and dislike of the norm suited him down to the ground, even though he always wore a suit himself, he used being a private taxi driver as a cover for visiting so many properties in the area. He wouldn't sell Heroin, Bob hated the stuff, he would bring speed, acid and sometimes coke, but at that time cocaine was too expensive for the likes of us, we stuck to economy class and if ever we had any issues, Bob would give us our money back. I bought a load of Superman blotters from him one day only to find they were dud, when the 1st one didn't work I ate another and another, eventually devouring a whole sheet of 50. Bob gave me a refund and promised the next batch would be better. He wasn't wrong.

Now that I was back in London I thought I would see more of Andy, but that wasn't the case. I would often go to gigs asking if anyone had seen or heard of him lately, he was busy with his new band Brutal Attack, and was hanging around with a skinhead called Lance. I went to see him in Ealing one afternoon. He was pulling his boots on and lacing them up, sniffed loudly and told me that he was going up the West End, "Paki Bashing!"

There was nothing I could do or say, Andy was being directed by his association with the band and his friendship with Lance. I hated the idea of racism. I hate racists and their blind hatred of others for no reason than the colour of their skin. I had grown up as the victim of other people's hatred of 'The Other', Andy had too, but now he was jumping in line, doing as he was told, selling out to hate. In my time in Coventry I had known cultural diversity and unity, black kids hanging around with whites, mixed race couples walking the streets, it was normal, it was how it should be. Coventry was home to the 1979 resurgence of Ska music. The Specials and The Selecter had turned the music industry on its head with their wonderfully monochromatic style and musical energy. Black and white had united to fight back at the status quo that had kept them fighting each other. When Roddy Byers penned Concrete Jungle, it was about our lives, growing up as the oppressed, it was a punk anthem but the punks had not yet realised it. When The Selecter released their album "Too Much Pressure", it was ex-punk rocker Steve Eaton on the cover. The bondage trousers were gone, replaced by a mohair suit, but the sentiment was universal. Pauline Black spoke to all of us, punks, skins, black, white, everyone included under one banner, the sound of unity, togetherness, fighting together against the true oppressors, the governments and corporations set on keeping us warring with each other as they keep us in our places, powerless to fight back. And here we were, Andy and I, best friends through school but polar opposites in adult life, our common ground becoming harder and harder to define.

Sylvie was from Northern Ireland and lived upstairs from Major. She was tall with long black hair, backcombed and pale of skin. She reminds me of Patricia Morrison, (The Gun Club, Sisters of Mercy) whenever I look back and remember her. Sylvie was the only person in the building who seemed to have a job. We had no idea what she did, but she seemed happy enough and would often treat us to free drinks and food. Fiona and Raggitty moved out of Major's room. Raggitty was becoming too reliant on heroin and the pair would often fight. Fiona left, I think she went to live with her parents in Portugal, I never saw Raggitty again.

I came home from the King's Road one day and before I could sit down on my mattress, the doorbell rang. Major looked out of the spy hole in the front window, he had painted the entire room- windows included, black. He'd left a tiny spy hole about the size of a penny clear. This allowed him to see who was at the door without them knowing he was looking.

Outside stood two young punk girls he didn't recognise.

"Who's this?" He gestured me to come over. I looked out of the tiny gap in the paint and saw two young girls I'd been talking to earlier that day. I let them in.

"What are you doing here?" I asked, shutting the door behind them and showing them into Major's room. Willow sat up in her sleeping bag, half naked and barely awake.

"We need somewhere to stay for a couple of nights, and you said you lived in Earls Court, so we followed you, hoping we could stay with you".

I was stunned and had no idea they had followed me home. Willow chatted with them for a while and when they said they were big fans of, and friends with, Captain Sensible of The Damned, Major agreed to let them stay.

Later that night I found out the two were under-aged and runaways. They had fled their parents in the hope of living the Punk lifestyle with us, here. Willow wasn't happy and Major was worried about this. It was one thing for us lot to live as we did, drunken debauched and messed up on a regular basis, but this was no environment for minors. They stayed the night and as soon as I got up next morning I went to the call box in the station and rang the police. When they arrived Sylvie answered the door and panicked, thinking we were being raided, but the police were not interested in us, they just wanted to take the girls home. They cried as they were led out, begging us not to let this happen, one had written her name and mine on her ripped jeans, next to our names she had drawn a love heart. I hadn't touched her all night, we'd chatted and laughed a little, but for some reason she had become infatuated with me and I was sending her home to her parents, her hearts would wash out, and she would eventually forget her crush.

Sylvie began to pop her head in more and more. Eventually taking Willow to meet her boss, an Afghan who ran a small trading company from an office above a shop on Oxford Street. Willow got a job, then Major and eventually I was offered a job too, it was cash in hand, £10 a day to work in the office making goofy hats for the tourist trade. Once a fortnight we were allowed to start late so that we could sign on and continue getting our dole money. The extra money from this new employment kept us out of some of the trouble we would have otherwise got ourselves into, and allowed us to get out of the house more and more. Drink, drugs, gigs, clubs, we could afford them all.

Barry and Lou took me out to a club one night, a little place by the Embankment called Heaven, I'd never heard of it. Lou said it might be a good idea if I held Barry's hand as we got to the door, we might not get in otherwise. I could have sworn I saw Siouxsie and Budgie from Siouxsie And The Banshees, behind us in the queue. We made it in and no sooner had I entered the foyer, I saw my mate Paul.

"How you doing Ribs, you alright mate?" I gave him a hug and stepped back "How's it going, fuck, didn't think I'd see you here, how's the dog, what did you do with it? Do you want some acid? It's good to see you, here- have this, have a great night, I'll catch you in a bit".

Paul thrust a yellow tablet in my hand and I duly swallowed it, turned and followed Lou and Barry to the main hall. I had been lured to this place with promises of a great atmosphere, great music and friendly people. All this was true, it was a great club, good music and friendly people, so friendly in fact that when I went to the toilet I had an audience all around me. The acid started kicking in, but instead of having fits of giggles I was starting to get paranoid. I have nothing against gay men but suddenly this night I found myself clinging to the walls. I sat higher and higher up on the steps, until eventually I was at the very top of the room, my back pressed against the ceiling and wall, whilst all about me other people mingled, danced and enjoyed themselves. All I could see below me were 2-300 Freddie Mercury look-a-like's in leather chaps, hairy chested macho men, topless but for leather bondage gear and chains, all pushing and shoving to the sounds of Frankie Goes To Hollywood, testosterone surging as they gyrated to Divine and way above them in my little world of paranoid illusion, a little child curled into the corner wishing for it all to stop. I shouldn't have taken that pill, not this night, I wasn't prepared or in the right environment for it, and would spend many months to come in a state of high emotion, scared of people around me, unsure of anything, emotionally insecure.

I was well on my way to fulfilling the prophecy. I was using everything I could lay my hands on and from time to time my body would remind me of my fallibility, I would often get stomach cramps, always felt lethargic, weak and sick. My skin and eyes would be various shades of yellow, some days barely noticeable, other days I resembled a mustard pot on legs, yet still I spent everyday in the pursuit of oblivion. I was dying, bring it on.

In the little workshop above a travel agent on Oxford Street,, Major, Willow, myself, Sylvie and a girl called Pam sat day after day making hats to sell to tourists and anyone else with no shame. The hats were just cheap, plain baseball caps in a variety of colours, onto which we made and then attached felt novelties, like a frog for example, a seagull, hamburger or parrot. The more insane hats were those with huge elephant ears and trunks, and the unforgettable arm and hammer hat. Basically, an arm protruded from one side of the hat, elbow bent over the top of the wearer's head, to where the hand held a hammer against the other side of the head. Remember them? Yep, we made them. Everyday we climbed the narrow staircase up to the 3rd floor, where we took our places and sorted pieces of precut felt, glued them together, stuffed that which needed stuffing, glued some more, wound elastic bands to hold the assembled parts together until the glue set, poured more glue, and listened to tapes of either the Psychedelic Furs, Bauhaus or Joy Division- they were the only tapes we had in the room. All this was done with the windows firmly locked, deliberately. We would close and lock the windows when we arrived in the morning, the fumes from the glue would fill the room and before we had time to say 'Dead brain cells' we would all be giggling and talking nonsense. By lunchtime we would have slowed production down to such a level as to be non-existent. The windows would be opened whilst we went for lunch, a big mac meal from the Mcdonalds next to the Tottenham pub, on the corner of Oxford Street and Tottenham Court Road. We had just enough time for a quick pint of John Bull bitter, before climbing back up the stairs for another lung full of evo stick and an earful of President Gas.

Our boss Sami, also had a couple of stalls on the street, not table tops but everything on large boards in empty shop doorways, illegal street trading, fly-pitching they called it, selling badges, t-shirts, sunglasses, watches, umbrellas and silly hats with elephant trunks, seagulls or hammers on them. We made the hats and got stoned in the process, the stalls sold the hats, the boss got paid, we got paid and then went out and got stoned. The circle of life was complete.

There was a punk band playing at the 100 Club, I bumped into them outside and was having a laugh with them before the gig. "Here, have some of these" I said and handed over some of the little blue microdots I'd bought earlier that day. "Enjoy!" We went downstairs to see their support act and soon enough I was bouncing around with everybody else. By the time the band came on it was obvious to me that at least 2 of them were tripping. They struggled through their playlist and at the end of the gig the band split up. It was their last gig for a very long time.

I bumped into a mate on the King's Road one day when I wasn't working. I'd known Spit for a while, he was a regular face at gigs and around town.

"My mates band are playing tonight in Victoria, fancy coming along and helping out with stage security?"

Stage security meant getting in for free, thumping people if they try to wreck the show and standing around all night acting like a skinny version of Del and Tim in the 100 Club. I could do that, well, all but looking like Tim and Del, they looked the part naturally, I looked a prat, naturally.

We arrived at the venue to find a hundred or so Goths and Alternative looking fans hanging around outside. Spit and I strolled up in our ripped jeans, jackboots and mohawks. The great unwashed amongst a sea of black and purple perfection. I switched on my best "Got a spare fag?" voice and soon had a pocket full of 10p coins, several marlboro and an offer I really had to refuse- he just wasn't my type. Spit checked at the door to see if his friends were in the venue yet, we were told they'd gone for a bite to eat around the corner, so we went off and found them in the wimpy bar. Spit introduced me and got straight into talking about personal stuff and asking how the band were, they were definitely old friends and very familiar. I sat quietly and chewed some fries wondering when would be a good time to have the bag of speed I had in my pocket.

We were taken through the stage door and glared at by the black clad crowd, all gathered round to catch a glimpse of me.......*cough!*................*who?*.........

Ok, the band, whoever they were.

We headed upstairs and I popped to the loo to powder my nose. Spit was busy backcombing and spraying the singers' hair, I was offered a drink from the pile of cans on the table and duly obliged. Everyone was busy with stagegear and make-up while I continued to drink my way through their rider.

"Here, have some of this"

A big bag of white powder was offered to me, there was more contraband in that bag than I could consume in the whole of the remainder of my days.

"Cheers, but I just had some".

We made our way downstairs and onto the stage. The band took their positions and Spit and I squatted by the side of the curtain so as not to be in the way. There was a full house beyond the curtain, people cheering, shouting and having a good time, whoever these people were-and I had no idea who they were, they were popular. The curtain went up and the first notes of a song I'd heard many times before rang out. I had danced to this song, many many times, in clubs, punk discos and pubs all over the place, I loved this song, I loved this band. I was on stage, doing security for Alien Sex Fiend.

Spit stayed the night at my place. He was still asleep on a spare mattress when I got up and went to Coventry. Before leaving I swapped jackets and took his, leaving him mine for the weekend. We used to do this back then to stop ourselves from being too easily recognised at times, if the face fits but the clothes don't match, the witness is weak.

I spent the weekend with my friends, hung out with Helen and Clare and headed back to London, blissfully unaware of what I had missed.

Sylvie opened the door and let me in.

"You better come upstairs, I have something to tell you".

I doubted she was pregnant, and if she was-it sure as hell wasn't of my doing. Major hadn't come to the door so maybe he was dead, but that being the case Sylvie would have blurted it out already. I followed her upstairs to her room and sat on a stool in her living room.

"Your Mother has been here, she's been in your room, and Major is pretty pissed off because the Police were with her".

I could think of no reason on earth why she would come here, what had happened?

Who'd died?

What the fuck was she doing in my room?

"Spit got busted Saturday night. He beat up an undercover cop on Oxford Street and then overdosed on his way to the station. The Old Bill knocked the shit out of him before calling an ambulance. When they searched his jacket" -*My Jacket.* "-They found a birth certificate in the inside pocket and thought he was you"

"Holy shit, so….?"

"So they knocked your Mum up in the middle of the night and took her to see her dying son in hospital".

I guess that proved our theory about swapping clothes actually worked, but in this case it seemed to have backfired. It brought the Police right into our home.

"So what happened when she got there?" I asked.

"Apparently they took her to his bed- he was still out of it, wired up and all sorts. She went ballistic, pulled him out of bed by his throat demanding to know what he'd done with you, the Old Bill didn't know what was happening"

"Oh my god, poor Spit" I laughed

"Aye, well it wasn't so funny when they turned up here, Major thought we were being busted".

My room, I thought, she went into my room, oh fuck, she must have seen all my drugs paraphernalia, oh bollocks!

It was one thing to have slipped into a sleazy lifestyle, playing with amphetamines and heroin, being a naughty boy in a big bad world and believing you can handle it, you don't have a habit, you just have bad habits. It is another to find your mother had walked in and found you out. I never got caught by my parents masturbating in my room, but I imagine the shame must have been equal to how I felt at that moment.

I went downstairs to check my room and sure enough, she'd seen everything, my bed was made, clothes put away and in the drawer next to my bed, my spoon and 'works' neatly lined up next to my matches and filters. For as long as my life had been compartmentalised and separated, I could lie to myself about what and who I was. I could pretend the person who turned up to visit family was one character in the film of my life. A misunderstood child wanting to find adventure in the big wide world. The one that would turn up in Coventry was another, a happy-go-lucky carefree wanderer, doing my thing, my way. No ties, just me and my now yellowing eyes, out there and free. Neither of these were the useless, insecure bag of flesh that woke each morning to an amphetamine fix, then puked into the toilet before getting dressed to go to work, making stupid hats in a toxic fume filled room. I was a junkie, lying to myself about everything in my life and seeking comfort in the arms of oblivion. The white light I had touched in my unconscious state had become my goal, my ultimate destination. I was not flirting with death, this was no show, I was actively chasing it down the street. The scar on my wrist and the holes in my arms were evidence enough of this. Once the boundaries had been crossed, the imaginary walls tumbled and I saw myself for what I really was, I hated myself. I hated that I had become this person, hated that I had allowed myself to get this low, this ill, this pathetic.

I wanted love, to be loved and to give love. To feel content that I was alive, to feel the joy of my own heart beating in my chest, the beautiful taste of life in my lungs. I had thrown it all away for momentary madness, a quick fix to my desires that left nothing in the morning after, nothing but regret and inevitable decline. I wanted out, but the door was firmly locked and bolted, this was my lot, my world, my life- what was left of it. Nobody would mourn, nobody would miss me, nobody cared because I had cared for nobody myself. I had only sought my own pleasures and frustrations, the one exacerbating the other, with no direction in mind, no destination, I was free to create a prisoner of myself. This was what I had become, what I had made of myself. I had done this to myself and only I could make it stop.

Major and I were as bad as Andy and I had been at school, we would play up to each other and drive ourselves further and further into trouble. Our job was now keeping us at bay a little, with less time on our hands we could get up to less mischief, with more money in our pockets, we could get up to more. It seemed as if we were destined to be casualties of our own making. But the battlefield had changed somewhat. Instead of sitting around all day and night, we were out and about. After work we would grab a burger and then a drink or two in the Tottenham. When I say two, I meant two at a time, one for him, one for me. John Bull bitter, from the Romford Brewery Company. Every night we would go into the pub and order 4 pints to begin with. The first two poured would be gone by the time the others were put on the bar. We decided to time ourselves one night, Major downed his pint in 2 and a half seconds. I swallowed mine in 2. I had learned to open my throat and just throw the liquid in, no pouring, no gulping, just open and down it went. Major was a little slower, which I put down to the fact that he had a cirrhotic liver, TB, Hepatitis and Pleurisy, and I was just quicker than him anyway. It was normal for us to have about 10 pints and then go home or out to a club or gig for the night.

Whilst waiting to be served in the burger joint next to the pub, I caught the eye of one of the servers, a French girl called Delphine. Each day after, I would say hi and eventually we met up for a date. She and her sister came to visit one evening and the next day were both absent from the restaurant. I asked after them and was told they'd had to go back to France suddenly, their brother had an accident and had lost a leg in a traffic collision.

Sylvie had become closer and closer to our boss Sami, but he had a girlfriend and in time the inevitable row erupted and Sylvie left her job. Pam stayed on and both me and Major were taken downstairs to work on the stalls, serving the public, taking money and getting arrested for Highway Obstruction or Trading without a Licence, whenever the police wanted to nick us they did. Sami would give us the fine money before we went to court and we would be back on the street an hour later. I loved working the stall, selling to customers, watching the world go by, I would often see famous people rushing to and fro, Shane MacGowan, Christopher Biggins and others. I was chain smoking all day long courtesy of the money in the bag. We would also help ourselves to a note or two at the end of the day, a bonus for all our hard labour. Sami never knew, he was pleased with our sales and according to Sylvie, his flat had rolls of cash thrown all over the place, thousands and thousands of pounds in rolled up bundles held in elastic bands were left on the floor, on surfaces or anywhere he felt like dropping it, even his bed. He literally was rolling in it.

One day I served a young girl with bleached white hair and a leather jacket, I saw her again in the 100 Club and we started talking, her name was Fiona and she had just finished with her boyfriend, a lad called Vulture who I had seen out and about. Fiona and I got together and she started to stay in Earls Court with me. I was a mess and she tried to help me straighten up but she was just as bad as me in reality.

Fiona was a huge David Bowie fan and introduced me to his earlier work. At Lou and Barry's we used to play his Ziggy Stardust album all the time, that or Lou Reed's Transformer album along with The Velvet Underground. Fiona got me to listen to the Lyrics of Bowie's Wide eyed boy from freecloud, and the incredible Cygnet Committee. I listened to the words, again and again I listened until I knew them by heart, she had given me more than just new songs to listen to, she gave me hope, the feeling that I may just get out of here alive,how I might do that I didn't know, but there was hope and that was enough.

My birthday was coming up soon and even though it didn't mean a great deal, I was going to be 19 and all I wanted was to enjoy myself. I invited Andy round and was looking forward to seeing him as we hadn't seen each other for a while.

Back at work a dispute had broken out between Sami and the boss of a rival gang of Fly-pitchers over an empty shop doorway along the street. It had been vacant for a few days and I had been sent over with a load of stock to run other stall. Sami put a new guy Dave on the pitch and I went back to my stall for a few days until things kicked off. The other team had claimed the doorway for themselves but we had beaten them to it, then Sami stitched them up on a deal he made with their boss. Sami told me to keep an eye on Dave at all times as the other crowd were looking for a fight and later one afternoon, it came.

I was on my pitch when Sami came over to me.

"I'm getting the girls down from upstairs to look after the stalls, I need you boys to be behind me" He said.

Major, Dave and I did as we were told and watched his back. Sure enough, the other crew turned up, their boss and Sami met between the two groups, one on one, to talk. There were three of us and Sami, against their five.They were mostly Asian, and a big bigger than us. Dave was stocky and from Stratford, he could handle himself ok, but we didn't know how ready the opposition were to start throwing punches.

We all held back while the bosses talked, watching from about 10 yards away when Sami raised his voice and then there was a slap as his head moved backwards. He had been punched in the face. We lept into action I grabbed the other guy off Sami, someone landed a punch to the side of my head and I moved sideways turning to land a fist straight into his face. Major and Dave had piled in too and shoppers ran panicking from the scene. I felt something hit my back and turned in time to see a huge Indian guy clutching a baseball bat. He pulled it back up and prepared to swing for my head.

"Not with that!" I shouted, pointing at the bat. He paused slightly confused and in his hesitation Major came in from his side with a clean punch that knocked him off balance. We both dived on him kicking and punching as fast as we could, whatever it took we did not want him getting back up still wanting to have a go, he was huge and we we were not.

It was 3pm on a Thursday afternoon. Oxford Street was heaving with people and traffic and yet not one policeman could be seen anywhere, it was as if they had been told to leave us be. We fought it out and were victorious, the rival gang routed, Sami took the first punch but won the fight, the pitch was ours now, and Sami bought the beers.

Every night Sami would meet us in the Tottenham at 6pm. He would sometimes come early and watch us shut up shop, putting the boards of badges, sunglasses, watches etc. away in the back of the store downstairs from where we made the hats, but usually would arrive at the pub and collect the day's takings from his cousin Pascha, who oversaw the operation when Sami was away all day doing business elsewhere.He would also always pay for the first round of drinks, as a good boss should. Pascha and Sami would always rush off and leave us once they'd paid the barman. We would hang around, have more drinks and usually go out for the night to a gig or dancing in a nightclub. The KitKat Club at Studio 21 on Oxford Street was a regular haunt for Major and I. There was always a good mix of Alternative music, Joy Division, Killing Joke, Billy Idol, Wasted Youth. Some nights we'd be on the dance floor for hours on end, not getting home until around 4am or later, then having to be up again at 8 to go to work and start it all anew. Sleep was delayed and avoided at every opportunity both because of our hectic social life, and secondly because of an unspoken fear that soon I would be sleeping enough anyway. I was determined to live and breathe every moment I could for as long as I could, I may have been dying, but I still had to squeeze in as much life as I could.

Fiona and I were in Major's room with him and Willow, we had few drinks and had just taken some acid when Andy and Lance arrived. Andy's hair was gone, he was a fully fledged skinhead now and Lance seemed to spend too much time trying to chat up my girlfriend. Maybe it was just my paranoia, maybe it was the trip, but they starting playing mind games with me, saying things that would confuse and scare or disorientate me. I started feeling very isolated and alone in a big room. Major and Andy were whispering, then smiled and were quiet for a minute. I didn't know what was going on as I couldn't really hear anything properly and it seemed as if everyone was plotting or laughing at me. It was my birthday and I was being ridiculed by my closest friends. Something was happening and I was not included.

Andy and Major left the room together and Fiona continued to talk across the room with Lance. Willow was in a world of her own and I felt totally alone. Outside I could hear voices in the hallway. Andy and Major were talking but their voices were getting louder, I couldn't make out what they were saying and I wished I hadn't taken the acid now, this was turning into a bad trip and I was getting unsettled. Fiona had just dyed her hair pink and each time I looked at her she looked like a creature from the children's TV show, Fraggle Rock. Cute, but a monster all the same. Lance was slithering closer to her and leering at me each time I looked. Their conversation full of double meanings, way beyond my understanding, I had never experienced this before and it was frightening.

The voices in the hallway rose to a full blown argument and suddenly the door flew open. Major fell in backwards, his arms and legs flailing. He hit the floor with a crashing thud , rose to his feet and dived at Andy as he entered the room. They fell back into the hallway and the walls banged with the sound of their fists and feet. Andy fell into the room. I tried to get up from my place on the floor but couldn't feel my legs.

"What are you-?" I tried to call out but everything was happening too quickly, my brain could not keep up. My best mates were fighting and I didn't know what to do.

Major jumped over Andy as he lay on the floor, Andy's leg rising to kick him in the stomach. He flew across the room and hit the wall next to me. I was frozen, unable to move.

Fiona screamed "Kill him!" as Major grabbed the Samurai sword he had hanging on the wall. Andy jumped up as Major lunged at him, the sword swung towards Andy's neck and I screamed "No!"

As the blade came down both Andy and Major froze simultaneously, the blade touching Andy's neck. Major turned round, dropped the sword as Andy put his arm around his shoulder and pulled his head down to kiss the shaved side of his scalp. They were both laughing.

"Got you!" they said simultaneously.

What did they mean, got me? This was a joke, they were laughing, laughing at me, I was the brunt of the joke, me.

I had no tools with which to deal with this, my head was shot and my brain in turmoil. I felt betrayed, I felt scared as I had never known fear in my life. I felt abused and foolish and thought the whole world was out to get me. Was this what had happened to John Hall, one of the punk's I'd first met in Coventry, was this what it felt like to take one too many trips, was this permanent insanity? My mind raced and I could do nothing to calm myself down. This birthday prank, a joke, mindgames, just a laugh, I could not process this, I was not equipped to handle it. My friends had seemingly turned on each other for no reason and I didn't know who to help, how to stop it. Nor could I stop my girlfriend from drifting into the arms of another. I couldn't blame her, I had little to offer and would not be around for too much longer, but still, what had I done to deserve this? On my birthday of all days.

In reality, nothing was going on with Fiona and Lance. Andy and Major were only joking and I was suffering the effects of a bad trip. Paranoia and feelings of inadequacy controlled my mindset and I could not shift them. The insecurity I'd first felt after seeing Lynn with Andy and Paul subconsciously haunted me, I didn't feel safe, I was sinking into a self destructive, self loathing that could so easily destroy me mentally and physically.

Fiona tried to talk me out of my crazy mindset, as strong and capable as she was, she could not bring me round and we separated a few days later. This was the straw that broke the camel's back, this was the proof, the justification that I was right all along and I sank into an almost catatonic state. I could go through the motions of getting to and from work but the spark of life inside me was gone. I wanted only to die. I wanted my diseased liver to explode and be the end of my self indulgent pain. I hated myself, the world, life. I wanted to die.

Sylvie was keeping an eye on me. She kept checking I was ok, asking me stupid questions, did I want anything?

" Let me know if there is anything I can do, say, buy, sell, beg, borrow or steal to make things better". Nothing could ever make things better. This was not me sulking because my parents wouldn't buy me an ice cream in Italy when I was a kid on holiday, this was me, an adult thinking I had nothing to live for, nothing to look forward to, nothing to lose.

I bought a load of trips with my dole money, 18 blue microdots, went back home and swallowed the lot in one go with a glass of water. This was it, this was the end, no turning back. I walked upstairs to Sylvie's room and knocked her door. She let me in and taking one look at me realised what I had done. My entire body was starting to tremble, my hands and legs were shaking.

"You've had that acid haven't you, oh my god Ribs, how much of it did you take? She was holding my wrists and staring straight into my eyes.

"All of it" I replied, my vision drifting out of reality and into hallucination. Sylvie's face cracked, green shoots of Ivy rising up from the neckline of her T-shirt.

"Oh you stupid fucking boy, stay here, I'm calling an ambulance".

She left the room and I entered a world of my own. A Jumanji like universe where walls breathed and floors sagged when touched. Major came bursting in to the room but I couldn't see him, I was lost in my fantastic world of fantasy and colour. Everything was bright and crystal clear, oceans of yellow flowers turning red, inanimate objects came to life, faces came at me from all directions, some human, some animal, others monstrous beings growling and snapping at me. Lights began to flash all around, bright white flashes, blinding white snap, snap, snapping all around. Press reporters shoving cameras into my eyes and the continual whirring and clicking of the mechanisms, my eyes burned as I tried to look away.

Major and Sylvie were dragging me down the staircase to meet the ambulance as it came to collect me. The walls were lined with reporters and fans, hundreds of fans reaching out to touch me, screaming for my autograph. I looked down to avoid the bright lights and was suddenly out of my own body, looking down at its limp form, laying on a stretcher, being carried to the street outside.

"And here comes the body now" a reporter cackled into his microphone, "Ribs is dead and the whole of the music world is shocked by his sudden departure, the greatest musician to ever live has been taken from us, never again will his style and charisma be reproduced" *(can you believe this shit? Really?)*

The eulogies kept coming as my body was slid into the back of the ambulance.

I was sitting on a stretcher in the back of an ambulance. The technician opposite held a clipboard and pen. He began asking me questions about myself as I looked out the window.

"Could you give me your name please…..

Date of birth…..

Your home address…..

Who is your next of kin…….

And what exactly have you taken today?"

Outside the ambulance I could see the entrance to Earls Court station go past. A few moments later it passed again, I looked at the technician with his clipboard and once more the station entrance passed us by.

"We're going round in circle here, we are aren't we? We're going round in fucking circles" I shouted at the driver, "Stop this fucking bus, let me out now, you don't know what you're doing, we're going round in circles because you don't know what to do. I am not staying here and waiting for this trip to end". I tried to get up but my legs failed me.

"Mr Reid, please bear with us, we are trying to….."

I was in no mood for bearing with, I wanted to get out, I wanted to run, my legs trembling with adrenalin needed to move, I had to get out of there. I reached for the door handle and blacked out.

I slept for an eternity, a million years of darkness passed before me, untouched by the universe about my being, I knew nothing of what I had been, what I was. I was aware only of my breath. I opened my eyes to see bright lights all around me. No sound, no colour, no distractions. Slowly I made out shapes beyond myself. I saw a curtain but did not know what it was. Above me, the tiled ceiling looked down and I didn't know what it was. I knew nothing. My entire mind had been wiped clean, I had no memory of anything. I didn't know who or where I was, how I got here or what here meant. There were no words in my head, no names, no knowledge, memories or thoughts. Everything was gone. I looked around me for the longest of times, searching for clues, stimulation, guidance and comfort. Everything was sterile and cold. I was naked but didn't know what it meant.

In time, I became aware of something at the end of my arm. It was solid, I could feel it to touch and lay on my side for the length of time it took for the universe to form, rubbing it between my thumb and forefinger. In my mind's eye I watched as the Earth was formed, still rubbing the item gently as the gases that swirled about slowly mixed and created the primordial soup in which life on Earth began. I saw bacteria, fish, dinosaurs and birds as they multiplied and grew, inhabiting the jungles, swamps, forests and seas all about me.

Volcanoes came and went, storms blew and seasons changed from moment to moment. I was reliving the history of the world, every minute detail passing through my mind. My memory reprogramming every thought and learned morsel as I relived the world.

I could make out this thing on my wrist now, it was a plastic band, a hospital name tag but I still did not know what that was. It was just a thing, on my wrist, something not of me but important all the same.

A door opened and a nurse pulled back the curtain.

"The doctor's coming to see you in a minute" she said and turned back out of the room. I looked all about me but nothing looked familiar, I didn't know what or where I was.

When the doctor finally came into the room he was carrying a clipboard like the one from the ambulance.

"Could you lay back on the bed and pull your trousers down slightly for me please?"

"WHAT?" I shouted back at him. He stepped backwards and I lunged forward punching him straight in the eye.

"Fuck this shit," I said, "Fuck the fucking useless fucking lot of you". I stormed out of the room and somehow found my way out of the hospital.

Not too far away in a waiting room, Sylvie and Pam were waiting patiently for news of my progress. Nurses had come and gone asking questions about what I had taken and how they could counteract its effects. They heard a kerfuffle and a short while later were approached by another nurse.

"I'm sorry to have to have to tell you, but your friend has left, he is no longer on the premises".

There was no more they could do, and so they left for home.

I was now alone and back out on the street. I too was heading home. I didn't know where I was or how to get home but I had help. Above me in the sky were my friends, huge towering giants up above the buildings. They were watching my progress on a huge TV screen, guiding me home with taunts and directions. 'This Way' signs illuminated the way before me, arrows pointing towards home.

"Get out of the road" someone shouted. I looked towards the car in front of me and roared from the pit of my stomach. I was a werewolf, just like in the film An American Werewolf In London. I fell to the floor and screamed. Pangs of agony wracked my entire being. My hands grew in front of my face, my feet twisted and my arched back popped as my spine curved and hairs and muscle burst through my clothes. My face contorted and I felt the searing pain of my nose and upper jaw extend. Every inch of my being was stretched and contorted into this new shape with agonizing effects.

A car horn sounded and I pounced on the bonnet snarling at its occupants, I crossed the road barking at pedestrians as they hurried by. Up in the sky the arrows still directed me onwards. I came to a road junction and looked up. There were arrows in all four directions. Confused, I looked to my giant friends in the party in the sky.

"Hahaha, you're fucked now aren't you?" a voice said. I didn't know what to do, why were they doing this to me, what was I meant to do? I reached out and touched a lamp post, I needed to support myself, I was no longer a werewolf but my own pathetic self, clinging to a post for sanctuary. I went to let go and immediately was hit by a jolt of electricity in my arm, right up to my chest. It felt like a bolt of lightning hitting me, like a sledgehammer in full swing colliding with every nerve in my body, the pain seared through me and I screamed out as I grabbed back at the lamp post, the pain stopped immediately as soon as I came into contact with it. A moment later I tried to let go and again was hit by searing pain. I tried again and again, each time with the same result.

"What do you want of me?" I cried, looking to my oversized friends up above. I was stuck to the lamp post and could never let go,whenever I tried, the same agonizing result. Above me I was humiliated, taunted by everybody I had ever known in my life, one by one they came forward to look down on me, each with the same or similar words.

"Look at you... Pathetic

You're an embarrassment...

I said you would never amount to anything....

So this is what became of you....

What a waste.....

What a miserable sack of shit you turned out to be...."

(I was kind of getting the idea that I was not popular....)

I had sunk to the floor and was crying, still clinging to the lamp post. This was my eternity, this was how I was destined to relive my dying moment for all time, a lonely pathetic sack of shit, huddled on the street, crying.

"There he is" a voice called out. A police van had pulled up at the junction and a side door slid open spilling 4 uniformed officers onto the street.

"Come along sonny" one of them said.

I rose from the floor and let go of the lamp post, there was no electric shock this time and as I stood up I continued to rise. My chest expanded outwardly and my arms bulged, I had turned into an oversized John McVicar, an uncontrollable tour de force, yep, you guessed it, I wasn't coming quietly.

I don't know who hit who first, or what happened next. I blacked out or was knocked out, both were feasible, both had the same result, oblivion.

I next became aware of being in a bare walled cell. It was windowless except for the tiny shutter in the big metal door, it kept opening at regular intervals, the shutter sliding back angrily and a face appearing in the gap.

"What d'you want?" It shouted.

"Fuck off" I replied, again and again this scenario played out.

I was huddled by the door, my arm up-stretched and seemingly glued to something on the wall. There was a continuous noise outside the cell, the sound of a bell ringing constantly that seemed somehow related to the vibration in my arm. Whenever I tried to remove my hand from the wall, the bell stopped and I felt a jolt of electricity up my arm again. "What d'you want?" Angry face was back.

"Fuck off". I let go of the bell button and punched the door. There were no more electric shocks, but I felt caged and wanted to get out, but out where? I didn't know where I was and again had no memory of what had gone on before. All I knew was the here and now. The 4 walls around me moved and breathed, hands pushed out stretching the elasticated fabric of the brickwork, faces came and went, trees grew from the floor and outside my cell was a an unknown universe, a place full of angry faces behind sliding shutters that would ask "What d'you want?" and then disappear.

 I stepped away from the door, huddled on the bench seat and looked around the room. There was a little side room, I could see the toilet rim but didn't know what it meant. I was a blank sheet, my mind once again swiped clean and once again I became aware of the thing on my wrist. What is it, what does it do, what does it mean? I knew it was important but couldn't work out what it was. I rubbed it as I had before, between my thumb and forefinger. I kept staring at it willing it to reveal its mystery, hoping it would be a clue to something. In time I began to focus and could see some markings, something written on it. I couldn't read it as I has forgotten how to read, I didn't know what they markings were. I worked my way deep into my memory and began to pull out snippets of information. I sat there alone and relearned from memory what the letters were, eventually working out that it was a name, my name. I was alive, I was a person, a real person with a name. The sense of relief and joy that flooded through me was surreal, like a relative being told their child had survived surgery and would make a full recovery. I existed, and I had a name, I was a real person.

"Now that you've calmed down, the doctor will be here in 10 minutes to see you".

Doctor? What Doctor? I looked around the cell, of course, I was here in this castle full of angry faces and mad doctors, to be operated on, to be experimented with. That was why I had no memory, that was why I was here, I was an experiment.

I could see now beyond my cell were a hundred more like it, each one containing an experiment, human heads transplanted onto the bodies of Pigs, animal limbs sewn onto people like me, people with no memories, people with no history. I had to remember, I knew now that I had to remember something and the clue began with my name tag. Staring down and concentrating as hard as I could,I pulled back more details, my date of birth, my place of birth, my childhood and more. Things were coming back in a flood and then the door opened.

"Good afternoon, I am the doctor on call", a short tanned man in a brown check suit jacket entered the cell. "How are you feeling?" He asked.

"I'm fine" I said guarded and suspiciously. "Yes, I feel fine"

"Are you seeing things, anything at all?"

"No, everything is just fine" His face was turning into that of Vincent Price, but I wasn't going to admit that, he was trying to catch me out, trying to trick me.

"Okay, I shall recommend that you are released now, it may take a while but not too long now". With that he left the cell as abruptly as he'd come in.

Released, I thought, released from where. This is a castle on a mountainside, am I to be fed to the wolves, thrown out into the night as a peace offering? I sat on the bench, nervously awaiting the door.

It wasn't long before 'Angry Face' came back and led me out of the cell. He was a big stocky fellow in a dark uniform with a white shirt, a policeman's uniform. What is a policeman? He told me to stand in front of a desk, another policeman was writing in a book. He didn't look up as he said "Sign here" and thrust a large book toward me. I took the pen and awkwardly scribbled in the manner of the other markings in the book.

"Here's your stuff" said Angry Face placing a bag on the desk. "Don't come back again-Ok?"

Don't come back? I didn't want to be here in the first place, or even know where I was still as I was shown out of the door.

I stepped outside and the bright sunlight hurt my eyes, I had no clue where I was or where I was going to so I turned left and started walking with my bag in my hand. At the next corner I could see nothing familiar and again turned and walked. At the next junction I turned again and was back at the door I started from, I did this twice before changing direction and heading away from the place of my recent incarceration. I kept walking, not knowing where to go but continuing forward, all the while the street moved and sucked my stride, walls rippled and animals people and monsters came and went by in a continual flow.

"Hey Ribs, how are you mate?" Someone in a shop doorway knew me, a familiar face, a voice I knew but didn't know.

"I'm good mate, but look, I'm tripping and I don't know my way home, where do I live?"

I took his directions and was soon knocking on the familiar front door of our house. Sylvie opened the door and with a shout of relief hugged me and pulled me into the hallway.

I was home.

It was to be another two days before I fully came down, no more visual hallucinations, no more bright colours and rubbery pavements and walls. I was finding it hard to work on the stall with the constant distraction of weird things I was seeing. Famous people walking by, dead people walking by, people with animal or monster-like faces and bodies asking "How much is this…."

"Do you have that in pink….."

"I want to buy your soul……"

"The Devil's coming to get you, but in the meantime, can I have an umbrella, I left mine at home….."

It was difficult at times but it was also what I needed to do, I needed the security, the routine and the income it gave me, all of which were essential to my well being and recovery.

Close To The Bed

Close to the bed there lies a candle
by the fire there's a stone,
In the mirror a reflection
flickers all alone.
In the cup is last night's coffee
and crumbs wait on a plate,
the clock ticks slowly backwards
as the TV sits and waits.
A crumpled sock-a damp old towel
and toothpaste wall to wall;
There used to be a carpet
but that lies in the hall.
A broken chair-an empty box
cigarettes and stagnant booze;
The only sign of human life
is a pair of worn out shoes.
And yes I am hungover
so no you cannot scream,
but should you leave then lock the door

And leave me to my dreams.
By the bed there lies a candle
by the fire there's a stone,
on the wall a simple message
"This is home, sweet home"

Gotta Getaway

No sooner was I back to normal then I was back at the
hospital again. My eyes had been hurting and what I thought
may have been the onset of conjunctivitis, actually turned out
to be Herpetic eye ulcers, I had cold sores in my eyes and was
in a lot of pain and discomfort. I wore sunglasses constantly
to help with the light sensitivity, but daylight burned as did
bright stage and disco lights.
 I travelled back to Romford one night to see old friends,
ending the night by staying with Mark Burns and a pot of
glue in an abandoned building near St Leonard's, the homes
where Adrian White had lived before being sent away. Mark
and I got on well, everyone loved Mark, he was a good guy
unless you crossed him, which didn't happen often. He was
there for everyone, a big brother, a middleman when things
went wrong and good company when you needed a laugh. I
needed that back to roots grounding after my recent
experience, and Mark was a good company. I left him in the
morning and headed back to the West End.

Major wasn't allowed on the street like I was, he wasn't trusted on the stall and spent more time upstairs, making hats with Willow and Pam.I liked being outside and was pretty good at selling. A new guy was taken on when someone left, Pam's boyfriend Des, a Psychobilly from Portsmouth. I got on well with Des-Pam too, they were a lovely couple and lived just up the road from me in Earls Court. Sometimes they would have the occasional domestic row and one or the other would come over for some sympathy or a shoulder to cry on. For some reason they thought I knew the answers to all their problems, me- the most useless inept person in London, I was their rock of salvation and sensibility whenever they had an argument. Also living up the road was Del, from the 100 Club. He had an apartment nearby and when I went to see him I met his new girlfriend Maz. It really is a small world.

Big Donna and Annie used to come round, they'd been regular visitors since the days of the old squat. I really liked Annie, she was sweet but something of an acid casualty, she was very sensitive and hard work at times, she was also much older than the rest of us, having been old enough to take part in the hippie revolution of the late 1960's. She lived with Donna, somewhere near Shepherd's Bush. Donna was on a mission to get really stoned this day, and ignoring Sylvia's warnings, managed to overdose in her room. Del set about bringing her back to life, I called the paramedics and Major disposed of the evidence in case they came with Police assistance. No doubt about it, Del saved her life and the paramedics just made sure she was ok. Seeing her laying on the floor, her lips turning blue, her skin paler than ever, life fading in front of me was a scary sight. Donna had been greedy, that was true, but this could have been any one of us, at any time, it was a warning.

It was good to have Pam and Des working with us. I didn't like the idea of strangers or any of them weird straight people working with me, you needed to be a little eccentric to work the stalls, the tourists and overseas visitors loved appearance and would often ask me to pose with them for photos as they bought our silly hats and other goods. I was posing for one such photo with some French kids, when a couple of mates from Romford appeared.

"Hey, how you doing mate?" I greeted them.

We chatted for a few minutes before one of them mentioned Mark, had I heard?

"Heard what, what's he done now mate?"

Mark was dead. He had been killed in a car crash. The day I left him he'd gone out in a friend's car. The car hit a lamp post which came down and decapitated Mark in the passenger seat. I was numb. I didn't know what to say or do. It was ok for other people to die, people outside of my hometown, people I knew in other circles, but this was someone close to me, I had only just been with him a few nights before and I found it hard to process that he was gone.

I attended his funeral a little while later, there were many people there, many familiar faces, Mad Max, Tony Barbara, most of the local punks, skins and kids from St Leonard's Homes. Mark was well loved, a popular guy, and he was gone.

Summer was fast approaching and nightlife in London was gearing up. Clubs were better attended, the good weather bringing people out more often. Near to my stall was under 18's Hip-Hop club on Saturday afternoon. Queues of young kids from the East End would practice their body popping moves as they warmed up on the streets. I wasn't a fan but appreciated their passion. They would often stand in line, pointing and whispering about the weird looking guy on the stall- "See him, look, he's got a tattoo on his head".

There were always opportunities to chat to customers, passers by would sometimes say hello if they were regulars, so being on the stall was never lonely. Sometimes people would flirt, or laugh and joke around, sometimes they hurried by. I never called out to people like the barrow-boys and proper market traders. I kept a low profile, let the display boards do the talking and would never push anyone into buying something they obviously didn't want. My style seemed to work and my takings were good, better than the guy who'd been on the job before, even with me dipping into my bag to buy cigarettes and lunch, I was doing well. I was smoking around 100 cigarettes a day, you can when you chain smoke for free and are busy all day serving people. I would light one up and then get sidetracked to serve somebody, the cigarette burning away in my fingers or between my lips, by the time I went back to it, it would be just about finished and so I would light another and repeat the process, from 9am to 5.45pm there was a cigarette constantly burning in my mouth.

Sometimes there would be a pause and I would get to see the people walking by. I would look at them and wonder what they were all doing day in day out. People watching became a byproduct of being on the pitch, watching, waiting for the next customer, the next sale.

A group of young Americans approached the stall one afternoon, it was late June or just the start of July. I had noticed a lot of Americans around, it was 1984 and almost the anniversary of their Indepence Day. I had spotted these teens on the other side of the road a few minutes earlier, especially the one girl with long black and purple hair. Our eyes had met from a distance and there was an instant attraction. I made some small talk with the rest of the group, trying to be polite and not too obvious, but I wanted to get to know this stranger, and I wasn't going to let her walk away without arranging to meet up with her later. Our eyes kept meeting, it was obvious we both wanted to get to know each other and before long we were talking openly. They were part of a group of competition winners from Los Angeles. KROQ radio station had run a competition, the winners were brought to London for a 2 week vacation with spending money and invited to a special US Citizens only, free entry event at the Hippodrome to celebrate Independence Day on July 4th. Rodney Bingenheimer, a famous presenter and radio DJ had come over with the group and was showing them around the West End. Some of the group were getting ready to move on and wanted to get to the HMV record store, I kept talking and soon Deanna and I arranged to meet up later, after work. I wasn't sure if she would turn up or not, maybe I had been too up front, maybe she would see someone else and forget about me.

My luck was in and Deanna did not forget about me, we hit it off immediately and by the end of the evening were holding hands walking back to the hotel they were staying in, The Tower Hotel, by Tower Bridge. Deanna was sharing a room with another girl who had also acquired a new boyfriend, a male model and restaurant worker called Tony. As we were not hotel guests we had to be careful getting in and out of the hotel by pretending to be with the others, maybe no one would notice. We got away with it for a couple of days but were caught out went the housekeeper came into their room and we were made to leave the premises. Undaunted, Tony and I slipped back in though the staff entrance an used their lift to get back to our girlfriends room.

July 4th came and with it I was invited to tag along to the Hippodrome. I had acquired a T-shirt from the stall that was printed like a dollar bill, so long as I kept with the others and kept my mouth shut, and as long as Tony did the same, we should be able to bluff our way in. The deal was that the venue would open from 7pm to 10pm for Americans only, the bar was free until 10pm and then it was open doors to anybody that wanted to come in, and all drinks thereafter had to be paid for. Having made it in through security and up to the bar, I was now determined to drink the bar dry.

"6 beers and 6 white wines please" I took a tray of drinks to a table near the dance floor. Having drunk my first beer, I headed back and ordered another round. Soon the table was full and a polite member of staff asked me if all the drinks were mine.

"Of course not, these 2 are mine, that is my girlfriends, these are for that couple over there and…." I kept pointing to random people on the dance floor and the bouncer cut in "It's ok sir, we just didn't want anyone to be abusing our hospitality this evening, that is all". They were obviously on to me and so I stayed away from the bar for a while.

Over on the dancefloor I did my bit for international relations, I didn't hit anyone and managed to funkily shake my tush in time to the music of Grandmaster Flash and Melly Mel's big hit of the summer, 'White Lines', Billy Idol's 'Hot In The City' and many other tracks I had heard in the clubs around town.

By 10pm the place was heaving and I was running out of drinks. I was feeling pretty drunk when then main entertainment of the night came on stage, The Psychedelic Furs. Pretty drunk, didn't really describe it accurately enough. I was blathered. So much so that I remember nothing of the bands performance. I know we left at some point and ended up at The Bat Cave, a famous nightclub for goths and alternatives. Here, all I recall was falling asleep in front of a stack of speakers. Somehow Deanna got me home to Earls Court and I was out for the count.

Because our girlfriends were friends, Tony and I became mates pretty quickly, and when it was time for the group to fly home I offered for those that wanted to stay, to stay in my place. There was plenty of room for everyone and so tickets were changed and trips extended. The main group flew home and those that didn't moved in to stay with me. This meant Deanna could stay as long as her money lasted, along with her friend, Tony, a guy called Mark Gazda from Marina Del Mar and 2 or 3 other people who'd chosen not to go home just yet.

I continued to go to work each morning, leaving my guests to sort themselves out, often going sightseeing around town, sometimes staying in bed all day. Most days Deanna would come to visit me on the stall once she had got herself up out of bed. She turned up one day with Tony and his girlfriend, looking somewhat confused and flustered.

"What are you doing here?" She asked.

"What? I'm working, you know that…"

"That's not what I meant" she said, her tanned skin looking a little pale. Something was definitely wrong. "I just saw you in the subway going down the escalator as we were coming up and you ignored me,I called you and you kept going. When we got to the top we chased down after you but you were gone, you'd already got on the train"

"But that's impossible, I've been here all morning"

"It's true mate" Tony butted in, "It was you alright, I saw you"

"But I've been here, I haven't gone anywhere- how could I have got back here before you if I had got on a train?"

"We came here to ask if anyone knew where you were going, but you're here". Tony looked as stunned as Deanna did. And then it dawned on me- my double, the guy I had seen in the pictures on a kids wall in Honiton a couple of years ago. It was him. Whoever he was he had not only fooled me in the pictures, he had made my girlfriend believe she had seen me on the escalator in Tottenham Court Road tube station. We had been only a couple of hundred yards from each other, me and my double.

Deanna stayed in London for a couple more weeks, as long as her money and Mother would allow. She was 16 and still at high school in California. Her parents divorced and so she lived with her Mum Joy, in a 2 bed apartment complex. We talked a lot while she was around and having asked her mum if it was ok, she invited me to go to Los Angeles and stay with them once I had the money to do so.

We eventually waved goodbye and I started planning my trip. For as long as she had been with me, it was easy for me to stay clean. I had something to look forward to, someone to look forward to, somewhere far from the city that I blamed for my own mess. Now I had to man up and start saving some money, I was finally going to Hollywood, not as a stowaway on a ship from Southend, but on a plane, as a free man, a guest of my girlfriend and future Mother-in-law. It was easy. Tony had done all the inquiries, we just needed to get the money to get out there, get a visa and ticket, a few hundred dollars to live on and we could go, get married and stay, or just work on the black market, whatever it took to get out of this filthy place, we were going.

I struggled once I was alone, I found the days drag and the nights were awful, I wanted so much to be gone but was a slave to my own vices. I could not stop going out. Going out meant distraction from my wanting to join Deanna, distraction from my increasingly poor health. I was getting severe cramps, wind and abdominal pains. My back was hurting and I was forever lethargic. The only thing that got me up in the morning was the shot that waited by my bedside. At night, another to put me to sleep. I saved what money I could and called her on the phone as much as possible, pushing a pile of 10p coins continually into a slot to say "Hi, I miss you, yes I am being good, I got my visa, no-I'm not going out" before going out.

A customer came up to my pitch on Saturday afternoon, we had another 10 minutes until closing time and I was already starting to tidy things away .

"How much are these watches?" He asked holding one out from the board.

"£2.99 or 2 for £5" came the standard reply.

"How much if I want to buy many?"

"I'll give you some discount, it depends, how many do you want?" I was now interested, this could be a good sale.

"I am flying out to Abu Dhabi tomorrow at 10am to go to my brother's wedding, I thought I would take some gifts for everyone. How much for 40 watches?"

"Forty watches, christ that's half the board, alright, look, not a problem, because I'm about to close up I will do you a good price, give me £60 and I'll get you 40 watches from the box out the back here, does that sound good to you?"

"That sounds very good, my friend, I will take them"

The box out the back there was either the box of new watches ready to go up on the sale board, or the box of broken watches we would cannibalise into working units. I shall let you decide which one I counted out into the bag for him before shutting up shop in record time.

It was a friday morning when Sami came over to see me.

"I have to go do some business today, Pascha is leaving early tonight so can you collect the stall money and pay everyone? I will see you in the pub later tonight"

"No problem boss, I'll see you later". With that Sami walked off up the road and I carried on as usual. Pascha came down to see me at 5pm when the hatmakers packed up for home. I gave Pascha his money and he hung around talking with me between customers. Pascha was Sami's cousin, an Afghan, but he and his wife had recently moved to London from Los Angeles. He knew I was saving up to go and told me about where he used to live, a place called Silver Lake, in the Valley. "Sometimes it gets so hot there man, you cannot breathe" I was liking it already. We shut up shop and stashed everything away inside the travel agents store as we did every night. I took the cashbags and paid everyone their money, finally holding out a large wad of notes to Pascha.

"Here you are" I offered him the money.

"No, I can't take it home with me, you have to have it and give it to Sami". This made no sense. Why was Sami letting me take the money when his own cousin was still here. I hadn't thought about it all day, but suddenly now it seemed odd that he wanted me to take it and not his own cousin. Pascha walked off and the rest of us crossed the road towards the Tottenham.

"If I were you…" Des started.

"No" I said firmly.

"He's right though Ribs" Major added.

"Don't……" I warned, putting up a hand.

"There's enough there to get you to America" Said Pam.

"Look, it's bad enough I'm thinking about it without you lot piping up, I'm not doing it okay?"

We walked into the pub and I ordered the drinks, Major and I downing the first pints in our usual custom, then taking the next one to our regular seats near the back of the pub. An awkward silence fell between us as we sat watching the clock, looking to the door and back at the clock. When our glasses were nearly empty I went back to the bar and got another round, courtesy of the boss, well, he was later than usual. I took the drinks to our table and passed them round before downing mine in one go.

"Have fun guys, I'll see you later" I smiled and turned away. As I passed the barman I called over to him,

"When Sami comes in, tell him I'll see him in the morning" and headed out the door.

I virtually ran down the stairs leading into Tottenham Court Road station. My heart was racing and my eyes darted around looking for Sami, I knew he would see me, I knew this couldn't be happening really, could it? Me, with a pocket of cash, more than I'd ever held in my hands in my lifetime, heading off to a new start. Tony had already left and now, out there with his girlfriend, he'd proved to me it could be done. I wanted it so badly, I needed it, I knew I would not survive the summer if I didn't do this. I had no choice.

My mind was racing, plan I needed a plan, what was I going to do? It was friday night, Dad would be out and I could pop home to see mum before I go. I had to her for the last time. It was only right. I pulled a ticket from the machine and headed for the central line, all around me people were walking to and fro, I kept looking, and still saw no sign of Sami. Jumping on the first train that came I checked all about the carriage, he was still not here and I was getting further away, the further the better. I had nothing against Sami, but I was holding his money. It had felt like a golden handshake to me. The odd way he had said about Pascha leaving early, and him still being there and not taking the money himself, it made sense to me. Sami knew I was trying to save up, he knew I was going away, he knew.

I got off the train at Hornchurch, and almost ran home to the house I had grown up in. Mum answered the door.

"What are you doing here?" She asked.

"I'm going to America" I said.

"I know that, but what are you doing here?"

"I'm going now, tonight" I pulled out the wad of notes and her chin hit the floor.

"You ain't going nowhere like that, you get in here and have a bath, you can't go to America smelling like you do, here, get your clothes off and I'll wash them while you have a hot bath. Joanne, your brother's here, put the bath on for him will you?"

I was sitting on an armchair watching Hawaii 50 on the TV. Mum had made me some tea and toast and I felt clean and warm, dressed in a bathrobe as my clothes sloshed around in the washing machine outside, in the kitchen.

"That's better, you couldn't go away looking like you did without clean clothes and a bath" Mum said "Loanne's gone over the road to ring the airport, find out when the next flight is, now where did you put your money?"

"I gave it to you" I said, pulling at the toast with gritted teeth.

"No you never, I ain't got it"

"Then it must be in my pocket, in my jeans"

You wouldn't think that a simple statement like that could bring the world to a halt, but it did. I froze. The TV seemed to be silenced, nothing moved. Nothing but my Mum running faster than Wylie Coyote with an Acme parcel for Roadrunner. I sat in the chair and laughed at the obvious outcome, no money, no ticket, no ticket no flight, no flight no money to give back to Sami…. Bollocks!

Joanne came back into the house just as mum pulled the door of the washing machine open. Water poured out over the floor and the two of them pulled my jeans out of the machine. The money still in an inside pocket, was damp through, we had to dry it out, and spent the next couple of hours with hairdryers and an iron, drying and pressing the notes out on an ironing board, notes spread about all over the living room in various states of dampness.

 We were about halfway through when the door went, it was the police. Well sort of, you see, this was the first time I ever met Joannes boyfriend, Chris. He went on to become a policeman, so in a way that counts.

 The next flight I could get was the following afternoon, standby. I headed back to Earls Court but fell asleep and went straight past it on the train, waking up near Ealing I managed to jump across the platform and onto the last train back to Earls Court.

 In my room, I packed my clothes and important bits into my backpack. Fiona, Pam and Paul stayed in my room with me that night. My backpack, ready to go, sat by the bedroom door. I had a hit and finally fell asleep about 4am.

 I awoke with a start, I'd heard a noise upstairs and knew something was wrong. Instinctively I dived out of my pit and grabbed my boots. There were loud footsteps and voices coming down the stairs into my basement flat, it was Sami. As he came across the empty living room at the base of the stairs, I fled to the toilet at the far end of my bedroom. There was no way out from here, no windows, no doors. If I had to get out I would have to fight my way through Sami and whoever was with him. As I pulled the toilet door to, I could see the bedroom door opening inwards, pushing my backpack behind it. My passport was still sitting on top, clearly visible, behind the door.

"Where's Ribs?" Sami demanded looking at the half asleep, bewildered faces laying around the floor.

"We haven't seen him since last night" Pam said in a voice heavily laden with yawns. "He hasn't been home, why?"

"He stole my money, £1,000. The police are on their way, they have a warrant for him, he won't get away with this, you tell him, you tell him I want my money back".

I was rigid, ready to pounce, ready to fight to the death if I had to.

'If he sees my backpack, if he touches my passport or comes near this door….'

"You tell him I want my money back!" Sami's voice was louder, as if he knew I was there, but he turned and left, stomping loudly back up the stairs. I waited a few moments until the street door slammed. Fiona went to check he'd gone as wasn't just waiting upstairs for me. She came back down. "Coast is clear" She said, "but we better get you out of here quick, before the police arrive".

I took my backpack and passport, climbed the stairs and was out of the house as soon as I could. The girls came with me and waited on the platform until my train came. They took it in turns to kiss me goodbye, wish me luck and say they loved me, even Pam, who was crying her eyes out. I felt guilty at leaving and for one moment thought that maybe I should stay. The moment passed and I stepped on the train, nervously looking around, checking for Sami or the police, neither were in my carriage and so I smiled, waved at my friends as the doors closed and I wondered if I would ever see them again.

It was probably somewhere over the North Atlantic, around Iceland, approximately 38,000 feet above the sea that I began to sweat. I wasn't scared of flying, I had never been on a plane before and I don't like heights when I'm standing on buildings and cliff edges. I was sweating because I had acquired a habit. I had been using more frequently than I had realised and was now going 'Cold Turkey' on the plane. My legs and stomach were cramping, I was in so much pain that I couldn't sit still and as much as I tried not to bring attention to myself, I'm sure the other passengers must have noticed something was wrong, but nothing was said and until I made it through immigration, I was not going to believe that I had made it.

My first sighting of Los Angeles was through the window as we were coming in to land, acres and acres of houses, every other one with its own swimming pool, streets lined with palm trees rose up to greet us as we came in to land, falling steadily from a clear bright blue sky. The air tasted hot and thick, my ears hurt from the decompression and my body ached. My passport was duly stamped with hardly a word and I was free to go. I had made it, I had escaped. Whatever happened now I knew I could never go back to where I'd come from, not London, not England, just the me that I had been. I could never again allow myself to go through this again, I wanted to live, I had known it from the moment I first woke up in Earls Court and wished I hadn't. When Helen, Clare and Lisa had come for the weekend, we jumped on the train to go somewhere and my head turned purple, my blood pressure so high I should have just popped like a zit and bled out where I stood. I knew from the look of fear on Helen's face. I knew I could not continue to pretend I was happy with my lot, that I could accept this pathetic way of life as being all I would ever have. I knew I wanted more, I wanted and needed to live, to live beyond this one year, this one room, one town. I needed to get out and now I was free of my own self inflicted shackles. I was in America, the U S of fucking A, California Uber Alles, the city of angels.

This was the start of a new beginning, a new me.

I stepped out from immigration to find Deanna waiting for me, her mother Joy too. We threw our arms around each other as if we hadn't seen ourselves for years not just a few weeks.

Joy hugged me and looked me straight in the eye,

"I know a good clinic" she said, she was serious, we had spoken a few times on the phone, but these were her first words to my face. I looked back at her and smiled.

"Thank you, but no, I don't want to go to a clinic and to be around the very same temptations I've just left. I'm going to beat this, without substituting one thing for another, I am getting clean, the only way I know I can".

She squeezed me tightly and smiled.

"Good boy, now, let's get you home".

It was to be another 2 or 3 nights before I could actually sleep. I laid in bed hour after hour staring at the ceiling, tossing and turning, my body in cramps, my legs aching. I would get out of bed and walk around in circles, feeling exhausted and sweating, my body burning up but cold inside and out. There was no respite, no comfort. I was sick, vomit and diarrhoea tearing my insides apart, breaking every opportunity for rest. Deanna gave me some sleeping tablets, when they failed to work, I took more, and more again. I took the whole packet and still found no comfort. I wanted to cry but not be heard. Joy, asleep in the next room had to be at work in the mornings, and I didn't want to be a hindrance. I smoked my way through cigarette after cigarette, the hours passing so very slowly as I watched the sky outside. One night there was a lightning storm and the sky flashed so beautifully over the mountains. I watched silently, like I was the only person in the world to be watching the sky at this time.

It was August 1984 and the Olympics were in full swing. The whole of Los Angeles was in full party mode, everywhere was clean and spotless, the most beautiful city I had ever seen.

Once I was feeling well enough, we started getting out and about. Joy took us to Santa Monica beach in her car, not a huge petrol guzzling Chevy but a little blue Toyota. I sat in the back of the car like a kid in a candy store, my eyes darting all around, big cars, trucks and motorbikes came and went, nothing like the traffic we had in England, these were the vehicles we'd only ever see in films, or on TV. Big, wide shiny motorcars, the brilliant blue sky reflecting off their chrome, driving along spotlessly clean roads. Behind them, the brown hills, fringed by lush green trees and the iconic Hollywood sign looking down at me. The familiar letters I had seen all my life seemed so surreal in the reality of every moment I saw them. This was a dream come true, paradise. The little kid from Mardyke, the snotty nosed urchin, now grown up, with the sun on his skin and hope in his heart.

 I had always been a keen swimmer, a good thing if you were planning for a life on the ocean waves. I would often go to the pool in Hornchurch when I was growing up, spending hours on end in the water. I had managed to pass my Bronze and silver swimming awards at school, I loved to sit at the deep end, on the bottom beneath 12 feet of water, holding my breath as long as I could before eventually rose slowly to the surface for air. I could swim 2 whole lengths of the pool, hugging the bottom, coming up to breathe and feeling accomplished. I could do anything I pleased in the water, but stepping into the ocean at Santa Monica beach was a whole new experience. Waves hit the beach clawing back about 12 inches of the sand and stones beneath my feet, pulling the ground from beneath me. I lost balance and fell backwards, the next wave crashing onto my face as I tried to rise and again lost my footing. I was pulled further out into the ocean and was unable to surface for air before being hit by the next wave, and the next. Sand and shingle pelted my skin, my eyes closed I couldn't tell up from down. I had never believed that the ocean could be so powerful, not like this, not when it looked so calm, when so many other people were able to swim, bathe and surf all around me.

I fought to reach the surface and my face hit the air as I gasped for breath, but was again spun in the water like a rag doll. I was so weak I couldn't fight back, I couldn't hold my own against the deep blue ocean and was expecting any moment now to be my last. Just when I thought it was game over, my arms were seized from behind, my head pulled up above the surface and I gasped for air as a lifeguard pulled me back to shore. It wasn't Pamela Anderson or David Hasselhof, but it was a genuine California Lifeguard doing their job, saving the life of someone experiencing the power of the ocean for the first time.

One of the biggest film releases of the year was Gremlins. Joy took us along to Mann's Chinese cinema on Hollywood to see the film and I loved it, I wanted to be a Gremlin like Stripe, bad to the core, but cute and cuddly in a reptilian kinda way. I had the hair for it and probably the teeth too. I was in Hollywood baby, Hollywood, the city of Angels, surrounded by sinners and not a sign anywhere of the ferry from Southend that would have brought myself and Chris Lacey to international stardom.

I soon started to feel better, no more withdrawals, but my liver would often remind me who was boss. Joy took us out for breakfast in Glendale one morning and although the food was delicious, I physically felt sick trying to eat my hash browns. I had never had them in the UK and even though they were only potatoes, they seemed oddly alien to me. Something else that seemed odd to me was how approachable and interactive people were. Strangers would talk to me, compliment me on my hair, tattoos or piercings. In England nobody said anything unless it was to start a fight. Sitting having our breakfast, we were approached by a young guy with a beard, he was wearing a bandana on his head. He introduced himself as Michael and complimented me on my image.

"Hey, you're from England, that's so cool,man" It was starting to become a bit of a routine, I would say something and suddenly everybody wanted to listen to my accent. Deanna took me to a club in Hollywood one night, the Cathay De Grande. It was like the 100 Club was in London, but the venue was on the street level, upstairs was the kitchen, changing rooms and general hangout area for those who wanted to smoke a few joints and have a laugh amongst themselves. The bar downstairs was a great place to mix and meet people, watch the bands and just have a great night out. We had just sat down at a table with about a half dozen other punky types when somebody caught my accent.

"Hey, are you from London?" She asked across the table.

"Yeah, I just got here a few days ago"

"Do you know Dave?"

There were about 6,000,000 people in London, and of them I could estimate about 300,000 were called Dave.

"Er, Dave who- you'll have to give me a bit more to go on, where in London, who does he hang around with, where does he drink?"

"He goes down the Kings Road a lot, his best friend is a guy with red and black hair, kinda like got all red one side and black the other, they call him Eagle or something like that"

"You mean Vulture?"

"Yes that's him, do you know him?"

"Yes" I knew Vulture, he was Fiona's ex before we met, I had seen him quite a bit out about, hung out together at gigs and on the Kings Road. "Yes I know Vulture, and Dave, that's his mate, Dave Ferguson"

"You know Dave, that's awesome, he was my boyfriend when I was in London".

Never be fooled into thinking it's anything other than a small world we live in. Here I was 8,000 miles from home, talking to a group of people I'd never met, about a couple of guys I was in the 100 Club with, watching The Soldiers Of Destruction, only a week before.

The Cathay De Grande had been recommended to us by Louis Elovitz, a punk video maker. We met him outside of Loves Burger restaurant on Hollywood. Louis seemed to know everyone and everyone knew Louis. He told us the Cathay De Grande was the best venue around for cheap punk gigs, beer and a cool place to hangout. Years later I learned it was a favourite hangout at the time of another ex-pat, Slash from Guns and Roses, though I can't honestly say I did or didn't meet him. I got to meet a lot of people at the Cathay De Grande, Louis had definitely pointed us in the right direction. He invited us to a party at his apartment too, this was a while later, I don't remember much, except that it was hot, really hot, no air conditioning, the beer in the fridge was warm and there were a lot of cockroaches, big creepy crawly things that seemed to click their heels as they ran up the walls with bellies full of Louis's food. One person we did meet there was a photographer I got chatting to. He was looking for a couple to be in a photo shoot he was doing. An advert for the Dr Pepper's New Generation promotion. He had the job of putting it together and wanted to do a shoot with me and Deanna next to a big motorbike. Topless, but with a big silver chain covering our shy bits. He was going to put us on billboards all over the states, were we interested? Hell yeah, we swapped numbers and waited for him to call, he rang a few times but was having trouble fixing dates with the studio he wanted to use, so we kept waiting.

We had tried getting hold of Mark Gazda, one of the guys who'd stayed at my place in Earls Court, we kept calling and eventually found out he was not very well. He had been in an accident and crashed his plane. Had I known he owned a plane, I would have charged him rent.

We found another club to go to, one that was a bit more upmarket and full of well-off kids dancing out of time to the latest 'Indie' tunes, it was a cleaner, more sterile environment but the sort of place where as much money had been spent on hairspray than the GDP of a small African Nation. A little too clean for me and my Dr Marten boots.

The Cathay De Grande was a great place to hang out, it was full of my type of people. People who swore, liked beer, loud punk music and having a good time. I saw a lot of bands there and got to be pretty good friends with many of the regulars. I was told on my first visit to be careful on the streets, how I dressed could be a health hazard. In Los Angeles, punks at the time didn't wear all the studs and big boots, belts and chains that had become the uniform of London's punks. Dressing too outrageously could get a person killed, there were drive-by shootings happening regularly. Punks in LA wore baseball boots, checked shirts tied around their waists and very few dared shave their head into a mohawk, I was lucky because I wasn't local, I wasn't part of one gang or another, I was 'The English Dude' - Ribs, the guy from London. I could get away with more than most, usually.

We had been at the Cathay De Grande one night and were walking home around 2am, somewhere down the bottom end of Hollywood, when a car pulled up alongside us.

"Hey, Punks, dirty mother fuckers" came the catcall.

"Don't say a word" Deanna squeezed my arm.

"Hey punk!" I ignored it a second time. Deanna told me not to react, she'd lived here all her life and knew the score, so I had to follow her lead.

"Hey mother fucker, I'm gonna kick your ass you chicken shit, mother fuckin' punk"

Enough was enough now and I couldn't hold back any longer, if I'd had a bag of chips I would have thrown them on the floor by now, instead I spun on my heel and pointed my finger at his face, hoping it was loaded.

"Think you're fucking hard do you, with your mates in that car,think it's fucking tough to call people names and drive away? Get out and show us what you're made of, just you and me, hands and feet, come on, right here now!"

I think that was meant to be both barrels and in any other circumstance may well have caused him to think twice. Only this time, I wasn't in Romford or Hornchurch being punched over a garden wall, this was Hollywood, a car full of Mexican cholos and I was out of my league. The guy in the passenger seat smiled, his thin moustache spread from one ear to the other as he leaned forward almost sinking below the door frame. The blacked out rear window concealed his friend and an automatic rifle. There was a loud click as the weapon was cocked pointed straight into my face.

"Ok, Ok,Ok!" I put both hands up, "Yeah, you win ok, you say what you like, yeah, just don't pull that fucking trigger ok?"

Every inch of my body tensed at I swang from fight mode to flight without being able to move. One step out of place now and I would cut in two in a hail of flashing lead. For one moment, I was more scared than I had ever been at any time in my life. Deanna was behind me, I couldn't protect her from this but she had known what was coming, she warned me.

There was another loud click and a hail of laughter, no bullets, just a group of young Mexicans raucously laughing at the Gringo from London with the funny accent. The car's wheels screeched as the window rose and the vehicle pulled away, Deanna and I suddenly alone on the sidewalk, chips all over the floor.

I got a phone call from Tony one day, he had split up from his girlfriend and was in a bad way. Having left her home he was hitchhiking through the desert, from Las Vegas to Los Angeles and been mugged at gunpoint. Everything was gone, money, passport, the lot. There was nothing I could do for him and I never heard from him again.

I was alone in the apartment one day and came across a celebrity gossip magazine containing an interview with a pop singer from the UK. I recognised him straight away obviously, and was intrigued to read the interview. One of the questions asked was "Have you ever owned a pet"

"Yes, I had a dog once but somebody stole it".

Joy took us up to Melrose one day. She dropped us off and left us to go window shopping, looking at the vastly overpriced horrible wares in the stores we'd never be allowed inside were it not for my smile and obviously British accent. (He's British and dressed like that must- be a wealthy eccentric rockstar) We gazed in through a few shop windows, entered one or two doorways, basically killing time before wandering off somewhere else. The sunshine was beautiful, dry hot air enveloping my skin, I felt so comfortable here, day and night I usually wore just a shirt or sleeveless denim. No need for layers here, no extra vest incase the weather turns. No shivering in the bus shelter, hiding from the snow, just sunshine, palm trees and more sunshine.

We stepped out of a doorway and were surprised to see a photographer pointing a huge camera at us, the type you see on TV that look more like a rocket launcher than a soul catcher, the type with the long fat lens that can pick out the spinach in your teeth from 300 yards, in thick fog. I didn't challenge him, just acted casual and continued on our way.

A few weeks later I was stopped by a girl in the Cathay De Grande.

"It's you, isn't it?"

"It is me, yes" I didn't have clue what she was on about.

"You're the guy from the Enquirer" she yelped, "can I have your autograph?" I still was none the wiser.

"What do you mean, what Enquirer?" I asked.

"The National Enquirer, you were on the cover last week, they had a photo of you outside a shop on Melrose. The headline said 'And they wonder why they're unemployed!' I saw it, you're the guy" I was? Possibly, but I've never seen it. She promised to send me a copy but never did.

There was a party at a house one night, someone Deanna knew. The host was a young woman whose partner had died about 6 months previously. I found her crying in a room and tried to cheer her up, make her see that life goes on, that he wouldn't want to see her upset or committing suicide, she was too good for that stuff, I knew it and she needed to know it too. A little while later, we all ended up at the Cathay De Grande. Donna, the girl whose party we'd been at had become a little worse for wear and we needed to get her home. We had come in her car and she refused to leave it behind saying she was ok to drive. However, before we could go we had another problem. The Cathay De Grande was frequented by two rival gangs, The LADS (Los Angeles Death Squad) who were a pretty hardcore bunch of guys I had come to know, and the XIIIth Street, tonight they outnumbered the LADS by about 8 to 1, meaning about 8 of them turned up and there was only Jerry from the LADS in the bar. I had gotten on well with Jerry and didn't want to leave him alone, so I offered him a lift home. I looked around and Jerry was not in the bar, someone said he'd gone outside, around the back street. I went to find him and sure enough there he was, surrounded by the rival gang, it was 8 against 1, they should have brought reinforcements. Jerry was a big, muscular, bald headed hispanic guy with a head shaved so close you see your own reflection in it. He was a one-man army and busily knocking 3 barrels of shit out of the XIIIth Street guys, all by himself. I called out to him and he didn't respond, so I got closer. He had one guy under his armpit, another in his hand being punched in the face by his free hand, a third guy lunged at his head with no effect, two lay on the floor out cold, the others circling, unsure what to do. I walked over to him and touched his shoulder.

"Jerry, we gotta go mate, so if you want that lift you'd better come now" I said.

"Just give me two minutes, I'll be right with you".

Jerry was good to his word and about 5 minutes later, we were in the car heading back to Donna's house. We came to an intersection on Hollywood, just where we needed to turn left and the light was red. Donna kept going and as we turned I saw a police cruiser sitting at the opposite light watching as we cut across in front of him.

"OH shit, there's a cop, we're going to pulled" I warned Donna. She was over the drink drive limit and had been smoking pot too, this was not going to end well. Sure enough the flashing blue lights came up behind us and we pulled to a stop. Donna was taken out of the car and subjected to a sobriety test. She was struggling to walk in a straight line and kept saying the cops were "Assholes". I got out and tried to apologise for her.

"Look mate, she's upset, her boyfriend died recently and she's trying to cope on her own, it's not easy for here".

"Where are you from boy?"

"London, England, I'm here with my girlfriend there" pointing to the back seat of the car.

"Can you drive this car?" he asked.

"Pretty sure, yes" I said.

"If you can drive these folks back home then we'll let you go, but if you can't, you're friend there is going back to the station". No pressure then.

I had never driven left hand drive, on the wrong side of the road, and automatic too. And where the heck was I going? None of this mattered, right now, I just had to concentrate and get everyone home, safe, without getting nicked. The Cops followed me for about a mile, I didn't hit anything, I didn't drive too fast or weave all about the road, I just drove normally, on the wrong side of the road, in the wrong side of the car but somehow going the right way.

Louis told me the Dead Kennedys were playing at the Olympic Auditorium and I had to go. I had seen them play 2 or 3 times in the UK, but I wanted to see what they were like on home turf, how the crowd reacted in a bigger venue, how Punk in the USA compared to back home. What I saw took me by surprise. In England, kids would bounce around in front of the stage, jumping up and down, flailing arms and legs around, sometimes pushing into each other, falling around. There would be crowd surges, when the guys further back pushed towards the front, or even sideways, people would fall, get up and continue to push, surge or bounce around until the end of the song, at which point everyone would catch their breath, throw empty plastic beer cups around or punch someone who'd annoyed them. A fight broke out in the Music Machine one night, at a UK Subs gig. A pair of skinheads, both topless but for their braces were competing for bragging rights. As they were seperated and calmed down one had got his braces caught on somebody behind. He walked hastily across the gap between himself and his adversary and the elasticated braces stretched 4 feet, 5 feet,

6 feet before they were released and pinged at a huge rate of knots into the guys back, sending him skywards in what must have been excruciating surprise.

In Los Angeles things were done differently. In front of the stage a group would form and run in a circle, pushing, pulling, kicking and punching whomever they could reach whilst still maintaining the circular flow, anyone who faltered was trampled and kicked by those behind them, it was like watching a massive Conga train on barbiturates, eating it's own tail, swallowing itself as it spun into certain self-destruction. Those in the centre were unable to get out, those outside could only step back and hope not to be dragged into the affray. Nobody stopped to pick up the fallen, nobody danced, they ran in a circle punching and kicking as they went, and that was it. I watched the spectacle from the sidelines.

"Do you want to go join in?" Deanna asked,

"No it's ok, I'll just sit this one out, I don't know what they're doing out there but it sure looks weird to me".

When I wasn't hanging out around Hollywood at night, I would be trying to find a job. I wanted to work but daren't do anything that would get me kicked out of the country. I couldn't work without a work permit, and I couldn't get a work permit without either a job that only I could do, like maybe being an actor, musician or artist, brain surgeon or astronaut, none of which I was actually any good at. I could bake bread, but not without a visa. The only other course of action would have been for Deanna and I to marry. This wasn't going to happen as it was obvious Deanna was still too young. She was still in school and due back there any day now. There was only one other option. I could marry her Mother. Needless to say, that was never going to happen either, and as the days went by, my money went down and it was obvious I would be heading home when my time was up. In the meantime, I was determined to enjoy every moment I could in this beautiful place.

Billy Idol was playing in Orange County, some big open air arena somewhere I had never heard of. Joy knew where it was but wasn't willing to drive us there as she had to go to work in the morning, but she allowed me to take her car instead. This meant I had to drive Deanna and myself halfway around the city when I didn't really know where the city was. Our instructions were clear, don't break or loose the car, don't get arrested or lost, and be back before morning or the car will turn into a pumpkin and Halloween will be the least of my problems. Joy made it clear, her car meant the world to her, and she needed it more than I could ever understand. I felt pretty honoured to be trusted with such a responsibility. I knew I would be fine getting us there and back in one piece, I just wasn't sure of where the hell there was. Los Angeles was a maze of freeways to me. Roads going here, there and just about everywhere, nothing seemingly making a lot of sense to me. Joy gave me directions and I assigned them firmly into my consciousness. It was one straight road apparently, straight there, straight back. Joy was right, sure enough, I managed to get to the gig unscathed, one straight road there, and one straight road back.

The gig itself was another new experience for me. An outdoor arena. I had only ever been to one outdoor event in London, a CND march from Battersea park to Brixton and a free gig in Brockwell park featuring The Damned, Hazel O'Connor, The Style Council and Madness, amongst others.

I spent much of that gig perched up in the scaffolding to the right of the stage, refusing the requests from security to do so, that was after we had bombarded The Style Council with mud pies, much to Paul Weller's disdain.

In Orange County there were no mud pies, no clambering up the scaffolding, just tier upon tier of well behaved fans sitting in their seats and singing along to the songs. I have to admit, I was like a petulant child that night. Billy Idol put on a great show, Stevie Stevens was fantastic too, energetic, raucous, they played some of my favourite songs of all time, Rebel Yell, White Wedding, Ready Steady Go. I loved it, but I also hated it, nobody was dancing, there was nobody bouncing around, jumping over seats to get to the front, no po-going in the aisles. Everyone just stood in their place holding their lighters aloft. This wasn't Yelling in a Rebel like manner, it wasn't Kissing anybody Deadly, it was Dancing With Myself at a White Wedding with 20,000 fucking candles on the bastard cake, where were the 100 punks of old, where was the Youth, Youth, Youth? Was this it, was I the only one left, or was I the only one refusing to move on, grow up and adapt? I sat in my seat and looked around me at the rest of the audience, these were not my people, this was not what I had expected. I was alone in a sea of faces, a lonely voice saying "This is not alright".

Louis was filming another video in the Cathay De Grande one night. Rigor Mortis were playing on stage and I was upstairs with friends, smoking and drinking when Louis appeared with his camera. He asked me what I thought about the venue closing down. We had heard rumours, and let's face it, 5 bands on a tuesday night for $3 was never going to turn a profit, even with beer sales, it would be hard to stay ahead at the best of times. Now it was being confirmed, Cathay De Grande was closing soon, the best little club in town was to be no more.

(Louis's video is on YouTube now, my words immortalised on the little screen, thank you mate, so little exists of my past on film or photo, seeing a 19 year old version of myself feels strange, but always makes me smile)

Time was ticking on, Deanna went back to school and I was left to wander the streets at my own leisure. I had seen an advert for budding actors, it was in a local newspaper. Free screen test, $200 for a week's training and then guaranteed jobs in advertisements. I booked an appointment and went to see what the score was. By the time I had been promised megabucks in monthly TV royalties, $800 a day for each day in the studio and had I heard of this company before, surely I had seen their name in the credits of half a dozen shows I had never heard of, except for Chips, Hill Street Blues and some other show that made him sound as if he was pulling names out of the air to sound good.

"Look kid, once you pay the 200 bucks, I got you a slot now as an airline pilot for an advert I'm shooting next, you just gotta pay up, we then take a percentage of your next few checks, until the true cost of the schooling is covered, you get a green card and everyone is happy, whattayer think?"

I didn't know what to think, except that I had yet to see an airline pilot with a black and white mohawk and ring through the centre of his nose. Something didn't add up.

I had much to think about, little to do and even less to do it with. It was obvious I was going to have to return to England, especially once my liver played up. I was thrown into excruciating cramps again and my eyes and skin were yellowing. Deanna took me to an emergency hospital but there was nothing they would do for me, I had no travel insurance and no medical cover, I had no right to treatment. All I could do was return to England and hope to get treatment before it was too late.

It was a sullen return as we drove back to LAX, I couldn't think of much to say except to thank Joy for her hospitality, for all she had done for us, to promise to return as soon as I was fixed and had enough money to stay next time. Deanna was too young to marry me, she was too young to be burdened with my problems, my needs, my inadequacies. Maybe she was better suited to somebody else, possibly the pen-friend she had in the Navy, a guy who'd call her at all hours of the night for a chat. Maybe better suited for someone more local, someone who knew her needs better than I could, we came from different cultures and I was too damaged to change, I wasn't ready for the sort of life I would have to live here, or anywhere really. We still promised to wait for each other, there were tears in amongst the lies, and eventually the inevitable departure.

It was true we had been in love for a short while, it was also true that without having been invited to Los Angeles, I would never had made it through the summer of 1984, Deanna and Joy had saved my life, something for which I would always be truly grateful.

"He who conquers others is strong,
He who conquers himself, is mighty."

Lao Tse.

Holidays In The Sun

Touchdown in London was smooth enough and within a couple of hours I was back in Earls Court. Major had heard no more from Sami after I left, all my friends had been sacked from the job and the police did come to look for me, leaving empty handed they made it clear I was a wanted man. My freedom was short lived. I left the house to make a phone call to Deanna, I wanted to tell her I was back safe, but no sooner had I exited the front door, a police van pulled up beside me and I was surrounded. I was only going to the station to use the phone, 20 or 30 feet away, and I never made it.

"That's a nice tan you've got there Son, been on holiday?"

"I was in Los Angeles" I replied, " had a great time…."

"Oh I bet that was lovely there, my Mrs wants to go, I don't know if I want to fly that far to be honest, so what's your name?".

Think quickly or else it's curtains.

I gave him Animals' name and date of birth, I knew I was busted but had to try to get out of it.

"Sorry mate, but I've checked the details you gave me and you have too many tattoo's, your friend doesn't have any, so I will give you one last chance to come clean or I'm arresting you, do you understand me?"

"Yes I understand" I told him the truth and in return he gave me some new jewellery, matching bracelets and a free ride to Hammersmith Police Station. I was busted, strip searched and processed before being shown to my room without a view.

Yesterday I was in Los Angeles, a free man with the world at my feet, today I was a prisoner in a cold grey cell, in a cold grey city, looking at a very short, cold, grey future.

I stood before West End Central Magistrates the following morning, they asked me to confirm my details and having read the charges the Crown Prosecutor moved that as I had already fled the country once, I was deemed a flight risk and bail was refused. I was to be held on remand for 28 days. I had never been refused bail before, I had never been held on remand or imprisoned for more than a few hours or a couple of days at most, this was not in the script and I had but only one choice, adlib and play it by ear, this was going to be a new and scary experience. I was taken down, literally, via a doorway in the dock, back down to a holding cell beneath the court, where I was joined by several other prisoners. Some had been sentenced, others, like me had held on remand. We were taken to Brixton Prison and kept in a holding cell there until allocated a place at another hostelry of equally ill-repute. For me, it was Chelmsford Prison, a much better choice than Brixton, a far less dangerous place for a first time remand prisoner, let alone convicted inmate.

I arrived at Chelmsford later that afternoon, there were 6 or 7 of us arrived on the same van. Each handcuffed to a bar inside a locked cell, inside a closed van, watching the world go by through the windows. I could see Barry's face in every other truck window as they passed, his voice cheerily blasting - "Go do your bird, you miserable fuckers, I've done mine!"

I had never done bird before, but I had been schooled plenty by those that had. I firmly intended to keep my head down.

At Chelmsford the dehumanisation process kicked in, stripped, left standing naked, searched and double searched, quizzed, poked and prodded, I was to be kept on suicide watch, fed a fat-free diet and have regularly visits to the prison doctor and psychiatrist. That actually sounded like a good regime, I might get myself fixed up and shipped out in better condition than when I arrived, ready to get back to Los Angeles before the end of the year, if I could get some money. The reality of it was to prove somewhat different. The fat free diet meant no fried food, no bacon, eggs, cheese, chocolate, milk, yoghurt, cream or fizzy drinks. I was to have salad, pasta without sauce, no butter, no fun. 28 days of this and I may just have to kill someone.

I was given my bunk in a cell and informed I would be getting a cellmate later on that evening. I expected some half mad, inbred of a skinhead, maybe even a psychotic nutjob with a very short fuse. Whoever he was, I was going to have to make sure we got along just fine, no bragging, no big stories, just keep him friendly and ride out the time.

Sure enough, I wasn't far off. When the door eventually opened and my new world shrank by 50%, I was joined by a young guy with a bald head. We had an awkward moment of neither knowing what to say, then we broke the ice and slowly got to let our guards down a little.

Pete (I shall call him him that), came from Basildon and was on remand after committing ABH, Actual Bodily Harm. He'd had an argument with his girlfriend, they split, someone stepped in too quickly and Pete lost his cool, battering the guy and breaking his arm in 2 places. Like me, Pete had been put on suicide watch because of answers to the questions on our intake sheets. Neither of us was a threat to anyone else, but we both had scars on our wrists, therefore we could not be left alone for more than 30 minutes, day or night. Pete's baldness was not down to him being a skinhead, he was in fact, suffering from a disease called Alopecia, where one's hair falls out due to stress. Pete was very nervous about being inside, and between us, we were both able to help each other get through. I could reason with him, and he understood what I had done and how we had both come to be in this awful place.

At lights out, we were all meant to be quiet. Some of the new arrivals hadn't got the memo and thought it a good idea to keep shouting out of the windows, either to other prisoners, themselves or Santa Claus on his fucking sledge, either way, it was a big no-no. Cell doors suddenly burst open and shouts rang out into the night, the commotion repeated several times in that first night of my incarceration.

At Slop out the following morning, we were reminded that a very dim view was being taken of the amount of noise continuing after lights out, should it continue, there would be repercussions and a loss of privileges. I had little idea what this meant, but it couldn't be good.

Chelmsford being an older prison, didn't have all the modern facilities of some newer jails, here we were each given a bucket and would have to use that as our toilet whenever we were locked in our cells. Each morning we would have to slop out the buckets in the wing toilets on the ground floor, before returning them to our cells, going back to shower, and then breakfast. Ideally both you and your cellmate would hold on to your solids until slop out time so as not to have to suffer with the smell of it in the cell all night long. God help anyone with diarrhoea or any sort of overly fragrant waste system, you really could find yourself on the wrong end of a very unhappy cellmate.

On my way down to breakfast, I caught a familiar voice behind me and when I turned to see I saw my old mate James from the squat in Earls Court.

"James?" I prompted him to look around, he was talking to another prisoner.

"Fucking hell Ribs, what are you doing here? I thought you had escaped to America"

"I did, I just got back day before yesterday, the old bill must have been waiting for me, pounced the moment I showed my face out of the house again, put me on remand in case I do a runner, bastards, what about you, what you doing here?"

"Got done for burglary and possession of smack, now I have to get to the hospital wing and hope they'll give me some methadone". Later on that day James was taken to the hospital wing for treatment, not for his withdrawals, but for having slashed his wrists.

Being on remand meant 23 hours of cell time everyday. 23 hours a day in a cell the size of an average bathroom, no flushing toilet, no TV, no Radio. 2 prisoners, 1 small window with a limited view and enough tobacco to roll a match thin cigarette 10 times a day for the next week, until we were allowed to buy our next supplies. The one hour a day association we were allowed was given as either time to play sports, football, gym or running, or time in the yard, where we could walk in a circle and talk with our fellow inmates. It was the most important hour of the day. Other times we were let out of our cells were for slop out, shower, breakfast, lunch and supper. All meals were taken into our cells and again we were locked in, our used plates etc collected from our doors by inmates lucky enough to have jobs within the wing, they got out of their cells, were paid extra for working and got better credits towards their prison reports.

Once again after lights out the shouting continued. Pipes connecting cells were being tapped in a morse-like way as people pretended to send coded messages into the depths of the old building. Again came the noise of the Screws kicking in doors, roughing people up, shouts, counter allegations. It seemed almost endless.

When our door was opened for slop out next morning, a large Prison officer, a Screw, stood by the door to block my exit.

"Just a quiet word," he said, his mouth barely moving. "We know who's been doing the shouting out of the windows at night, we caught him last night but couldn't prove it. The lad in cell number 8, on his own".

"What's this got to do with me?" I asked, "I don't know the guy".

"Just a little tip off, in case you were to get upset when we cancel association for this wing later, 3 days of 24 hour bang up, courtesy of cell number 8".

The tip off had it's desired effect. Word got around that we were all to lose our association and were all being punished for the noisy antics of a single person. By the time we were due to take our showers, passions were running high. In one of the cubicles I saw the back of number 8's head and automatically punched him at the top of his neck. I walked away immediately but my action was followed by another attack, someone hit number 8 square in the face, another kicked him before he hit the ground and so it continued until finally his head was pushed face first into the shower wall. A puddle of blood washed itself away down the drain as a Screw appeared to move everyone back to their cells. Number 8 had apparently slipped and fallen on some soap in the shower. He was quiet at night after his little mishap, Association was reinstated after 2 days instead of 3 and no-one spoke a word about it ever again.

James was not the only person I knew from the outside, in Chelmsford. Luke turned up soon too. Luke was a mate of Spit's I had met several times, he'd stayed at my place sometimes too, a black punk rocker with a bleached white curly mohawk. A lovely guy, but an animal when he had to be, maybe we all were nice really, we just didn't know when to stop sometimes. Tony from Romford, was another fellow inmate. Purebred psycho was Tony, last I heard of him he was living in Scotland breeding fighting dogs. There were 2 lads from school in there too, from the year above me, they weren't on remand like the rest of us, they were already sentenced, they were doing life for Manslaughter.

 Once I had got myself settled in I wrote home and sent Mum a Visiting Order. I wrote to Deanna too, it was a very hard thing to have to tell her I was in Prison. It was a very hard thing to accept. One day I'm being touted as the New Generation of Dr Pepper's Model Citizen's, the next I'm doing porridge and can't even have a plate of chips for my sins. I had a great suntan, but my legs were so weak I couldn't even kick a ball clear into an open goal from the penalty spot. My eyes were yellow and the outlook remained the same, I would have only a year or 2 to live, maybe 10 at most if I am very lucky. I didn't care how long I had left. I knew I wanted to live now, I knew I wanted to survive this awful disease and live life to the fullest I possibly could. I had seen a taste of paradise, the deep blue skies, palm trees, Hollywood by day and night. I knew there was more than the dirt and filth of the London I had fled, the hopelessness that strangles youth and perverts the needy. I knew I had to get out again, and somehow I would, some day.

 Mum came to see me. She only came once, long enough to bring me some cigarettes, drink a cup of tea and tell me I had to straighten up now.

"You can go and live with your Sister when you get out, over in Buckinghamshire. That way you'll be out of harm's way and you can straighten yourself out". I was grateful for the opportunity, but worried about the prospects. I had no job, no skills, nothing to offer, and I still wanted to get back to California, once I was healthy again.

The following morning there was an incident in the kitchen. After we had collected our breakfasts, it was normal for the sex offenders to be brought in for their breakfasts. They were kept away from the general population for their own safety, but sometimes even that wasn't enough. Apparently all the screws walked out of the canteen, the inmates working in the kitchens took their cue and leaped over the counter attacking the Nonces with everything they could hold, hot trays, pans and saucepans of boiling liquid. Once more nobody saw anything, the Nonces must have slipped on the floor, a shame really, because there was nothing left for them to eat either.

I was taken back to Marlborough Street Magistrates Court and after hearing my reports and plea, I was given 2 years probation and ordered to pay back the money I had taken from Sami. I was freed and sent on my way. After 28 days in prison, I swore then I would never return to that awful place. I have never been the type of person that can sit and waste away in an institute like prison. I am a freebird, a wanderer, a person always looking, touching, feeling, seeking life and it's myriad sensations and opportunities. Prison is death. Prison is torment and degradation that destroys the essence of human spirit. It is hopelessness, it is finality, it is crushing. I would do all I can to never have to return to that dark place, if I had to turn my back on all my friends, family, loved ones, anything, I would do it to avoid going back, such is my lust for life.

I moved out to Aston Clinton but before a month had passed I had relocated to East Ham, to live and work with my uncle Rob. Sitting on the bus back to London, with just a rucksack to my name, I felt free, free to live and be as I chose.

Rob was recently separated from my Aunt Julie, he was a labourer and jack of all trades, master of none. We had been promised some building work and if I helped him out, I could live with him, we could work together and keep an eye on each other. Rob had been staying at my parent's house for a bit but now had an apartment over a shop in East Ham. Rob and I worked well together at first, we did a couple of artex jobs, decorating peoples houses with swirly lumps of thick plaster decoration. We then went on to work in the shop downstairs, rebuilding the inside to make the store larger and more open, as well as the shop next door, our landlords' Son Zia, was turning it into a custom tyre and wheel supply store. We worked day and night to get the shops done as quickly as possible. Our rewards included more work from friends of the family, rent free accommodation for a while, and an almost non-stop supply of home made Indian/Pakistani food.

We established our own franchise of the Bodgett and Leggett Quick standard of cowboy builders. Neither of us having ever had any real training or qualifications, but both having used a shovel and hammer enough through our lives to know how to break things, mix concrete and threaten anyone who owed us money with a wet paint brush and half a bag of ready mixed artex. "Pay up or I'll stipple effect your toilet seat".

We built a new garage extension on a house, big enough not for a large family car, but a full size mechanic's workshop. The customer was a pain in the backside, he was always in the way but disappeared when it came to collecting money from him. We took out part of the rear of his house to build an access room to the garage. Removing the door and window frames was easy enough but calamity struck when I went to render the walls. Armed with a shovel full of mortar, I stepped on the wooden door frame as it still lay on the floor, I had been in too much of a hurry to get on with the rendering to bother clearing the woodwork out of the way, and suddenly found myself stuck to the spot. Each time I lifted my foot, the door frame rose and creaked a little but my foot wouldn't budge. I tried 3 or 4 times to move before realising that I was actually impaled on an old nail in the framework. The rusty piece of metal had passed through my foot and out of the top of my boot, securely fastening me to the spot. I carefully placed my other foot on the frame so as not to drop my shovel or spill it's contents, and then used the extra weight to lift my impaled foot from the nail and continue with the job in hand. It wasn't until about 10 minutes later that I realised I was actually in pain and thought I should pop to the hospital for a tetanus injection and clean the wound. I excused myself and drove to the hospital, but by the time I arrived I was in agony, each time I touched the brake or accelerator pedal my foot burned as if a whole new nail had been hammered into it.

The next 3 days were spent in bed, foot rest, Karma had brought to me the pleasure of it's revenge for what I had done to my Sister Anne, all those moons ago with the garden fork in the backyard, digging holes for our rubbish.

We finished off the garage and the customer suddenly became very unavailable when we asked for our money. After several visits to his house, more broken promises and passed deadlines, I eventually walked into his house and removed the family TV, if nothing else, he would pay attention now the kids had nothing to watch. Within an hour he was banging the door of our apartment armed with a knife, I let him in and told him he could have his TV once he paid us his outstanding balance. A few choice words were exchanged and he eventually left with his TV set and a much lighter wallet. Another satisfied customer.

I had been on probation since leaving Chelmsford, paying back the money I had taken from Sami, trying to keep away from my old life and building a new existence for myself. It wasn't easy, temptation was always there throughout the cold winter months of 1984. I stayed away from Earls Court, I knew I couldn't trust myself in that environment, that it would be all too easy to step back to where I had once been such a brilliant failure. I had planned on getting away, getting back to California, to Deanna, only by now, she too had moved on. She had told me she was seeing another guy now, a local punk who kept snakes, someone I could not compete with, someone better than me, someone else. I was hurt by this but had to move on, I had had my time, my chance.

I had also had regular check ups for my liver and the Hepatitis that had been such a blight on my health. Monthly blood tests were taken and the results eventually came back through my GP. The first tests were as expected, there was scarring on my liver and traces of Hep A and B. I was told to keep off alcohol, cigarettes and all drugs. To keep to a fat-free diet and that I may live a few more years if I were very lucky. I considered myself to be very lucky indeed, I had already made it beyond 1984 and into 1985, despite having done the very best I could to bring about my own demise. California had given me a new outlook, a new start if I wanted it, and I wanted it so very badly now. I had seen a new life, a better existence, a dream come true in my own lifetime, and I wanted to live now more than at any point in my life before.

When I returned for my follow up results, my GP was confused.

"This doesn't make sense" She said, "I am going to send you back for more tests, these can't be right, there must be something wrong here, we'll have to keep checking you each month". I duly obeyed and returned again the following month having donated yet another armful of blood to the testing Lab.

"I'm totally at a loss here, your results are back and it seems that you have no Hepatitis A or B in your system".

After all this time it now appeared that I was cured, I had some antibodies in my blood, signs of having had an infection, but no disease, I was cured of an incurable disease. The idea that one day I had only months to live, and then suddenly I was cured, having had no treatment whatsoever, was baffling.

"The liver is a wonderful organ" my GP said, "it can rejuvenate itself every 7 years or so, which means, sometimes it will cure itself of some diseases if given the right foods and conditions to do so. We will have to keep an eye on you, but it seems that you're in the clear now, just take it easy as you are, no more drugs, avoid alcohol, cigarettes and fatty foods".

I had in essence, been given a new lease of life. My short time in Chelmsford and abstinence upon release, had been enough to cleanse my system. I was still smoking but I had given up drugs and my alcohol intake was minimal, hard work and clean living were paying rich rewards and I was happy to be given another chance.

Rob and I needed another works van. Our finances were limited which meant we were pretty skint. The quickest, cheapest way to get a new van was to buy one at auction. Neither of us had a clue when it came to vehicles and we bought the first ex-Post office van that we could afford. It made the journey home from Chelmsford, barely. Just as we stopped outside the shop, the radiator drained itself into the engine block and our new pride and joy was now little more than an elaborate wheelbarrow.

We had been asked to quote on another shop development, in Stratford. A customer arranged to meet us on site late one evening so that we could price the job up. Just after accessing the property, a car came screeching past the shop, it was obviously being pursued by the police who pulled up to ask which way it had gone. A few minutes later another officer stopped by the shop and asked me for my details. I gave him my Date Of Birth and all the usual stuff, but rather than just thanking me for my assistance, the officer informed me of an outstanding warrant for my arrest, in Northampton. Before I had chance to say anything to Rob, I was cuffed and placed in the back of the police car. The arresting officer poked his head inside the shop and told Rob I would be back in due course. He stepped outside laughing as I was driven away, not a care in the world. I looked back out of the rear window, wondering what the hell I had done this time.

At Stratford Police Station I was told of an outstanding warrant in Northampton, it was an old warrant, the charge relating to the day I had broken down on the M1 a couple of years previously. I was charged with having no car tax and a fraudulent tax disc. Calls were made as I waited in a cell and within a couple of hours I was on my way back up the M1, handcuffed in the back of an unmarked car.

In court the next morning I pleaded guilty but because the tax disc had been from a previous car I had owned the charge of fraudulent use was dropped. I was ordered to pay a fine and costs and then set free back into the public, in Northampton, 100 miles from home, with no money and only 3 cigarettes. I found the local probation office and after hearing my plight, was given £10 and a coach travel ticket to London, to be repaid through my own probation office. Everything has a financial value, especially law enforcement.

Back in London, Rob and I decided to go out one night. We headed off to a club in Rayleigh and I ended the night travelling home in the back of the van with a newly acquired girlfriend, Plig. We had only met that night but I may have known her before, she had been a long time girlfriend of my mate Mad Max.

Plig was an art student, she lived in a very well to do area of Hornchurch, Ardleigh Green, with both her parents and little sister Roz. We met up a couple of more times in the following days before she was due to go to Paris with her college on a field trip. This coincided with her birthday and so I decided to surprise her and myself, by going to Paris to be with her on her birthday.

I had never been to Paris, I had no idea where it was or how to get there but was determined to do so. I wrote Rob a note saying I was running away to join the French Foreign Legion, threw some clothes into a bag and headed off to find a tiny hotel, on a little backstreet, in a city I didn't know, where the people speak another language, and all I had to go by was an address I had obtained without Plig knowing.

I headed into London and got a train to Dover where I then got a foot passenger ticket for the ferry to Calais. I had remembered to bring my passport and managed to exchange some money on the ferry. I also found a street map of Paris and as the ship rolled in the waves, I drew a hasty map on a scrap of paper I had in my pocket. Things were looking good. Customs was a breeze, nobody asked me where I was going, who I was or what was in my backpack. I found the train ticket office and bought a ticket for Paris. By the time the sun was setting I was pulling into Gare Du Nord Train Station, taking in the change of smells in the air, the warmer temperature and the strange cacophony of languages around me. Paris was vibrant, different to London in sights and sounds but also the smell, there was something sweet and intoxicating in the air, a sense of life and love.

I stepped out into the busy dark streets, strutting my way like Sid Vicious in the Great Rock 'n' Roll Swindle, each step an invitation to verbal confrontation, I was alone in a strange city and my best defence was to front it out, be mean and stay safe. I followed my little map straight out of the station and down to the Arc De Triomphe. It was a long walk, but it was worth it, I knew now once I had made this first landmark, that I would find the hotel I was looking for. Sure enough, it was exactly where it was meant to be. I went inside and inquired after Plig, she was out with the rest of her group having supper, I left a message to say I would return next morning, her birthday, walked back outside and waited around for an hour before deciding to find somewhere to sleep. Beneath the Arc De Triomphe was a subway under the road, suitably fitted with stone benches and well lit through the night, I was warm, dry and safe until morning.

I returned to the hotel in time for breakfast, Plig had been given my message the night before and was pleased to see me. She could not believe I had found her, on her birthday, in a backstreet hotel, in Paris. We ate breakfast together and spent the day walking around the city, visiting various landmarks, including the Louvre, which was part of the field trip Plig was on with her college. To me, it was all an adventure, being in a strange city for the first time, not speaking the language or understanding the signs, I loved it and wanted more. Back at the hotel Plig went to her room to get ready for her birthday dinner at Chez Maxim's, a huge, warehouse like restaurant where hundreds of diners were served by an army of waiters. I sat alone in the reception area and was soon joined by an Egyptian man who claimed he owned a string of shops in Paris and Cairo. If I was interested in doing so, he would pay for me to go to Cairo to collect a suitcase of Women's clothes to deliver to his Paris store, it would save him a small fortune in import tax and I could get to travel for free, and earn some money doing it. I told him I would think about it and was pleased to finally get away from him when Plig and her fellow students arrived, everyone ready for an evening at Chez Maxim's. I had always wanted to visit Egypt, I had a lifelong fascination with the ancient world of the middle east and now

I was being invited to go there, I just had to bring back some womens' clothes, yeah, right?

I returned to London alone the next day, instead of going to East Ham, I went to stay in Dagenham, at my brother's house. Les was away in the Navy and I stayed with his wife Debbie. I also found work with an agency run by a friend of my Mum. I started working as a labourer and was sent to a building site in Earls Court. The world suddenly shrunk again, I was back on familiar territory but determined to stay straight. I worked hard on site, sweeping, shovelling, lifting and shifting all manner of goods. I spent a lot of time watching the plasterers at work, watched them mixing and spreading, day after day. I watched and learned as best I could, for some reason I thought it may be useful someday.

Plig and I became closer and closer, I had started staying over at her parent's house and eventually moved in to share her bedroom. Max had lived here for a couple of years and stories of his misdemeanours hung around the house like favourite photographs. Plig's mother, Julia, enjoyed telling me about the night she woke to find Max in her bedroom, he'd been drinking and took a wrong turn, choosing to urinate in her wardrobe instead of the bathroom on the opposite side of the hallway. Max was a big act to follow.

Life with the Pellings was a good life. Julia and Chris were members of the British Humanist Association, they campaigned for a better society and moved in influential circles. Chris, Plig's Father, was a chemist and had a shop nearby. Julia was an Antique Jewellery trader and had a stall at Covent Garden Market. Chris was a very quiet man, he spoke little but ruled overall. He had a great sense of humour and I would often not get his jokes until much later, such was the cryptic nature of his humour. Julia was more forthright, and open- straight talking, we had many good conversations about life, the world, politics. She was a very welcoming and warm person, a surrogate mother to all who came under her wing. Roz, Plig's little sister, was also a student. She was a big fan of alternative music and comedy too. She was the only person in the house to understand Vic Reeves and Bob Mortimer, to laugh at their moments of silence and understand what the hell they were even going on about. She was happy-go-lucky and great fun to be around. There was also Nik, he lived in the flat above Chris's shop, he was a brilliant computer programmer and created his own video games that he sold worldwide. In many ways, I was part of a happy family, solid, respectable and for about the first time in my life, productive.

Life in Hornchurch rolled along quite happily, I continued to work on the building site, and Julia and Chris invited me along to the Humanists' annual convention in Nottingham. I had never been to a convention and had no idea what to expect. We arrived on campus, at Nottingham University and after settling in attended our first meeting. After an hour of listening to people talking about homelessness, I had heard enough. I took advantage of a coffee break to sneak Plig and myself out of the building. We hit the city centre, treating ourselves to some new clothes and Red hair dye. We dyed our hair in our room on the campus, then sneaked out again to Rock City nightclub for the evening.

Our absence did not go unnoticed and the return drive to London was an uncomfortable one. I felt like a naughty boy who'd been caught bunking off school, which in some ways was exactly what had happened. Julia and Chris were upset at our shenanigans and they let it be known. However, they didn't stay angry for long, Roz brought home a new boyfriend, Skinhead Pete, a huge guy with a chest like a beer barrel had been rammed down his throat. Pete was from New Zealand, had lived in Australia for a while and was now currently staying with us. He was meant to have run an agency that hired out skinheads to film producers, his greatest achievement being the film Breaking Glass, he organised the Rock Against Racism crowd and revelled in telling me how they'd swapped their dummy rubber bricks for the real thing, making many of the injuries seen on the film a little more realistic. He also knew Andy, and Lance. I hadn't heard from them for a long time, Andy was now playing bass for a band called Skrewdriver, as racist a band as one could imagine. They were later disbanded after their singer died in a car crash on his way home from a gig. I never saw Andy alive again, so I could never ask him about this time. I heard he had gone to Sweden to marry a blonde haired, blue eyed Aryan woman. I eventually met his wife,Catherine at his funeral in 2014.

Pete and I would often meet in the kitchen, I would be putting the kettle on for morning tea, Pete collecting a bottle of Malibu from the fridge.

"I don't drink anything other than alcohol" he informed me, "best way to cure any thirst I ever had".

Whilst helping Julia in the garden one day, Pete climbed a ladder to trim some bushes. As he rose up the steps he let rip an almighty fart.

"Squeaky steps you've got here, Mrs P!"

I took Plig to Coventry for the weekend, to meet some of my old friends, and have a night out in the town. We stayed with Helen and her new boyfriend H. Helen swore I knew H from the Lanch when I used to see bands there a few years before, I didn't recognise him but we got on really well all the same.

A month or so later they came to visit us in Hornchurch, Helen was pregnant and didn't know what to do. H didn't seem too bothered but eventually, when they left to go home, they were determined to make things work out for themselves.

Pete and Roz split up in time and I felt a sense of relief, Pete seemed a nice enough guy by I wasn't convinced he really was, there was a lot about him that didn't add up.

Chris and Julia had another house, in a little village in France. I was invited to go with them on their next holiday and looked forward to getting away again. I had no idea where we were going or what to expect.

"It's a little village in the south, near Montpellier" said Plig, I had never heard of it.

"South of Lyon".

Never heard of it.

"It's near Beziers and Clermont L'Herault".

Never heard of it.

"Bélarga"

Still nope, never heard of it.

"France"

"Yes, I've been there, is it far from Paris?"

"Nearer to Barcelona than Paris"

"Barcelona isn't in France is it?"

We didn't have Google in 1985, I didn't have many maps either, nor much of a clue where anywhere was beyond the London Tube map.

I told my boss I was going on holiday and that I would be back in a couple of weeks. I was grateful he paid me my holiday money up front so that I wasn't owed any outstanding pay, I had money in my pocket and an adventure on the horizon.

We left late on Friday night, Chris liked to drive through the night to get to the house at around tea time the following day. We drove to Dover and caught the ferry to Calais. From Calais we headed south to Paris and around the notorious Periphérique ring road. I had never heard of it, but it was notorious all the same, accidents were commonplace and drivers drove like absolute maniacs getting on and off the various slip roads linking the city of Paris. I compared the Periphérique to Coventry's own ring road, both were too close to the city centre, too fast and overcrowded, but Paris was definitely the more dangerous of the two roads. By the time we reached Porte D'Italie my nerves were pretty shot, and I was just a passenger, in the back, not knowing where we were.

We took the A6 south to Beaune, Macon and Lyon. Most of this leg of the journey I spent asleep in the back. When I woke up, we were stationary. Chris and Julia had left us in the car, on a back street in Lyon, while they went in search of croissants.

"Where are we?" I asked,

"Lyon"

"Oh, where's that?" I still had no idea.

We followed the Rhone south heading to Nimes and then Montpellier, the air outside the car getting warmer and warmer the further we went. When we stopped for fuel I could hear grasshoppers, their crackly buzz almost drowning out all other sounds around us. The sky was deep blue, the same colour of sky I had seen in my Asterix books as a kid, the same colour of sky I had seen in California, but rarely ever noticed in England.

Bélarga is a little village on the Herault river. Some 200 or so houses built for farm labourers and rural workers. Some of the houses have now become second homes to foreign holidaymakers willing to pay higher house prices than the local economy can afford. The name translates through the old Languedoc, language of the Occident, as Beautiful Water, Belles Aigues, Belle Aqua, Belarga. The River itself, L'Herault, lends it name to the French department in which it flows, a department rich in history, famed for its native accent, L'accent du midi (the accent of the Midi), its wines and agriculture. Surrounded by fields of grape vines and asparagus, the village sits alongside a quiet road between Gignac and Pezenas, across the river a few miles south of Clermont L'Herault, its nearest large neighbour.

The house itself sat on the main road, a terraced property with a neighbour on one side and his garage on the other, the only noise was the infrequent passing traffic and the neighbour Henri, whenever he started up his tractor in the mornings. Breakfast was courtesy of the village shop, bread and jam, washed down with strong black coffee and a selection of fresh fruit and yoghurt. Other than the obvious language barrier, my only reservation about our holiday had been the fear of going to the beach, or rather, the fear of having to visit a nudist beach, something I had never been exposed to in my life. The thought of getting my tackle out in public, of being naked, vulnerable and even suntanned in places the sun should never see, was anathema to me. Add to that, the thought of my girlfriend and even worse, her mother getting stripped and topless in front of all Europe was both horrifying and a typically British reaction. We don't do naked, not in England. Even though this was not England, this was France, a liberal and open society, I was English and I was not keen on the idea one bit. At least, not until we arrived at Marseillan Plage.

Between Marseillan Plage and Cap D'agde, is a naturist beach, an area where it is perfectly legal and accepted to be totally naked in public. A place where keeping one's bra or pants on is tantamount to heresy, where nobody cares if you have a fat stomach, little willy or boobs like pancakes. People on the beach do not stare at each other, compare bits, watch the 'crumpet' walk by with a nudge-nudge wink-wink. Benny Hill doesn't chase women between the dunes, nor does anybody else, nobody cares what is on show, because nothing is on show, everything is just there, in its natural form, in its natural place, in nature. Something I had never experienced before, something I had never considered because of preconceived ideas about nudity, of relating the naked form to sexuality, of seeing the naked body as an invitation to sexual activity, not as just a naked body in the sun, in nature, as it should be.

I arrived at Marseillan Plage as an insecure young man, afraid of my own body, afraid of the bodies of others, fearing my vulnerability, without the armour and protection of clothes, my fear of being unmasked, being seen naked from all angles, being seen. Therein lies the rub, nobody saw, nobody cared, nobody noticed. Within a few short hours, I had removed my trunks and for the first time in my life, with the waves of the Mediterranean washing the family jewels, I felt truly liberated.

Suntanning my backside was fun and all, but there was much more to being in France than just sunscreen and sand. I was introduced to local produce, fresh foods, fruit, wine, Pastis. Flavours and smells I'd never experienced. I was falling in love with my surroundings. In London, Chris and Julia were friends with a couple called Aggie and Alan. Aggie was Armenian, married to Alan, a groundhog who would only ever eat one meal, roast beef, potatoes, peas and gravy. Every bloody day of the week, the same meal, day after day after day. Here I was being introduced to Ratatouille, artichokes, cheeses and wines, my taste buds were loving this, everyday something new, something different.

In the village, almost opposite the house, was the cave of the local winemaker, a label called Domaine Des Amourettes. For the princely sum of around 5 Francs, 50p in English money, I was able to buy 5 litres of red table wine in a reusable plastic tub. 5 litres for less than the price of a bottle of cola, it's no wonder the French were always tipsy, at that price I could bathe in the stuff and still have change for a bag of chips every night. Monsieur Maffre-Bauge was the owner of Domaine Des Amourettes, he was also an MEP. A smart, well spoken man, he spent very little time in Belarga, usually he was away in Paris, Brussels or Strasbourg. I met him on a couple of occasions whilst buying our wine, one day he asked me if I would like to return to the village and work for him during the vendange, the wine harvest. I checked with Julia and Chris, between us it was agreed that Plig and I could stay for rest of the summer, I could help out by doing some work around the house until it was time to work for Mr Maffre. He promised me 6 weeks work, solid, everyday working in the fields, cutting grapes alongside his migrant Spanish workers and other casual labour from the village. This was a fantastic opportunity but first we had to return to England. We had to collect our clothes, Plig's car and painting equipment, as well as sort out some money to get through until I got paid at the end of the vindange. We finished our holiday and headed back to London.

Roz had acquired a new boyfriend, a Psychobilly called Lurch. At first all seemed well, but Lurch was something of a dullard. His only desire was to plug himself in to his stereo and pull gurney faces at himself in the mirror. He had no ambition, no drive, no desire to get on. I could see this would eventually irk Julia and Chris, but in the meantime I had a job of my own to sort out.

I returned to the building site in Earls Court, the job had moved on a little but some tensions were rising amongst the plasterer's. One of the labourers Paul,was a former hairdresser from Rainham, he drove a TR6 and wore a long shaggy perm. He looked like a surfer dude from Southern California and regaled us with his stories of pulling birds with his car. Another labourer, we called Mad Malc, was a bodybuilder who spent all day humping bags of cement and plaster around. He would put a bag of plaster on each shoulder, one across the back of his neck and another in each hand, and run upstairs with them, the man was an animal. After work he would go to the gym, pumping iron and steroids all night in the quest for the ultimate muscle bound body. Malc thought Paul was gay and before anyone could pull them apart, the pair were swapping punches in a ferocious show of machismo. The leaner, faster Paul got the better of the slower, bulkier Malc. In the battle of the hairdresser against the bodybuilder, muscles were of limited use, agility won the day and Malc's ego took days to recover, the two of them kept working at opposite ends of the house. The lads at work had asked about my holiday, when I told them I was going back they all said the same thing, that I was crazy for having come back. Truthfully though, I didn't have much choice. I just hoped that nothing would get in the way of going again.

It took a few weeks to get some money together, and get ourselves sorted. Whilst we were around, we popped up to Coventry to see Helen and H, Pat and Scruff came round while we were there and we all ended up at Busters nightclub in town. Rich Mulligan was now DJing on a more professional basis, gone were the days of 10p on the door, calling him names if he wouldn't play your favourite song that nobody else liked or had even heard of, now it was £2 to get in and Rich had to keep punters both on the dancefloor, and handing over their pennies at the bar. He was good at his job, which really pissed off some people, they didn't understand he had a job to do, part of that being to keep a steady flow of cash going across the bar. Any DJ can fill the dance floor, but he's not going to be asked back if nobody buys any drinks. I liked Busters, it was a good venue and the walls were all made up to look like the inside of a cave. Rich did a great job of playing the music I loved, and some I didn't, but that meant I could drink beer and chat between dances. Life was good and I was making the most of it.

We also attended the End Of The World Festival at Bedfords Park, near Romford. !984 was meant to be the year that humanity destroyed not only itself, but the entire planet around us too. It was now 1985 and someone had worked out the original dates were about a year out, so we went to the park, drank beer, watched some bands play and waited for the End. It didn't come. I was bitterly disappointed but rather than demand a refund I thought I should be grateful, at least I could go back to France. I didn't know it at the time, but this was to be the last time I saw Mags, she died from breast cancer a few years later.

Belarga was still in the same place we'd left it, a good job really as I wasn't altogether sure where it was in the first place. Turn right at Calais, go through Paris and Lyon then turn right at the split as if you're going to Barcelona not Marseille. Simple enough I guess, if you know where any of those places are to begin with.

We spent a few days settling in, awaiting word of the start of my employment. Days passed at the beach, swimming in the sea or lazing by the river. A local builder, Henri, had been employed to build a patio on the top floor of the house. He took off the roof to the rear, laid a stone floor and put in a chimney breast to the back room on the ground floor. Doors and windows were fitted so that the front of the loft could be used as a bedroom, with external access to the patio and staircase down to the first floor. Henri and his labourer Claude, spent the next 3 months working on the house. It was noisy, dusty and hot.

I finally got word that the grape harvest would be starting the following week. I was meet the rest of the labourers in the town square, outside of the Mairie, or Mayor's office.

It was a cool Monday morning when we met up, 7am in the town square seemed an ungodly hour after my long break from the routine of a working week. We were about 20 strong, mostly spaniards, a couple of local youngsters and the lady who ran the village shop, as well as myself. The only english speaker in the group, also the only person who didn't speak spanish, or french. Learning the job I was expected to do was going to be a case of watching and copying everyone else.

We were herded into the back of an old citroen van, the suspension creaking as we pulled out of the village. I had thought I would just be in a field nearby, would pop home for my breaks and maybe lunch, but that wasn't the case. We were driven way up the road, almost to Gignac before we pulled off the main road and along a dusty track into the vines. We were each given a pair of secateurs, razor sharp cutters for snipping the grapes from their vine, then told to spread out in a line at the edge of the field, each person had a row of their own to cut, and each of us was expected to keep up with the others, both in the speed we progressed through the vines, and the amount of grapes we cut on the way. We were not expected to leave too much fruit on the vines, nor cut too much of the bush beyond each bunch of grapes.

Never in my life had I seen so many grapes. Each vine produced 6 or 7 bunches, some as many as 10 or more. We each had a bucket, or seaux, into which we would put the cut grapes. When the bucket was full, it was taken to a large plastic tub at the end of each row and emptied out. The bigger tubs held around 70-100 kgs of grapes. These were loaded onto the van and driven away to the Cave for turning into wine.

Once we began cutting, working our way through the rows of grapevines, it became clear I would have to up my game. I moved as quickly as I could but still fell behind the rest of the team. The spaniards seemed to take everything in their stride, they would walk and talk as if out for a stroll in the park, cutting as they went, their arms moving at such speed as to seemingly strip each plant without touching. Their rolling tongues masking the enormous effort being made by their arms to cut, catch and collect their bounty with apparently no effort at all, while I flailed around, leaves filling the air and ground about me, my cutting hand hacking away at stems, leaves and fingers with unforgiving aplomb. I cut chunks from the grapes, from the branches, from my fingers. My blood mixing with the purple juice in my bucket, offset by the green leaves it kind of pretty in a masochistic (watch me bleed to death) kind of way. My fingers stung. My hands were scratched to pieces and I was way behind everyone else by the time we'd gone half way up the line.

At 9.30 am we stopped for a rest. Bottles of water were passed around and we drank thirstily.

"Non, non, non, pas comme ça!" (*not like that!*) One of the villagers advised me. I was guzzling the water as quickly as I could, the cool liquid hardly touching the sides of my throat. He took my bottle and showed me that I should drink slowly, and then pour some over the back of my neck to cool the blood going to my brain. The relief was instant and I thanked him. He looked at my hands and made a noise.

"Ho putain!" He said.

"What? It's only a few cuts, just a few nicks that's all"

"Putain" he repeated, his accent making it sound more like 'Pooteng!' I had no idea what a Pooteng was. I'd never been to Nam, I didn't speak french and I was fine as I was, thank you.

"Ho putain"

Ho putain, hopiteng, hopital, the progression made sense, he wanted me to go to hospital, the little wimp, they're only nips.....

"No, no hopital, no hopital, only little cuts"

He stood holding my hand in his, repeating the call as I looked into face repeating my lack of desire to spend my first day at work sitting in A&E getting my hands stitched, even if they did warrant stitching, which I doubted. Gilles, our supervisor came to my rescue.

"He wants me to go to hopital" I said

"Ho putain" said the french lad.

"Putain" said Gilles and walked off to the van. He returned a few minutes later with an antiseptic spray an a pair of gloves. The spray stung my wounds more than the secateurs and vines had, but at least they were clean.

When we stopped for lunch, we were taken back to the village and told to regroup at 2pm. Once home I asked Plig, "What's a pooteng?"

"A what?" She asked, taken aback.

"A pooteng, I thought it might be a hospital, one of the lads kept saying it when he was looking at the cuts on my hands, Poteng, pooteng, Hopooteng, Hopooteng, something like that"

Plig laughed and then explained that 'Putain' was an exclamation widely used by the locals, a bit like saying 'Shit' or 'fuck' but it actually meant Whore. Apparently, I had the hands of a prostitute.

Day after day I returned to the square to meet the gang. Day after day we went through the same routine. Cut, catch, drop, move, cut, catch, drop, move, empty bucket start again. I got quicker and quicker, my hands toughened to the ravages of the vines but the secateurs were unforgiving. I would still cut myself on an almost daily basis, but no matter what I did, I could not catch up with the Spaniards, they moved through the vines at a breathtaking pace.

I became friendly with one couple, Manolo and his wife Maria. I invited them round one evening for supper and spent the whole evening watching Manolo's eyes get heavier and heavier as he drank more and more wine. I couldn't understand much of what was said. Plig spoke French but no Spanish, Manolo spoke Spanish and very little French, Maria spoke only Spanish and I knew only English and bullshit, neither of which were any good on this occasion. Manolo was happy though, he laughed and smiled all evening, he seemed very grateful to be welcomed into our house and returned the favour a few days later. Their accommodation was provided by Mr Maffre, a very basic apartment in the village with running water, gas and electricity, lumpy, dirty mattresses and a threadbare sofa. It made our place look positively regal, even with the builders in.

I worked solidly for 6 weeks, cutting and catching grapes, sweating profusely in the hot sun, loading bucket after bucket into the bigger containers. I was promoted to loader, my job was to put the large containers of grapes into the back of the van until it was fully loaded, then ride with Gilles to the Cave where I would unload them into a large concrete vat. It was here that the real work of turning the grapes to wine happened. The fermenting, the pressing, the bottling, it all happens in the Cave.

When I heard I was going to the Cave I had visions of the Grotte De Clamouse, a deep cavern under the hills carved out by the river, a dark dank hole in the ground with all manner of things lurking in the shadows. I was wrong, I was so wrong it is embarrassing. The Cave was a relatively modern building, it was essentially a small factory. The boxes of grapes were unloaded onto the top of the fermentation vat. A hole, the size of a manhole cover on a sewer was the intake. I would tip the boxes out one by one onto the hole and use a broom to push the remaining bunches down into the vat. The vat was solid box the size of hotel bedroom, maybe 10 feet high and 15 feet square. On the floor inside was an open drain running down to the entrance, a small door with a sliding hatch through which the wine would be drained and pumped into barrels for further fermentation or storage. Once the vat was filled, the weight of the grapes would crush themselves and once fermented, a Premier Cru would be drained out and pumped into barrels before the rest of the grapes were pressed to release more juice. Second and third presses ensured the fruits were dessicated and every single drop of wine collected.

We were on our way to the Cave one day when something in the road caused Gilles to swerve, the back doors of the van flew open and a ton and half of grapes spilled out onto the road. We spent the next couple of hours shovelling and sweeping the mess up off the road. I was loving working in the Cave. Watching Gilles do all the technical touches after I humped the heavy stuff around. Being out in the fields was good honest work, but it was hard and repetitive. Going to and from the Cave gave me a chance to see and learn my way around the area. It also meant that once the harvest was done, the last grapes cut, I still had work to do. The Spaniards were paid up and sent home. I would miss Manolo's ever happy smiling face, he was fun to be around, even though I couldn't understand a word of what he said.

Once the wine fermented enough, Gilles opened the tap on the vat and the first of the wine poured out, he dipped a glass into the liquid and took a drink. Passing me the glass, I did the same. It tasted like grape juice, only stronger. A very sweet, soft, fruity wine. I swallowed the mouthful I had just in time to see Gilles spit his out into a sink, he gestured at me to do the same but it was already too late. I had swallowed my sample and Gilles burst out laughing. He knew what was in store for me, and for the next 24 hours I belched, farted and vomited out of my backside. The unfermented yeasts played havoc with my insides and I lost a day's pay. Still, I soon recovered and was back in the Cave for the first pressings.

First press was done once the vat had been drained. This meant shovelling the grapes from the vat into a wooden frame. To compact the grapes we took off our boots and trod them down into the press. The grapes slipping between our toes, the juice soaking into our skin, just like when they show it being done on the telly. Once our weight was insufficient to make a difference, we climbed out and began the mechanical pressing process. The wooden tub had a central post upon which a pressing plate was fitted and a winding handle. As the handle was wound, the plate lowered and crushed all beneath it, the wine seeping out between small gaps in the frame and collected in a series of drains on the floor which fed into the barrels. As each barrel was filled, another was plumbed in.

As each vat was emptied and cleaned out, we moved on to the next. There were several vats in our Cave, each taking 2 or 3 days to clear. Eventually, the last vat was drained and my job was done.

Mr Maffre asked me if I wanted to work in the winter, out in the fields with his Grandson Blaise. I was offered the chance to cut back the vines, remove the oldest stumps and plant new. In effect I was being offered a year round job working for him. It was tempting, but I had other plans by now.

We had spent the summer wondering how we could finance ourselves to stay here. Chris and Julia had said that we could stay as long as we wanted, rent free, but that we would have to look after the house and do any decorating or modernising that I was able to do, to help get the place finished. Walls were in need of plastering, internal walls rearranging, timber ceiling joists had to be stripped of their plaster and treated, an electrical box needed fitting into the wall outside, and many other little bits that would keep me going for a long while, all whilst trying to earn a living. Throughout our conversations one thread kept repeating was the idea of setting up a market stall. I had experience in selling to the public, I knew where some of the wholesalers were in London, Chris and Julia took us to some others they dealt with, and before long, the decision was made, we would set up a market stall.

We toured the local markets and chatted with traders. Some were very helpful, others not so, but we found out how they worked, how we had to be registered and set about establishing ourselves as traders. Of course there were hiccups, teething problems with bureaucracy and attempting to find our way through the mess that was the French system.

We drove to London and invested £115 of my wages from the vindange in cheap costume jewellery. The remainder of the 2 liters of wine per day could not be exchanged, and therefore awaited our return in Belarga. I made up a display board that fitted onto an easel by covering an old length of plywood with a piece of shiny black felt, onto this I stapled some black thread creating rows upon which to hang the earrings from. We bought some wallpapering tables and extra black cloth to cover those with and were ready to go.

Our 1st market was in the little village of Paulhan, just over the river from Belarga. All was going well until two policemen asked us for our papers. We showed them what we had but that wasn't enough. After much consultation, it was agreed that we would return the following week with the required documentation.

In order to be a Market trader (*Marchande Ambulante*) in France, in 1985, a person needed to be in possession of a volume of different documentation, as well as the requisite customs paperwork for goods imported from the UK. None of which we possessed or even knew about at this point.

Our first requirement was to obtain a Carte De Séjour, (*Residence Permit*) this- we discovered, was awarded by the Prefecture in Montpellier. However, in order to qualify, we needed to the following :

Attestation De Domicile (*Proof of residence in a fixed address*)

Proof of payment of local (council) tax.

Register with local Doctor.

Register with local Dentist.

Register with relevant trade body (*URSSAFF*).

Register with state pension body (*CAMULRAC*).

Register with Tax office.

Open French Bank account.

All of which were to take many months to complete, undaunted by this we continued going from office to office in our spare time, filling out paper after paper, translation after translation, stamp after stamp. French bureaucracy was as much the nightmare as the rumours purported.

The following week we were back at Paulhan. We had made our first tentative steps towards getting ourselves a legitimate place in French society. We presented our papers, those we had that is. The two officers were not exactly impressed, but they could see we were trying, that we had progressed and were doing what we could. We had worked a couple of other markets, Gignac and Clermont L'Herault, and had sold enough stock to know that the efforts required to establish ourselves would be worthwhile, there was money to be made and the officers in Paulhan were less of a problem than a good source of advice, information and direction.

In order to fund our lives we needed to make a profit and these first little markets showed us that a profit was very possible. In our research, our trips to the markets prior to setting up, we observed the huge price differential between local traders and the prices I knew I could buy things for in London. We started off with the cheapest jewellery we could find, plastic studs and bangles, beads and feathers. Our first few markets showed us we could not sell too cheaply, the cheaper the goods, the more suspicious the customers were that things were 'too cheap', below standard, poor quality maybe. The bigger the price tag, the better the product. We had bought earrings for as little as 3p (30 centimes) a pair from the wholesaler, which we were having to sell at £1(10 Francs). Our more expensive purchases 70-80p were selling at 20-50 Francs, up to £5 or more. Dipping our toes into the water had proved to my mind that we were on the right path, this was a viable project, and so long as it fed us, we could stay here forever.

We returned to London and bought more stock, christmas was coming and we invested all we had in more jewellery, better products and new lines. Julia took us to a make-up wholesaler and we bought trays of Constance Carroll and Gallery products. I also went to one of Sami's suppliers and invested in some button badges, badges with the names, logos and pictures of popular bands and artists of the time. The badges were 3p each, I knew I could sell them 3 or 4 for 10 francs, the profits would be reinvested and our stock would grow as quickly as we could sell it.

The make-up was a hit, as were the badges and jewellery. I had built another display board and had 1000 badges on show, the local kids loved it. Plig was selling the cosmetics and jewellery while I concentrated on badges, we worked well together and I was starting to learn more and more French. The repetition of questions and descriptions working on a stall, gave me the best opportunity to imitate and learn.

When we first began, customers would be pointed towards Plig to answer their questions, sometimes I would joke with them and talk in English just to see the confusion on their faces.

"You want chips with that?"

" Should I wrap them or are you eating them now?"

"How much for these-how much do you want for your daughter?"......... *You really had to be there.*

For the most part, markets would start around 8-9 am, we would trade through to around 12-1 pm and then pack up and go home. Some days this meant we could be on the beach for 2.30 pm, not a bad life. One afternoon at Marseillan Plage I stepped out into the water, the beach was far from full as it was out of season, but there were people around. As I stepped into the waves something hit my leg, I looked down and saw what I thought was a bikini top in the water. I reached out to pick it up but recoiled immediately when I touched it, it wasn't a bikini top, it was an eel limp in the water. I slapped it to see if it was alive, no response. Looking about me I couldn't help myself, this was the perfect opportunity.

I shouted out something illegible and dived in and out of the water, my arms flailing, smacking and splashing the surface, rolling over and over, my body making the most awful fuss as thrashed and kicked finally reaching the crescendo of my performance as I dived beneath the surface one last time, pausing for dramatic effect. I finally surfaced, raising my arm above my head to reveal the barehanded catch I had just made. I had caught and killed an eel with my bare hands. I marched triumphantly up the beach holding my catch before me for all to see, the occasional shake to make it look like it was twitching, and the crowd was mine. People all around gaped with open mouths, kids applauded and cheered, I was Tarzan for a moment, milking it for all it was worth.

We were on the road to Montagnac, probably heading for the beach, when something caught my eye. Something moved in the brush at the side of the road and we stopped the car to investigate. Sure enough we found two little kittens, a ginger and a grey tiger-striped sibling. There wasn't anything nearby, no houses, no shelters, they had to have been abandoned.

"Can we keep them, pleeeeeeasse?" There could be no refusing a lady with a pussycat in her hand saying 'Pleeeeeeasse!"

Pud, the grey, and Kit, the ginger, moved in with immediate effect, our very own constant companions, our babies.

Work on the house had begun at the earliest possible moment. I wanted to show I was keen and productive, getting things done seemed an important part of being here and with each mission accomplished came the next one. I started off by fitting the electricity box into the outside wall of the house. A new meter was to be fitted into it by the electricity company, all I had to do ws fit the box into the wall. I started with a hammer and chisel but eventually had to hire a Kango hammer, the wall was solid stone, about 4 feet deep and no matter how hard I tried, I was never going to do without mechanical assistance. Once the box was in place and the new meter put in, I set about the kitchen, chiseling off the old plaster around the wooden beams. Once the beams were exposed, I sanded the timber and treated it for woodworm before coating it in dark varnish. The walls were stripped and painted and the whole room rejuvenated. Things were going well and I was as happy as I could be.

On subsequent trips to the UK we collected our clothes, books, paintings, record and tape collections. We moved in all our worldly possessions, Bélarga was our home now and between visits to different government offices, markets and the builders' supply merchant in Clermont L'Herault, most of our time was spent working in the house with the occasional day off for visiting local attractions like the Grotte Des Demoiselles, where two young children were believed to have got lost and vanished many years ago. We would often go to the beach, or the Devil's Bridge (*Pont Du Diable*) to watch the local kids hurl themselves off the rocks and the bridge itself, into the river below, they were fearless because they had grown up with it. With my head for heights I expect a pat on the back and a chocolate biscuit each time I hurl myself from a kerb when crossing the road. We would also go to the top of the mountain at the head of the valley, somewhere near Ganges, I never could remember it's name, but it could be seen from almost anywhere in the Herault.

We started making friends through our stall and also in the village. Blaise, Mr Maffres grandson, came round to the house a few times for drinks and food, as did Veronique, a young lady who'd worked on the vendange with me. There was not a lot happening in the village itself, but we did find out about a piano-bar that was opening soon in Clermont L'Herault. We attended what I think was the grand opening, maybe 20-25 couples mostly, seated at tables around a room with some very impressive and atmospheric wall art, depicting cartoon scenes reminiscent of an early morning in Hollywood, as members of the Rat-pack, stagger homewards, still clutching their cigarettes and whiskey tumblers. We ordered huge ice cream cocktails and listened to Matt Bianco in the background. It was all very kitsch, and expensive, but the proprietor was the son of the family who ran one of the best restaurants in the whole of France, The Hotel Terminus in Clermont L'Herault. His food, drinks, his art and his humour were second to none.

We heard a rumour that we could trade on Christmas Day at the Place De La Comédie in Montpellier. Knowing things would be quiet in the new year, many traders go on holiday

January and February, we decided to give it a go and set up our table in the centre of the city. Although we had a really good day moneywise, we found something more valuable, English speaking friends.

There were some traders we saw and talked to quite frequently at various markets. In the early days we were helped along by the advice and experience of other traders, people like Jean-Claude, a Belgian who looked like a real-life Obelix from the Asterix cartoon books I'd collected as a youngster. He was a huge man, with a large stomach, skinny legs and a fantastic ginger handlebar moustache that must have been great fun when negotiating a spaghetti bolognaise. He and his wife, a Danish lady with blonde hair, thick glasses and heavy accent-who just about reached his belly button, were a great help, always keen to help and advise.

Montpellier attracted a lot of expats. Drunks, junkies, travellers and people who had fallen out of love with the modern world. There were punks here, living in squats, some beggars and all manner of other people in the shadows.

One couple we befriended were Nina and Cali. They were both about 4'6" tall in high heels, standing on a step, at the top of a small flight of steps. Perfectly suited for each other, they were little but perfectly formed. Cali had short bleached hair, blue eyes and an almost permanent smile on his face, nothing seemed to ever get him down. Nina looked like a French Nina Hagen, short with long dyed black hair and enough eye makeup to paint the ceiling of Canterbury Cathedral. Here bright red lips made sure she could never be run over in the dark on a quiet street anywhere. Between the two of them there were many laughs to be had.

Montpellier was also home of Dave (*not that one*) a former candlemaker from north of Watford Gap. He lived with Patrick and a couple of other young men, they'd somehow followed different paths and ended up in an apartment in Montpellier together. They made a living by selling bootleg tapes on markets and on the streets of the city. Dave was selling Mother Of Pearl jewellery on the day we met, the next time he was selling cassette tapes. They bought the tapes from London, as soon as they were available on the market, usually just days after a gig. There would be one they would keep as a master, and they would copy as many copies from it as they needed. Some bands would have people running for the bootleggers more than others. I bought a Killing Joke and an Alien Sex Fiend tape, then others. I knew they were illegal recordings, but it was nostalgic to listen to them live, what I didn't know was how many times Dave and his mates had been busted. They were arrested on a regular basis, their apartment raided and all recording equipment confiscated, they were all on their last warnings, next time they would be imprisoned and then deported.

There was a flea market in Montpellier, *Marché aux puces,* which had recently moved to a new venue, the sports stadium, Stade Richter. It was held on Sunday mornings and was an ideal place to sell our wares. Because we were not allowed to sell anything 'New', I had to made sure that all my invoices were marked as 2nd hand, Clearance stock, Bulk lots, by doing this I could prove the stock was second hand and passed inspection each time customs or the tax office, Gendarmes or local police inquired about the stock. I had one more hurdle to cross too. The car. Nowadays, anyone within the EU can drive to another state and use their own vehicle for trade. In 1985 that was illegal.

Nina and Cali became regular visitors to our stall, along with another friend, Acide who was no taller than the other two. I did start to wonder if there was a law in France disqualifying tall people from being punks or whether it was pure coincidence. I struggled to break through Acide's strong accent, I thought he was from the south unlike Cali, who was from Bourges, while Nina was from Rennes, both of whom I could communicate with fairly well. I was picking up phrases, learning words and generally just interpreting situations to understand and make up what I thought was being said.

Chris and Julia had invited friends to stay at the house. It was put forward that their Son Richard, may be able to stay on with us to help out with the house and maybe even work on the markets with us too. This sounded like a good idea until they turned up. As small a world as it is, I couldn't believe it when I found out that our guest was none other than the retired commander of HMS President and HMS Chrysanthemum, the 2 ships moored on Embankment, where I had trained on several occasions, when I was in the Sea Cadets. Having found out that I had once been under his command, Richard's father took on an air of boss about the house, the Commander was back in command and he let us know it by eating all the grapes in the fruit bowl, in one sitting, without offering any around. Uncouth and terribly bad manners, this just wouldn't do. I was glad when they left, though not too happy they'd left their spawn behind. Richard was ok, but he was there, you know, in the way more than of any use. He'd never used a shovel in anger and was just looking for something to do in his gap year.

We had to find some use for him and so decided to split our stock and let him do the market at Gignac, while we went to Pezenas, but in order to do this he would need some help. We recruited Nick, an expat living in the squat in Montpellier. Nick was from Middlesbrough but had squatted in Brixton before heading to France. He was long haired biker/hippy type chap with a great sense of humour, a desperation to get out of his rut, and a willingness to work with us. Nick moved in and we set about conquering the world one market at a time. It wasn't to be however, we had overlooked the fact that Richard's car,as well as our own, was not allowed to engage in commercial business. His papers were checked and he was told to shut up shop, fined £130 on the spot, he could not trade and was given 30 days to leave the country. Richard's gap year had lasted all of about 10 days.

Richard headed back to England, Nick stayed on in the house but soon left to return to Montpellier, he had other work lined up working for another ex-pat, Graham, the Pizza guy.

I had to go in search of a new vehicle, quickly. I had to buy a French registered van before we were closed down ourselves. I had seen a garage on my travels, a place that sold old PTT (*Postal office*) vans. What attracted me to this place was that they would paint the vans any colour/colours you wanted. I ordered one to be sprayed black on the bottom with a pink bonnet and upper half. The finished item was duly collected and looked fantastic. Unfortunately, it broke down on its first trip to Montpellier and after much swearing and threatening at the garage, our money was refunded and we had to start afresh in our search for a new vehicle.

There was a Renault dealer in Clermont L'Herault and within a few days we were the proud owners of a brand new Renault 4TL van, the perfect tool for our requirements. Being left hand drive, and with a gear stick like an umbrella handle protruding from the dashboard, the van took a little while to get used to but within a few days I became a very competent driver, it was only when we returned to the UK did I struggle with which side of the road I should be on, normally only having a problem when turning into a street with no obvious road signs, the memory and natural instinct fighting to override each other.

We were now motor legal. Our vehicle held as much stock as we could need on any market. Our papers were in order as best they could be, being incomplete dossiers they would usually invite further questioning from anyone doing spot checks on traders, but as we were doing all we could to get ourselves legal, we were left alone, sometimes advised on where and what to do next.

There was a gig coming up in Millau, a town the other side of the mountains beyond Clermont L'Herault. Acide told me about it, some french band he loved and so I offered to take them to the gig, Acide, Cali, Nina, myself and Plig. We picked the gang up from Montpellier, as they clambered into the back of the van Acide said something about getting some beers. I offered to stop en route at a supermarket and he starting bragging about how much he could drink in a night. 40 litres he reckoned. The gauntlet was down and when I returned to the van with 40 litre bottles of Valstar beer and some more for the rest of us, I told him to let me know when he was done and I would stop for more.

We arrived over the mountain in the dark, the lights of Millau appearing like a UFO off to the side of us, rising up and down, turning and twisting with the course of the road. Cali was steaming drunk, Acide pissed as a coot and Nina flopped around in the back of the van like a rag doll rolling down the stairs. They hadn't even drunk half of the beer between the 3 of them, Acide and his 40 litres was busted.

When the band eventually came on, we all jumped up in our seats, Cali let out a scream and a look of sheer panic spread over his face, his leg was jammed between 2 seat and he wasn't enjoying it. When we took him back to Montpellier, he went to the hospital and had his leg x-rayed, it was broken.

We caught up with them the following week, Cali was on crutches, his leg in plaster. Nina was worried, they were struggling to survive in the squat and after a brief conversation, we told them they could stay with us until he was better.

Cali helped out with replenishing all the badges and jewellery on our sale boards. Nina helped around the house and for a few weeks we had a lot of fun together. Eventually things came to a head, Nina discovered she was pregnant and didn't know what to do, Cali couldn't provide for her and a baby, we couldn't help them out, we were all in a quandary Eventually we decided to call her parents, in less than 24 hours they were on our doorstep, Nina and Cali were taken home to Rennes, her parents thanked us for our help and we had our quiet little house back.

Nick was now working with Graham, making pizzas, merguez and burgers at the Marché Aux Puces. Graham was from Knaresborough originally, married to a local woman Claudine, they had 2 kids, a boy and girl, as well as a very volatile relationship. Nick also had a sideline, he was starting to sell cannabis and that was not going to end well.

I had my knuckles rapped by a customs officer *(Douanier)* at a market one day. He saw the cannabis badges I was selling on a board and was close to arresting me. I found out the hard way that not only was it illegal in France to possess, sell or use weed, it was also illegal to advertise it on t-shirts, badges etc.

"C'est vraiment interdit". *Very illegal.*

Civility

Bang, bang, bang- look at me
Smack you in the face with civility.
Bomb in a black bag-face on a screen,
Blast from the past in a magazine.
I could be Nero, a tourist or me,
I could be anything I wanted to be,
A dilute liberal with a face like your cause,
An Irate angel on a male menopause.
A land in the sky full of money and fame
A labour of love for conservative gains.
But down in the grass- where the hippies run free
The thin blue line sings for Anarchy,
As arm in arm the law is unknown,
And one for one- no mercy is shown.
Now bang, bang, bang- look at me
I am the future that you want me to be,
Thumb up your backside, head in a dream
Buxom bitch, blood group HIV.

Time Of My Life

Life in Bélarga was plodding along nicely, everything I touched seemed to turn to gold, fools gold maybe, but it looked alright from where I was standing. I had lots of work to do on the house, lots of work with the markets, lots to learn about the language, the paperwork and even life itself. I was happy and healthy, the sun kissing my skin almost every day, the warm air suited me, it made me feel happy and content. I was now the master of my own fate, I may have been living in a foreign country, in a house that wasn't mine, running a business with no guarantee of success-especially when the weather turned.

The worst weather for market traders are wind and rain. Rain will keep your customers at home, wind will send your tables, boards and parasols flying. Stock will disappear down the street as quickly as the wind will take it. Thankfully we were blessed with pretty good weather most of the year. The tourist season in our region lasted for around 3 months. That meant we would have 3 months of good sales to make as much as we could to get us through the lean winter months. However, we were selling to the local kids, the women and young men too, so our sales continued quite nicely out of season when the tourists had gone home. January to march were particularly lean months, the markets would be quiet, many traders on holiday, many customers stayed at home in the warm. We set up at the Marché Aux Puces one morning, it was -18 degrees overnight. I don't know if I had ever been wrapped up in so many layers, and still felt cold, in the whole of my life.

We were invited to a wedding in Geneva, this was somewhere I had never been, to the wedding of a couple I had never met before. We drove over from Bélarga taking the autoroute to Lyon and then up into the Alps. I had never seen the Alps, except as a kid so many years earlier, when we holidayed in Italy once. The wedding went smoothly and we stayed at the apartment of the bride and groom. Geneva was beautiful, crisp, clean and covered with snow yet the traffic moved freely and nothing ground to a halt. We walked around the shops, treated ourselves to some new gloves etc, sat by the lake for a while and had coffee in a restaurant/bar. As we sat cuddling our Grand Cremes, a couple who were sat behind us were conversing about their days' activities. As I listened in I became more and more fascinated, not in what he was saying, but how. He was skipping from English to French, German and Italian all in a sentence. Describing nothing more than his day on a building site, fitting bathrooms in different apartments, I fell in love with his ability to switch tongues, to talk all four languages at once, so fluently, I wanted to do this, I wanted to learn and use language as easily as this.

As the weather improved, we started to get calls and letters from home, people planning their summer holidays, wondering if they could come see us. Our first visitors were Roz and Lurch. Roz came to help and Lurch turned up for the free electricity. He spent so much time plugged into his stereo and headphones that one day I lost it and had a go at him.

"You need to get a grip mate, you can't spend all your life wired up to your stereo, don't you have any ambition, or drive, don't you have any goals in life?"

The hypocrisy, my own existence just a couple of years earlier was nothing to shout about, I don't even know why I had to say anything, I can only guess that I was trying to help him, stop him from making mistakes I had made that had led me to my own downfall. I was trying to make up for my own failings, something I have done a lot of over my lifetime.

Lurch had come to help me with the roof on the house, we had a leak and the old tiles seemed to be in a sorry state. It was decided to change the lot, put a whole new roof on, too big a job for me alone. Scaffolding was hired after a licence acquired from the village Mairie, there is always a paper trail in everything you do in France, permission must be sought for everything and a fee paid for more.

The old roof came down easily enough, the new roof however, that was a different matter. I laid and relaid the new tiles again and again, the roof still leaked. Thankfully it doesn't rain too often on Bélarga, but when it does, the house cries for better weather.

Tears for Fears were on tour and we were lucky enough to get tickets for their show in Nimes. I loved their first couple of hits, Mad World and Shout, both songs are wonderfully atmospheric, symbols of the darker side of life in an uncaring world. We arrived at the venue and every other person seemed to be english, it was as if they'd brought their own audience along and allowed a few natives in as well. Once on stage Roland Orzabal addressed the audience in French.

"Bollocks. Tell 'em in English!" I shouted, instantly regretting that I had. Roland looked into the audience, to where the call had come from.

"Did someone just shout Bollocks?" I shrank into the crowd, busted, I hadn't meant it to sound quite that bad. They played a great show that night, it wasn't like seeing The Dark play at the 100 Club, or Killing Joke blowing the roof off the Lyceum, it was just a good 1980's pop concert.

We had some friends coming over from Romford, girls Plig had been at school with. We met them at the station in Montpellier and went straight home. No sooner had they un-packed their bags than there was a knock at the door. I opened it to find Lucy and a friend, Sandra, standing on the street outside. I was stunned, I was not expecting them and suddenly had to rearrange the sleeping arrangements. Both couples stayed for a week, long enough to show them around the area and take a drive to the Toulouse Lautrec Museum in Albi. I loved having people at the house and found it very quiet when they all went home. Plig and I returned to our routine, markets, houseworks, portraits and knitting. I spent a lot of time sitting still whilst being drawn, charcoaled or painted. I was her muse, a live-in model. I tried learning to knit, both Plig and Roz were big knitters, they would always have something they were making, creating a new jumper or scarf. I tried for weeks, months even, and all I had to show for it was a pile of knotted wool stuck on a needle, it was interesting, but not for me.

Fiona was our next guest, I had stayed in touch with her after leaving Earls Court and always been good friends. She flew in to Montpellier and we were there to meet her. All evidence of the girl I used to know was gone. Fiona was no longer hanging around on the punk scene, she had moved on and it suited her. She looked healthy, happy and radiant in the mediterranean sun. Her hair was still bleached blonde but the thick eyeliner, the grouchy pout and threatening stance were gone. I was pleased to see her, it was good to have someone around who'd seen me at my worst and could appreciate the lengths I'd come to be here, even though it was still as a guest of my own girlfriends' family.

We'd heard about a nightclub that was opening at Marseillan Plage and decided to try it out. Living in the sticks is great for a while, the peace and quiet are wonderful until you want some excitement or to let your hair down. All our nights out previously had involved village halls, warm beer and a mix of 'Live is Life' by Opus, or bloody D-D-D-D-D-D Dixneuf, the French version of Paul Hardcastle's '19'. French teens from rural villages had little rhythm, or if they did, I never got to see it. I saw all manner of twisting, twitching and downright bloody awful dancing at events that were meant to be the highlight of the year for local kids. If this was their best, they needed to get out more often.

 Domino's was different, a young couple had invested a lot of money in turning a backroom area into a proper nightclub. Lights, dance floor, bar, DJ and sound equipment were all brand new, fresh, newly fitted and ready to go. We spread the word and looked forward to a grand opening night. We were not let down. Although turnout was low to begin with, the following weeks were more and more successful. We danced our socks off as the DJ blasted out some of our favourite sounds. Siouxsie, Killing Joke, Billy Idol, The Cult and The Cure. I had never heard The Cure played so much in all my life as they were in France. I made a shedload of money selling their badges and t-shirts, along with Madonna, Duran Duran and Johnny Halliday. I didn't mind that, but I have never fully appreciated listening to The Cure since, it was everywhere and it was overkill.

 There were some huge events taking place whilst I was in France. Coventry won the FA Cup, I wasn't a fan but it was huge for many of my friends back home. Live Aid happened and I wasn't there either. Nor was I there when Helen gave birth to her daughter Toni-Anne, the first baby of our generation, of my friends. It meant time was ticking on and I should be settling down too, I should be making babies and growing up myself, I should be settling down, although, in my head I already was.

The Market stall was growing all the time, I reinvested every penny I could into new stock, new lines. People would ask us for specific items from England and we would get them. Once a month we travelled back to London and bought more stock. We had gone from selling plastic earrings, to badges, t-shirts, jewellery, studded and bullet belts, wristbands, hair dye, make-up, sunglasses, the silly hats Major and I used to make, as well as leather biker jackets and Doctor Martens' boots to order. Anything I could get cheaper in England and sell at a profit, I did. I found a clearance lot 7" singles in a charity shop in Coventry one day, 200 records, £12 the lot. There were about 30 copies of the Toy Dolls' Nellie The Elephant, half a dozen copies of a Bryan James single, Split Enz and many others. I made a profit at my first market, the rest was pocket money. Not everything I sold went through official channels. Sometimes I would bring stock into France without declaring it, nobody would know as most of the invoices I had would be for job lots, no specific items, too many to count etc etc. The badges and t-shirts were posted out and I had to pay tax on those, thankfully the initial price was so low that the taxable value was affordable.

I had gone to see Toady, he was on probation after having just got out of Young Offenders' Prison. We cleared it with his probation officer and I took him by train to Montpellier. Unfortunately, the little bit at Dover where we were meant to declare our exports seemed like a little too much trouble and we might miss our ferry, so we hopped aboard and then walked confidently past the Douanier in Calais, I even stopped to nonchalantly adjust my backpack right in front of him. Once we got to the ticket office for the train to Paris, Toady asked me where we were meant to go for the customs stuff I'd mentioned earlier.

"Nowhere mate, we just got fast tracked through!" I reassured him, adding Smuggling to our list of historic misdemeanors.

Bérurier Noir were playing in Montpellier one night. They were a favourite band amongst the punks I knew in France. I don't think I have ever seen such a riotous, cacophonic sound in all my life. Nothing I had ever seen before compared to them, they were brilliantly chaotic, fierce and unforgettable, Acide had recommended them, Cali had said they were the best band in France, and I believed them.

Business was good and the stall had grown from one pasting table and a board of plastic earrings, to a 10 metre spread with parasols and canvas surrounds. We were doing well and other traders could see it too. Soon we began to sell to other traders, mostly just badges and sunglasses, then the cosmetics too. I heard of a wholesaler in Paris who sold the same brands of make-up and looked into the chances of buying in France instead of importing directly, after a brief conversation however, the Paris wholesaler laughed and said I was buying product from London for less than he was paying direct to the manufacturer. We parted on good terms but I was to hear from him again.

Supplying other traders meant buying more, which meant some goods were even cheaper. I was ordering 10,000 badges a month and paying 1.5p each. Retail I sold around 3,000 a month, the other 7,000 going in wholesale, the cosmetics sold well too, but in the summer sun we lost a lot of lipsticks to the waste bin, theft could also be a problem, La Paillade was the worst market for that, some groups of people feeling they had a right to just take what they wanted. It was the one market we felt uncomfortable at, we earned well, lost a bit and had to put up with more bartering and haggling than at any other market we did.

One regular market we did was Gignac on Saturday. We had a regular clientele from the local school when they finished early. In France, schools would be closed Wednesday afternoon but open Saturday morning. We would sell a lot of badges, jewellery and makeup there. One Saturday there seemed to be an absence of teenaged customers. I asked one of our regulars a couple of weeks later where they had been, "We've been on holiday, we went to England with our school."

"Whereabouts?" I enquired, "Anywhere nice?"

"It was beautiful, we stayed in a lovely town near London, it was called Romford, do you know it?"

I was expecting her to tell me she'd met Dave and Vulture, 'Do you know them?'- or maybe she'd bumped into my cousin Lyn, she had a stall on Romford market, anything is possible in this small world of ours, even me learning to speak French.

I was passing through Gare Du Nord one day, and asked the lady in the ticket office for a single to Calais. She smiled and then started giggling.

"Qu'est-ce qu'il y a?" *(What is it?)* I asked.

"It's very funny" she laughed, "I have never heard an Englishman talking with an accent from the Midi".

Inside the house I had worked my little butt off at every opportunity. I had moved a couple of internal walls, rendered and plastered throughout the house. It had been like living in a building site for much of the last year, but was starting to come together at last.

Dave and Patrick called by one day, they wanted to buy a some badges. I gave them a box that had recently arrived from my supplier and left them to choose what they wanted. It wasn't until much later that I discovered I was missing an invoice. I checked everywhere I could, it was gone. I thought back to when they came round and believed they must have gone through my box of paperwork. The invoice was from a previous delivery to the box that I had given them, there was no explanation other than they must have taken it. I called Patrick and he said had it, that it was in the box I had given them, that was not possible, I didn't believe him. Dave turned up at the next market in Montpellier and I asked him for the invoice, I needed it for my accounts.

"We didn't steal your fucking invoice, it was in the box, you gave it to us. We know what you pay now, and where to buy them so fuck off, we don't need you anymore now, you prick!"

You know what's coming next, don't you....?

Now, I'm not a betting man but I'm pretty sure that was not his finest moment. Two Policemen appeared as if from nowhere and pulled me off him, we were still trading insults and accusations when one of them interjected;

"En Français!"

As if a switch had been pulled somewhere, we both converted to French without pausing for breath. I had never heard myself speak so fluently, swear so graphically in another language, it was beautiful, it was also confirmation that I could now speak the language fluently, without thinking. I spoke French daily, not too brilliantly but enough to get by. I even dreamed in French some nights, a most confusing experience to say the least.

Dave was furious and demanded I be arrested. The Police gave him some good advice-

"If you don't want him to hit you, don't steal his paperwork".

I continued trading with Patrick, Dave kept a wary distance, all the while Plig and I had started growing apart. Our relationship seemed ok, but we spoke very little, I worked too much, she knitted, sang along to Nina Simone and the Cocteau Twins, ate cheese with chives. For me, it was The Ramones, Alien Sex Fiend and strong blue Danish, I didn't do delicate, my feet tended to get in the way when I pussyfooted around anything. I pawed over paperwork, counted stock, balanced bills and emptied the cat litter trays. One day she told me she'd made a decision.

"I'm going back to college, I want to finish my degree and become a portrait artist".

This meant going back to England, this meant, leaving the house unfinished and going back to working on building sites, smoking Benson & Hedges instead of Gauloise, drinking tea, having to say "No cucumber in my salad, please" everytime I ate out. No more markets, no more beach. No Pastis, no Vino. I was gutted but held it in, somehow, I felt as if I knew it was coming. We had drifted and our lives seemed to already be going in different directions. This was going to take a lot of thinking about. However I looked at it, I felt the decision was leading to a 'Dear John', that I was on my way out. I had nothing to go back to, no work, the agency I'd worked for before going to France had vanished, the week after I left the owners disappeared with a lot of money, leaving the guys I'd worked with unpaid. I had no faith in finding alternative employment, no desire to leave a fledgling business I'd put so much into. I couldn't leave. I just couldn't.

We talked about our position, Plig said she would come back during her holidays, and I would see her when I went to England to buy stock, it could work, we could make it work, but all I was hearing was various versions of a slow goodbye. Whatever I was doing wrong, I could not see, I didn't know why she wanted to go, but she did. France was not enough, I was not enough. She wanted, well, something other than I could give. We didn't argue or fight, we talked it out like adults and made preparations for the coming changes.

Nick got himself into a bit of bother. He had found himself a girlfriend, was working with Graham and continued to sell dope. There had been a party at a house in Bélarga and he'd been reported for smoking a joint. Two witnesses came forward and and named him. I was interviewed at the Gendarmerie, I was at the party but knew nothing about the illegal use of drugs. I confirmed only that I was there. I had seen nothing. I was cautioned and left alone, Nick was hunted down in Montpellier and given 3 months in Nimes Prison, on the word of 2 witnesses, for smoking a joint.

Graham was in need of a new worker, he asked me to help him but I couldn't, I had my own business to run. Eventually he took on Simon, an alcoholic ex-pat who'd just moved to the squat in Montpellier from living on the streets of Aix En Provence for the previous 6 years. He was a nice guy, drank too much but looked after his dog, an Alsatian he'd found on the streets a few years earlier. I too was in need of assistance and began to look at my options. I kept my eyes open for people I thought I could trust to help me at various markets, that way I could still continue and try to build on the wholesale more, that way I could make money without having to set up the stall and pay other people. There were several people I had in mind at different markets, people I had made friends with, who would hang around the stall most of the day anyhow. It would be a simple enough thing to give them 100 Francs to help out, maybe some free stock from time to time, as a 'Thank You'.

I had decided to cut out the smaller, less valuable markets, to concentrate on the bigger ones, as well as getting the house done and building the wholesale side of the business. I still hadn't completed my portfolio for my Carte de Séjour, and time kept running out, I had to complete it soon. I was going to be a very busy boy, alone in a foreign land.

Plig and I were invited to a party, we had made friends with Marianne, a popular figure on the streets of Montpellier at the time. She owned her own home, and a plot of land around it on the outskirts of the city. She had an open door policy, allowing homeless people to come and go anytime, so long as they behaved, they were welcome, fed and housed for a day, a night, a week or month. She had inherited money from her wealthy family but chose to live among the people, the drunks, the addicts, the drop-outs and mentally challenged. Marianne was the sort of woman you only hear about, but never see. Possibly the most beautiful soul I had ever come across, not in looks, looks are superficial, they fool you, trick you and deceive you. Marianne was beautiful of heart and had time for everyone who needed it. We sat outside all night, drinking, eating and entertaining each other. A fire burned near the row of tables at which we sat, hippies, drunks and punks of a million fables, all lost in a world that misjudged and cared so little for the most fragile.

Nick was eventually released from Prison, he was quieter upon release, but soon regained his old character. His girlfriend kept him in check, and he seemed to be happy. "Iron Maiden are playing in Montpellier man, you've gotta come see'em man, they're great!" I agreed and treated myself to a ticket. Plig didn't want to go, she was not a fan and was due to go back to England soon afterwards, her head and heart had already left.

Iron Maiden were absolutely brilliant live. Bruce Dickinson bowled me over, his voice was like an air raid siren, powerful and commanding. Some fool in the audience kept flipping him the middle finger and halfway through their set, Bruce dived into the audience and pummelled the guy into the ground. Security pulled him off and took him back to the stage but the guy on the floor was dragged out of the venue, worse for wear and no doubt regretting his stupid act.

Nick and I met up at the show, he was with a welsh girl called Sian, *(pro: Sharn)* he introduced her as a friend from the squat. During the evening she told me she had to go to Perpignan, to another squat there, she had been staying there and left her tattooing equipment and some clothes behind when she left for Montpellier. I offered to drive her and made arrangements to pick her up the next day.

On our return she offered to tattoo me for free. Anything I wanted. I couldn't think of anything and so settled for her blacking over Melina and Lynn's names on some old tattoos I already had. I gave no thought at the time to hygiene, it didn't crossed my mind that she could have been passing on any number of infections, that she could have tattooed anybody in the squat without access to sterilizing equipment. Sepsis, AIDS, Hepatitis, all manner of things. I had been in a bubble so long I hadn't given it a thought.

The time had finally arrived, Plig was heading home and I was taking her. I took her out to Gignac where we ate pizza in a small restaurant the night before leaving. I told her I wished her every success and we were very civil, adult, like friends parting company for unknown adventures. We both knew it was over, neither wanted to be the one to burst the bubble.

In the morning we left bright and early, Plig and I in the front seats, Sían and the luggage in the back. She had developed "Women's problems" and needed to get home for medical treatment, I had developed a problem of my own too, and when asked what the little creepy crawly things in my pants were I blamed the cats. Pud never did forgive me.

I dropped Plig off at Hornchurch and drove Sían home to her parents' house, in Swansea, where I was put up in a spare room before returning to Essex the next day. It had been a very long day, added to by a slight detour at Swindon to find a biker's pub her ex-husband used to drink in. I was shattered and slept like I hadn't slept for days.

I returned to Hornchurch to find Roz and Lurch were not getting on too well. A plan was quickly hatched and Lurch's attention diverted. Plig and I smuggled Roz out into the car and drove to Coventry. We took her to Rich, he had a new flat in Hillfields by this time and seemed somewhat bemused to see us.

"Can Roz stay with you for a few days mate, I know it's short notice but she's in a bit of a fix?"

Rich looked her up and down and opened the door for her to come in.

"No problem" he said, smiling. "She can stop in my spare room".

I thanked him and drove back to Hornchurch, Lurch was gone, he wasn't a happy bunny, but he was gone.

I shopped around London for stock, bought all I could for the business. Leather clothes, jackets, trousers, skirts. Lots of jewellery and all the other lines I needed to stock up on. Julia was coming back with me to help me settle once we'd gone to Coventry to collect her youngest daughter.

I filled the van with all the stock I had purchased, then Julia and I headed to Dover after saying our goodbyes.. I had filled out a customs declaration form, a T2, to present to customs. I was told I needed an agent but that we could get one in Calais if necessary. We'd arrived just as a ferry was due to load and so decided to do the papers in Calais. *Ooops!*

In Calais we were stopped and asked for our papers. I asked where the agents were and after much ado found out that they were all closed until the morning. *Ooops!*

"Can I find one in Montpellier?"

"Non monsieur, you cannot leave here until your vehicle has a plomb *(seal)* and has been cleared for inland customs clearance, I am afraid you are going nowhere until tomorrow at least". *Ooops, Ooops and big bloody Ooops!*

This definitely wasn't in the script, I had customers waiting for stock, I couldn't delay getting back, but it seemed I had no say in the matter. This was the way things were.

Julia and I spent a long cold night dozing on the upper floor of the terminal building in Calais Port. The hours dragged by slowly, very, very slowly. We were standing by the door of a customs agent's office waiting for them to open in the morning. We had chosen Jules Roy for no other reason than they were the nearest. After much explaining, much to and fro with the customs officers, we were told to unload the van and verify the goods corresponded with the paperwork. Everything had to be unloaded, presented, counted,checked and reloaded, everything had to correspond. I had declared approximately 40 cases of cosmetic's, but when it was unloaded there were 120, I had to get some tape and bind all of them together to bring the tally down. Hours were wasted under the watchful eye of the Douane, many of whom just wanted to collect the diesel money they were notorious for getting from the truck drivers as they passed through the port on their way into Europe.

Eventually we were cleared to go, but only to an address in Sete where the van would be impounded until it was cleared, taxes paid and the paperwork stamped. It was a long drive south, to Séte, a fishing port between Montpellier and Cap

D'agde. From there we got a taxi home and waited for the phone to ring.

It was 2 days and about £800 later that we were finally reunited with our property. Julia flew home and I set about getting the stock to my customers. The delays and added costs did nothing to help me, I needed to avoid this happening again. In future, everything had to be posted out to save on the cost and delays.

Simon

Nothing to give and much less to lose,
Save the sting of the snow as it entered his shoes,
Now all that is left of that cold young man,
Is the sign from his chest
"J'ai Faim"

The Fall of Because

Once Julia had returned to England I continued with the work on the house and trying to sell more stock to more traders. I could only do so many markets alone, or with the help that I had. In Montpellier I recruited a young lady whom I'd seen on another stall one day. I agreed to pick her up the night before the market so that it would save time on the day, she stayed in a spare room at the house and we left early in the morning. The day went well and I was happy with her work, she seemed to enjoy selling and takings were good. After the market however, I took her home and she invited me to come into the house. Half way through our coffee she took my hand and led me upstairs.

Alone in the kitchen a short time later, I heard the shower start and then a knock at the door.

Yep, THAT knock at the door….

"Where is she?" He was about my age, with a beard, leather jacket, long hair and an 'I want to punch you in the face' look about him. He was a biker, or more precisely, a pissed off biker who had a sneaky suspicion about what I had just done with his girlfriend.

"Come on in, she's in the shower". I offered him coffee, he just sat at the kitchen table looking at me, his face red and angry but I ignored him, I acted as though nothing had happened, and he slowly relaxed.

Eventually she came downstairs gave him a hug and kissed him. I had no idea he existed, I had no idea she had a boyfriend and would not have entered the house if I had. I felt angry at having been put in this position, and when I left, I didn't return.

I called in my back up plan, a young student called Fredérique. At first he wasn't too keen, but after his first couple of weeks he became more confident and competent. I had him take care of the badges, belts and t-shirts while I tried selling the cosmetics and jewellery. Things were going well, but I needed a female salesperson really, to sell makeup to women and young girls.

Palma was German, a school student in Clermont L'Herault. She and her mother lived by the Lac Du Salagou, an artificial lake created by the flooding of valley near Clermont. Local tradition tells that the church bells can sometimes be heard from beneath the waves. Palma's mother was a leather goods trader on the markets, she would make her own goods and sell them, a very talented craftswoman. When I heard David Bowie was touring, I invited Palma to come along and see him. I knew she was a fan, and the nearest show to us was on a weekend, in Toulouse, too far for me to drive back alone after a show, I thought it would be nice to invite her along as company. She was really excited and we took another of her friends along with us, I bought the tickets and we set off nice and early.

Toulouse was about 4 hours away, I took the autoroute and headed north west, passing the medieval fortress of Carcassonne. The show was easy to find, temporary signs had been placed all over the region and judging by the size of the place, I reckon everyone living south of Nancy must have have been there. I'd never seen such a huge crowd. Arriving early we were able to head close to the front to get a good view. Once in place, we stayed put.

The Glass Spider tour was a magnificent success, the show was amazing. David Bowie came down on a wire from the roof of the stage. David Bowie. DAVID BOWIE. Spelt G O fucking D! On stage about 20 metres away from me singing Heroes. I had died and gone to heaven, I must have. I will never forget the brilliance of that night, that song, that moment.

Graham had the pitch next to mine in Montpellier. We had become good friends and each sunday I would sit and eat a full english breakfast with him once I had set up my stall. Fred looked after the stall as I chatted with Graham about stuff, then I would send Fred over for pizza or a burger while I kept the stall before things got too busy. When we finished for the day, we would pack up and then sit and have a beer together.

"I've got some work to look at, how d'you fancy helping me out if we go halves on the proceeds?"

"What's it doing?" I asked.

"I got some old bird wants me to render the outside of her house, a lime render, then paint it once it's dry. Apparently she sacked her last builder, he was too slow and too expensive, fancy coming along to price it up in the week?"

"Sure mate, I'm up for that."

We drove over in Graham's van and priced up the job. A weeks' work we estimated, and we could start the next week. Graham brought Simon along to help out and we got stuck in.

Our client Marie-Claude was a retired travel executive. She'd spent her working life travelling the world and finding holiday hotels for the tourist trade, managing accounts and looking after clients. It had been a high powered position, demanding but also it had its rewards. She had spent most of her life in other countries and was now home to stay. Marie-Claude also kept rabbits, Angora rabbits. During our time working on her house, Graham became more and more interested in her rabbits, while she became more and more interested in Simon. Before we knew it, Simon and his dog moved in with her, Graham agreed to take her rabbits , all 40 of them,as payment for the work done. It had seemed like a good idea at the time but the thought of having to de-fur 40 wriggling bitey things on a daily basis sounded like hard work, and having seen how many scars Marie-Claude had on her hands, I thought it best to be a silent partner and let Graham take control.

The weeks passed quickly, working in and out of the house. When I was home alone the house seemed too big. I drank a lot of pastis, wine and whatever I fancied. I played a lot of records, Joy Division, Chameleons, Wasted Youth, Sisters Of Mercy. Loneliness was my constant companion.

Graham had another job in the pipeline, some kennels. A friend- Roger, from the same village Graham lived in, kept Alsatians, German Shepherd Dogs as some people call them. These were not cute family pets though, he kept the rejects, the biters, the killers, those that could be trained for Military use.

I hadn't realised the scale of what he had taken on, not until we visited the site and pegged out the footings. A row of 10 kennels in each of 2 buildings, plus an office. Each kennel was to be the size of a family kitchen, with a window and door to each and a long corridor the length of each building.

We set about digging the footings and then the concrete arrived, 3 truckloads for these alone. Next was the blocks, around 2,000 to start with, plus sand, 2 pallets of cement, a mixer and wheelbarrows. The site itself was just an empty field, there were some small shelters for the dogs that already lived there, one of whom was kept away from the others. Satan was nasty piece of work, all teeth and no smiles, one of the few dogs I have ever come across in my life that scared me, he was a natural killer, how anybody could train him was beyond me. One morning, shortly after we started, we arrived on site to find Satan loose. There was no way we were going in to the field while he was loose, so we sat and waited for Roger to arrive. Once he had retrieved Satan we had a look round the sit. What we found was pretty bad, Satan had snapped his chain and killed another dog, a third dog was also injured. He had been so desperate to get at a rival male that he'd ripped his neck open, front and back, two gaping wounds where his chain had cut him, but to have actually snapped that chain must have taken incredible strength. There was no arguing who was leader of the pack now.

Graham tried to collect payment from Marie-Claude on several occasions but was getting nowhere. I resigned myself to not getting paid, or rather, not collecting the rabbits, brushing out their fur daily, bagging it up and eventually selling it by the kilo, it seemed like a lot of work and gnawed fingers, it may have been profitable, by then why was Marie-Claude so keen of offloading them? Surely, if they were as valuable as we were led to believe, why was she living in such a small house, and with Simon and his dog?

The Damned were coming to Montpellier and I was looking forward to seeing them. I had a friend in Montagnac who had just started a small independent radio station, Phillippe was a

DJ and played all the bands I loved, plus The Cure, a lot. He was a big Cure fan and also a fan of The Damned.

We went to the gig together and he asked me if I could somehow get him backstage to interview them after the show. I spent the evening bouncing around at the front of the stage, from time to time I would try to get the attention of one of the stage hands, even the singer Dave Vanian himself. Eventually I passed a note I had hastily written to one of the crew, he disappeared behind the curtain, came back a few minutes later and said "Yes", we could interview the band, but would have to wait by the stage once they had finished, then we would be taken upstairs to see them. This was incredible, I really hadn't thought it would happen. I danced to the rest of their set with renewed vigour, Phillippe couldn't stop smiling.

Sure enough, after the show we were taken upstairs to meet the band. I had never interviewed a band in my life and had no idea what I was supposed to say. Thankfully, Phillippe had a whole load of questions set aside, all I had to do was translate and give him the answers.

Dave Vanian was on a post-gig high, running around the room unrolling rolls of toilet paper, he was manic and couldn't sit down. Rat Scabies was sitting on large padded chair, the other 2 members of the band sat on a sofa, each refreshing themselves with a can of beer, Captain Sensible was no longer with the band at this time having gone solo.

"Alright lads, my name's Ribs and this is Phillippe, he's got a radio show in the area and is doing a Damned special tomorrow, he's asked me to come along and translate for him, hope that's ok with you?"

"Yeah, no problem" They sounded bored, distracted. This was my first time but they had to do this day after day.

Phillippe was a little starstruck, he loved this band, possibly nearly as much as The Cure, he pulled out a piece of paper and started asking questions, I translated as best I could and all was going well, Vanian paced in and out of the room, toilet rolls flew through the air, Scabies sat up and cut me short half way through a question.

"Phillippe wants to know about the influences….."

"Tell him to fuck off" Rat said, "What are you doing here- do you live here, in Montpellier?"

"I live here yes, out near Clermont L'Herault, a little village by the river, a little village next to the river. I love it".

"It's beautiful here, I love this area" he replied.

"Have you been out and about around here then, where are you off to next?"

"Barcelona tomorrow night, we had a bit of a walk around the town centre earlier".

"If you get out into the country it's gorgeous…."

Phillippe wanted to know what was being said, he was trying to make notes.

"Ribs, demande si ils peut me dire…"

"Tell him bollocks" Rat interjected, "what do you do here then?"

This was hysterical, I was being interviewed by the band I was meant to be interviewing, at the same time being hassled by my mate for responses to questions I wasn't able to ask, making up my own answers as we went along.

Rat Scabies has got to be one of the nicest, most down to earth guys in the music biz. I got on so well with him I ended up giving him my phone number and inviting him and his family to come and stay once the tour was finished.

I am such a groupie, Lol….

The following afternoon we went live in Phillippe's studio. I was on the air answering questions that were never asked the night before. An entire generation of young Damned fans in the Herault have grown up believing the crap I made up.

"Mais c'est vrai, je l'écouter sur la radio….."
"It must be true- I heard it on the radio…."

Working with Graham was easy, we got on really well and he had a better knowledge of construction than I did, a friend in his family, or village, was a builder and gave him tips plus he was older than me and so had more experience. Graham was in his mid 30's, I was just coming up to 22, he was married with kids, a Yorkshireman through and through, I could tell by the way he rolled his sleeves up and wore his jeans baggy, "Harder to get your hands in your pockets when they don't reach", he said.

"Innit!" I replied, knowing full well that meant I was buying the drinks.

Each day was pretty much the same as the previous day. Get up at stupid o'clock, have a wee, get dressed. Downstairs for coffee and a light breakfast-usually some bread and jam or spicy ginger cake, a yoghurt and some bitter chocolate, empty the cat litter trays, feed the cats, put my boots on and jump in the van. Drive to Graham's, more coffee, off to work. Quick coffee and then we'd be ready to start. Graham laid the blocks, I mixed the muck and smoked Gauloises, filterless of course and in a soft pack, men were men in those days, we knew how to impress. We brought our own lunches, I'd usually make myself a salad with boiled eggs, black pudding and couscous. I loved working outside, the mornings were cool and by the time we'd had our 4th or 5th coffee, about 10 am, the sun would be warming our backs, or burning our necks. The afternoons were hot, the cement would dry quicker than we could use it if we weren't careful, and so we kept the mixer going, making sure the muck was always wet enough to last but not too wet as to ooze out between the blocks. We'd finish around 4 pm, have a drink at Graham's and then I'd drive home. Graham would change, shower and go off to his regular pitch in Montpellier, to make Pizza's until 10 pm. I would go home, say hello to Pud and Kit, pour a drink, make some supper while singing along in my head to David Bowie or Joy Division. Sometimes when I felt good, I'd put on one of my Rezzillo's albums, or Lene Lovich. I saved my Cult albums for doing the washing up, dancing from the ankle down whilst elbow deep in the sink, farting along to- "Just a revolution…." *Parp, parp, parp, parp.*

I tried going out alone, I drove to Montpellier one night and headed to a bar frequented by foreign students, the sort of place people went to when there were no bands in town. I ordered a beer and mingled. My shirt getting ever more damp, it was hot, it was hot outside even though it was night time, but inside a crowded bar the air was thick with tobacco smoke, laughter and perspiration, every face glistened, every armpit and back dripped quietly into loose clothing. It felt wonderfully exotic and mediterranean. I had visions of what it must be like in Casablanca, or Tunis on a hot summer's night. I also had an empty glass. I wasn't making any new friends, nor did I see anyone I knew, I had driven 30 something miles to drink beer alone.

On weekends we didn't work for Roger, we kept up our stalls at the Marché aux Puces. I would load the van at 4 am, have coffee and light breakfast, drive to Montpellier to be in place around 6 am. Set up the parasoles and tables, then have a quick walk around the market searching for records or anything I fancied. I would start setting out my stock about 7-7.30 just in time for the early morning rush. Fred would normally arrive about then and would get stuck in to help out. At 10, Graham would call me over and we'd have breakfast together, Simon would run Graham's stall as we sat drinking beer and eating bacon. Around 1 pm, the market would thin out and we'd start packing up, by about 2 pm all would be done and we'd share a beer or 2 before heading home.

I was driving home via Sete one day and the car in front seemed to be going way too slow, they were tourists from another department enjoying a Sunday drive down the coast. I sat behind until the point where I just wanted to pass them, put my foot down and overtook them. By this time we had entered the next conurbation and were in an area of no overtaking. A point brought to my attention by a local police officer standing on a street corner to catch people like me, doing what I just did. I was pulled over and issued a ticket, I had to go to the local Police station to pay the fine. By the time I'd finished ranting about the injustice of it all, paid the 20 francs and got my receipt, I had sworn at just about every person I could see in uniform only to remind myself on the way out that it was only 20 francs, and they hadn't said a word about my beer breath. I was lucky, very lucky.

Now that I was busy with Graham, I had to look after my wholesale customers as best I could, when I could. Sometimes sneaking off for an hour to drop stock off at a market, sometimes having customers come to the house in the evening or weekends. I had ordered some stock early in the year and was expecting it to arrive in April at the latest. It was May and not only had it not arrived yet, but my stocks of fast selling cosmetics was running low and my birthday was coming up.

To celebrate, I invited some friends for a night out in Montpellier, there were about 12-15 of us altogether. Even Simon came along. I kept everyone refreshed and made a point of trying to be inclusive with everyone, after all, those from the village didn't know those from the city and they sure as hell didn't know Simon. He got me onto the pool table at some point, winner stays on, doubles. Simon and I were about as practiced and professional as 2 ex-pat english guys who very rarely play pool could ever be, but somehow it all came together for us. We were winning game after game, either someone was spending a lot of money paying the regulars to lose, or we were natural winners on the baize. Either way, by the end of the proceedings, we hadn't lost a single game. We were very drunk though, pocketing shots we wouldn't even have tried if we were sober.

At about 4 am, Simon and I left the bar and took a slow stagger to where we had agreed to meet Graham in the morning. The sun was rising as we sat on the floor by Graham's Pizza pitch, our eyes were heavy, but we'd had a good night. Graham picked us up on schedule and having taken one look at the damage took us for coffee before work, it was going to be a long day.

Because my stock was held up, I was having some problems with customers I had made promises to. Jean-Claude went to Paris and bought stock, much more expensively, from the wholesaler I had spoken to a few months earlier. He in turn, wasted no time in calling me to say I should stop supplying the cosmetics to other traders, or else he would start legal proceedings against me. He had a Franchise and I was in breach of his contract. I didn't know it at the time, but he could not sue me as I was buying my stock as a retailer from a wholesaler in London. I was not in breach of his contract unless I was to buy from the manufacturers directly. It's funny how people start making threats when they perceive a threat has appeared, in reality he should have been thanking me for creating a customer base in the South. Again, I didn't know and I honestly thought I could be in serious trouble here. I promised to cease wholesaling and to stick to the markets, he promised he would start legal action if I didn't.

Simon and his dog moved in with me. He and Marie-Claude had parted over his inability to stop drinking. Simon was a proper alcoholic, unlike me who would go for days on end without, just enjoying it as much as I could as often as I could without it being my boss. Simon had no choice, he had to drink, his body was addicted. Every night he took a litre bottle of beer to bed with himself and I placed another next to his bed for when he woke in the morning. Every morning he would bring the empty bottles down to the kitchen and get another from the fridge. If he went for more than a few hours without a beer he would start getting anxious, confused, shaking. His shakes were real, they were disabling, the only thing he could do was drink himself straight again. Unless you have lived with this disease it is easy to condemn those that suffer it, it is easy to forget that it is no longer a choice. I had a choice, and I treasured my ability to say no whenever I felt I had to. Simon could not, his body would not allow his mind to overrule it, and that conflict was clear to see in the dark circles around his eyes. Simon was a wonderful guy, an educated man, talented artist and good soul, he just couldn't say no to drink.

Simon functioned quite well so long as he was close to a drink, he could work, talk coherently and crack jokes whenever the mood took him, we had a lot of laughs. He started taking the piss out of me because I was from Essex.

"Nah wot I meen? 'Ot 'ere innit? Hahaha, innit?"

I would try retaliating, reminding him of his own roots.

"Newark, Newark- the only town in England that's an acronym of Wanker!".

A couple of American students turned up in Montpellier one Sunday morning, a black girl and her white friend, they were pawing over some jewellery and moving on to the cosmetics.

"Ask him how much this is" I heard one mumble to the other.

"Shit, I ain't asking him, have you seen that guy?"

"I want to ask him but I'm afraid"

"Don't worry ladies, I won't bite" I joked. They both laughed and hit each others' arms, obviously embarrassed they'd said anything.

"Oh my god, you speak English?"

"I am English"

We chatted for a while and somehow I managed to keep them long enough to swap phone numbers and arrange a date. I had a new girlfriend, an American art student, called Marybeth. Over the course of the next few days we met up before she left to go to Morocco for a week, alone.

When she returned we picked up where we left off, spending as much free time together as we could. Marybeth started helping on the stall at weekends, but before we knew it, her time in France was coming to an end, her university course was to conclude in Delaware after the summer break. Once again I was having to say goodbye.

Not only was Marybeth's time up, but mine was coming to an end too. I had the threat of legal action from the Paris wholesaler hanging over me. Chris and Julia wanted the house finished and for me to move on, my wholesale business was struggling with getting sufficient supplies in time, deliveries of cosmetics were arriving with damages or missing goods and to top things off, I received a letter from the Préfecture in Montpellier:

Monsieur,

A la date du 29 décembre 1986, vous avez déposé un dossier de demande de carte séjour afin de régulariser votre situation administrative en France oú vous etes entré en touriste en juillet 1985.

J'ai fait procéder á un nouvel examen de votre dossier. Cependant, en l'absence d'éléments nouveaux, je ne peux confirmer ce refus.

Dans ces conditions, il ne m'est pas possible de faire droit á votre demande de carte de séjour.

Il vous appartient donc de quitter le territoire français dans le délai d'un mois á compter de la notification de la présente lettre qui vaut autorisation de séjour jusqu'á votre départ.

Passé ce délai, si vous n'avez pas regagné votre pays d'origine, je me verrai dans l'obligation d'engager á votre encontre la procédure de reconduite á la frontiere, prévue par la loi du 9 septembre 1986.

My Carte De Séjour had been refused and I had 30 days to leave the country or be deported.

I could easily have left for England and come back the following day, or gone to Spain for a few days, but all in all my will was broken. I wanted to move on, my time was up here.

Marybeth had invited me to Delaware, but I had to win her parents over to be able to stay with them, although the chances were slim that I would be able to. I would have to be prepared to stay in a motel.

I had a contact in Montpellier, a wholesale customer Arnaud, who was interested in buying the cosmetics I had, he was a small-fry trader, someone who wanted to put up a table and collect handfuls of cash. He preferred photography, but photos were not selling and he needed to find something to make money. In order to seal the deal, Arnaud invited me to his apartment to meet his wife and have a drink. On arrival I was invited in and briefly met his wife, who was very pleasant and sociable. A good looking woman in her 50's who took care of herself and her family. Arnaud decided that it would be preferable for us to talk business over a beer in his favourite bar. His wife gave him a sharp sideways look, but before she could voice her disapproval, I was being led out of the door.

Arnaud's favourite bar turned out to be a small backstreet bar with about 8 customers on a sunday afternoon, 8 customers and a loud music system. We stepped inside and he ordered 2 beers before introducing me to a couple of his friends. As we chatted a small woman in her late 50's, maybe even 60's came in to the bar through a back doorway. She was wearing a dressing gown, which seemed odd until she slipped it off and revealed some sort of skimpy stage outfit underneath. She approached Arnaud and kissed him a little too enthusiastically before climbing up onto the bar.

I had never seen a stripper before, not a real one, in the flesh, on the bar in front of my face like this. She twisted and gyrated in time to the music, Arnaud and his friends clapping and singing, their mouths gaped open as if hoping to latch on to an errant nipple as she twirled her way up and down the bar. When her panties came off she threw them at the baying pack creating a scrum of the depraved, undersexed middle aged men desperate for a souvenir. Someone had them safely tucked away in his pocket by the time she finished her set and stepped down from the bar totally naked, using the seats we were sat on as a step down to the floor.

Arnaud introduced me as his new business partner, I smiled politely and reached for my beer as she again kissed Arnaud before climbing onto my stool and sitting butt naked on my lap facing him. She ran her hands all over him while wiping her backside on the front of my jeans, I made a mental note to wash them as soon I got home, I had no idea where she'd been but I suspected Arnaud had been there with her.

After about 5 minutes of flirtation the stripper was gone, along with several of the notes Arnaud had previously had in his wallet, I was not in the least bit interested in the woman, to be honest, it was embarrassing. He had paid 700 francs for a bottle of champagne, most of which had been swallowed by his lady friend, the same champagne that could be bought in any supermarket for 2-300 francs.

We were finally able to discuss business. I had been through my stock and estimated the value of what was there. Arnaud agreed on the price and I told him once he'd paid me I would give him telephone numbers, addresses etc of my suppliers in England, plus all remaining stock minus what I had sold on what was to be my last market, the following weekend. This was agreed and I arranged to deliver everything to him once he had my money ready to collect.

The following weekend was a crazy day, I had put signs up on the stall, "Everything 50% off" and "Soldes" (*sale*). For some customers, this wasn't even enough of a discount, they would still barter, and for once I joined in and confused the hell out them.

"C'est combient?" (*How much?*) they asked holding a fistful of eyeliners or mascara.

"Vingt Francs" (*20 francs*) I'd reply.

"Quinze francs?" (*15 francs*)

"Non, normallement ça vous coutez 50 francs, donnez-moi 20" (*No, normally that would cost you 50 francs, give me 20*)

"Pas 15?" They smiled.

"Non, pas 15, 10 francs seulement!" (*No, not 15, 10 francs only*)

"DIX?" Confused.

"Non, 5 francs" I said, undercutting myself and smiling. The confusion on their faces was wonderful, I had them totally befuddled, nobody undercut themselves in this way, it made no sense. To me it made perfect sense, everything must go, the price was irrelevant. That I was giving people handfuls of stock they normally bought was more important to me, some customers had been regular and given me a lot of money. Today was my turn to say 'Thank You'.

I paid Fred at the end of the mornings trading. I gave him some extra money and told him to help himself to anything he wanted. We said farewell, me thanking him for his help over the months, he smiled and walked away with his girlfriend, his voice cracked and there were tears in his eyes.

I shared my last beer with Graham and Simon. Graham had finally managed to get the Angora rabbits we were owed. He kept them at his house in a shed he'd constructed specially for them, but late one night they were taken by someone with a balaclava and shotgun.

I delivered the remaining cosmetics as promised. Arnaud handed me a wad of notes and a bank draught. It was too late to bank anything so I put the draught in an envelope and placed it in an overnight deposit box outside my bank. I had already cleared everything in the house, my tools and cats all had new homes, the washing up was done, beds made and doors locked. I took my personal effects and climbed into the van for my final departure from the village. In front of me lay the long overnight drive to London, and the first flight I could get to New York.

Au revoir Bélarga- my beautiful waters, and bienvenue Delaware, bring it on baby, I is ready.......

ABOUT THE AUTHOR

"He's an idiot, ask his wife, she'll tell you."

Born in Romford 1965, I have lived a varied life done and
achieved things I never thought I could do, or had to.
Trained as a Baker after having been in the Sea Cadet Corps.
I have been married three times, have three grown up children
and still not managed to grow up myself.
I have driven trucks professionally across the UK, Europe and
Turkey. Trained as a yachtsman and sailed across the Atlantic.
Lived and worked in France and Israel and been awarded for
bravery by the Society For The Protection Of Life From Fire,
the highest award given to civilians following a fire.
Former owner of a Gothic Guesthouse in Scarborough, which
featured on the TV show, May The Best House Win, and
Eileen Daly's film, Daly Does The Dead-Exorcism.
Now living with my long suffering best friend and wife Laurel,
in Sudbury, Suffolk, England.

If you liked this book, Thank You.
If you bought it, Thank You Very Much.
If you want to know what happens next, watch this space,
there will be a sequel.

86548683R00165

Made in the USA
Middletown, DE
30 August 2018